The Hidden I
DERBYSHIRE
including
THE PEAK DISTRICT

By
Hugh Taylor and
Moira McCrossan

© Travel Publishing Ltd.

Published by:
Travel Publishing Ltd
7a Apollo House, Calleva Park
Aldermaston, Berks, RG7 8TN
ISBN 1-902-00783-2
© Travel Publishing Ltd

First Published:	*1991*	*Fourth Edition:*	*1999*
Second Edition:	*1994*	*Fifth Edition:*	*2002*
Third Edition:	*1997*		

HIDDEN PLACES REGIONAL TITLES

Cambs & Lincolnshire	Chilterns
Cornwall	Derbyshire
Devon	Dorset, Hants & Isle of Wight
East Anglia	Gloucestershire, Wiltshire & Somerset
Heart of England	Hereford, Worcs & Shropshire
Highlands & Islands	Kent
Lake District & Cumbria	Lancashire & Cheshire
Lincolnshire & Nottinghamshire	Northumberland & Durham
Somerset	Sussex
Thames Valley	Yorkshire

HIDDEN PLACES NATIONAL TITLES

England	Ireland
Scotland	Wales

Printing by: Scotprint, Haddington

Maps by: © Maps in Minutes ™ (2002)   © Crown Copyright, Ordnance Survey 2002

Editor: Hugh Taylor and Moira McCrossan

Cover Design: Lines & Words, Aldermaston

Cover Photographs: Monsal Dale Viaduct: Leanwood Pumping Station, Cromford Canal; Ramshall Rocks © www.britainonview.com

Text Photographs: © www.britainonview.com

All information is included by the publishers in good faith and is believed to be correct at the time of going to press. No responsibility can be accepted for errors.

This book is sold subject to the condition that it shall not by way of trade or otherwise be lent, re-sold, hired out, or otherwise circulated without the publisher's prior consent in any form of binding or cover other than that which it is published and without similar condition including this condition being imposed on the subsequent purchase.

Foreword

The **Hidden Places** is a collection of easy to use travel guides taking you in this instance on a relaxed but informative tour of Derbyshire, a county famous for its beautiful countryside which includes, of course, the 'Peak District National Park', the very first of Britain's National Parks covering an area of around 540 square miles. To the north of the county the High Peak is an area of windswept moorland and steep river valleys whilst further south is the undulating green landscape and gently flowing rivers of the Derbyshire Dales. Throughout Derbyshire the traveller will find attractive villages in beautiful settings but it is also a county that possesses a very interesting industrial and cultural heritage which should not be ignored.

This edition of **The Hidden Places of Derbyshire including the Peak District** is published **in full colour.** All **Hidden Places** titles are now published in colour which ensures that readers can properly appreciate the attractive scenery and impressive places of interest in Derbyshire and, of course, in the rest of the British Isles. We do hope that you like the new format.

Our books contain a wealth of interesting information on the history, the countryside, the towns and villages and the more established places of interest. But they also promote the more secluded and little known visitor attractions and places to stay, eat and drink many of which are easy to miss unless you know exactly where you are going.

We include hotels, inns, restaurants, public houses, teashops, various types of accommodation, historic houses, museums, gardens, garden centres, craft centres and many other attractions throughout the area, all of which are comprehensively indexed. Most places are accompanied by an attractive photograph and are easily located by using the map at the beginning of each chapter. We do not award merit marks or rankings but concentrate on describing the more interesting, unusual or unique features of each place with the aim of making the reader's stay in the local area an enjoyable and stimulating experience.

Whether you are visiting the area for business or pleasure or in fact are living in the counties we do hope that you enjoy reading and using this book. We are always interested in what readers think of places covered (or not covered) in our guides so please do not hesitate to use the reader reaction forms provided to give us your considered comments. We also welcome any general comments which will help us improve the guides themselves. Finally if you are planning to visit any other corner of the British Isles we would like to refer you to the list of other **Hidden Places** titles to be found at the rear of the book and to the Travel Publishing website at **www.travelpublishing.co.uk.**

Travel Publishing

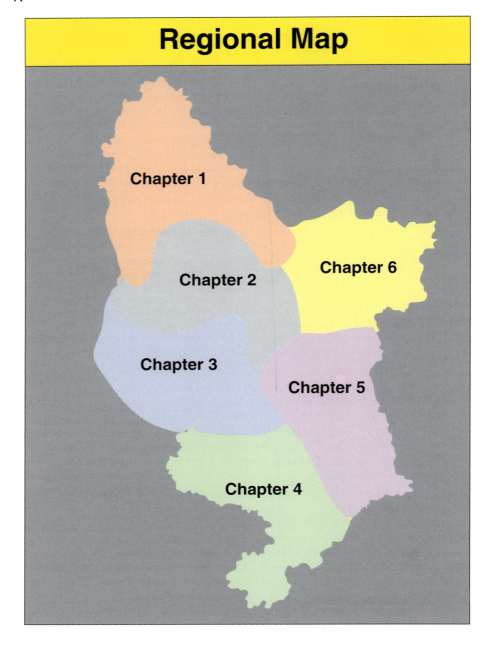

Contents

FOREWORD   III

REGIONAL MAP   IV

CONTENTS   V

GEOGRAPHICAL AREAS:

    Chapter 1:   Buxton and the Dark Peak   1
    Chapter 2:   Bakewell, Matlock and the White Peak   33
    Chapter 3:   Dovedale and the Staffordshire Moorlands   81
    Chapter 4:   The Trent Valley   107
    Chapter 5:   The Amber Valley and Erewash   131
    Chapter 6:   The Derbyshire Coal Mines   159

INDEXES AND LISTS:

    List of Tourist Information Centres   183
    Index of Towns, Villages and Places of Interest   184
    List of Advertisers   190

ADDITIONAL INFORMATION:

    Order Forms   195
    Reader Comment Forms   199

1 Buxton and The Dark Peak

The Peak District and the surrounding area, situated right at the centre of England, is truly a microcosm of the country. It divides the rugged north from the softer pastoral countryside of the south. There are spectacular rock formations, windswept moorlands, undulating pastures, picturesque villages and historic churches and castles. The Romans have left their roads and the remains of their forts and baths, there are Saxon and Norman churches and the Civil War raged through the area leaving a trail of destruction. Mainly agricultural for hundreds of years with some coal mining and ironworks, the industrial revolution transformed the area as mills, mines and works sprang up everywhere. As the population of the towns grew, the factory and mine owners built houses for the workforce, churches and grand civic buildings and left a rich legacy of Victorian architecture.

Black Tor and Loose Hill, High Peak

The first of Britain's National Parks, The Peak District itself covers an area of 540 square miles close to the large industrial conurbations of middle England. The National Park is scattered with the remains of ancient settlements. The northern area of the Peak District National Park, known as the Dark Peak or High Peak is a landscape of moorlands and deep valleys edged with escarpments of dark sandstone and shale. The rugged Millstone Grit moorlands and crags enclose the softer limestone plateau of the White Peak like a horseshoe. The southern section of the Peak District is the beautiful Dovedale. The River Dove is a famous fishing river, first mentioned in Izaak Walton's *The Compleat Angler,* in 1653. The River Manifold too has wonderful scenery including the beautifully preserved estate village of Ilam. The ancient custom of well-dressing is found mainly in these limestone areas of Derbyshire, where the streams frequently disappear through the porous rock.

The Amber Valley, the Erewash and the Trent Valley, to the east and south of Derbyshire, although not part of the National Park, have many pleasant walks and magnificent stately homes for visitors to enjoy. Derbyshire was at the forefront of the Industrial Revolution and its history is recorded in the Industrial Museum at Derby. It is reflected too in many of the villages with their rows of 18th and 19th century workers' cottages. To the northeast of Derbyshire is the heart of the coal-mining area, which prospered during the 19th and early 20th century. Sometimes overlooked, this part of Derbyshire is well worth exploring for its industrial architecture alone.

On the southern edge of the Peak District, the undulating pastures and crags of the Staffordshire Moorlands are ideal places to walk, cycle or trek. It is a mixture of

(Continued page 3)

2 The Hidden Places of Derbyshire

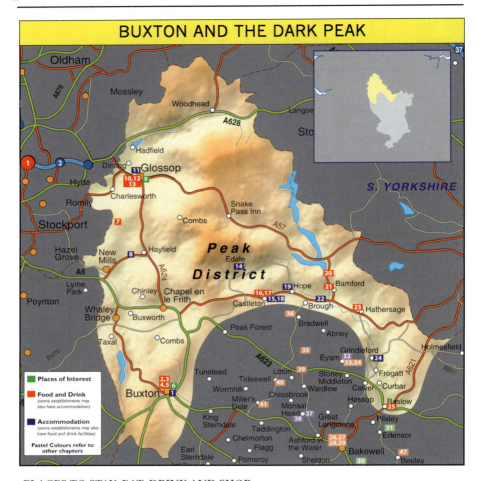

PLACES TO STAY, EAT, DRINK AND SHOP

1	Kings Croft, Buxton	Guest House	Page 4
2	The White Lion, Buxton	Pub	Page 4
3	The Miltons Head, Buxton	Pub with Restaurant	Page 6
4	The Robin Hood, Buxton	Pub with Food	Page 6
5	Café Nats and Bar Nats at The George, Buxton	Café with Accommodation	Page 6
6	Buxton Museum and Art Gallery, Buxton	Museum	Page 8
7	Little Mill Inn, Rowarth, Nr Via Marple Bridge	Pub, Restaurant and Accommodation	Page 14
8	Spinney Cottage, Birch Vale, Nr High Peak	Bed & Breakfast	Page 14
9	Glossop Heritage Centre, Glossop	Heritage Centre	Page 15
10	The Rainbow Bistro, Glossop	Restaurant	Page 15
11	Windy Harbour Farm Hotel, Glossop	Hotel	Page 15
12	The Queens Hotel, Old Glossop	Pub, Food and Accommodation	Page 16
13	Barista Coffee and Patisserie, Glossop	Café	Page 16
14	The Rambler Country House, Edale	Country House Hotel	Page 18

PLACES TO STAY, EAT, DRINK AND SHOP (CONT.)

15	Eastry Cottage and Hillside House, Castleton	Self Catering and Bed & Breakfast	Page 20
16	Ye Olde Nags Head, Castleton	Pub, Restaurant, Accommodation and Tea Rooms	Page 20
17	Rose Cottage Café, Castleton	Café and Tea Rooms	Page 21
18	Causeway House, Castleton	Bed & Breakfast	Page 22
19	Underleigh House, Hope	Bed & Breakfast	Page 24
20	The Ladybower Inn, Bamford	Pub, Restaurant and Accommodation	Page 24
21	Yorkshire Bridge Inn, Bamford	Pub, Food and Accommodation	Page 25
22	The Rising Sun Hotel, Bamford	Hotel	Page 26
23	Oddfellows Pool Café & Tea Rooms, Hathersage	Café and Tea Rooms	Page 28
24	Sir William Hotel, Grindleford	Hotel and Pub	Page 29
25	Garden Café, Baslow	Café and Gift Shop	Page 31

charming villages, historic market towns, ancient farms and relics of the Industrial Revolution including the reservoirs of Rudyard and Tittesworth, originally the water supply for the Midlands, now peaceful havens for wildlife and leisure.

Referred to as the Dark Peak as well as the High Peak, the northern area of the Peak District National Park is not as foreboding as its names might suggest. It is a landscape of moorlands and deep valleys edged with escarpments of dark sandstone and shale. The rough Millstone Grit moorlands and crags enclose the softer landscape of the White Peak like a horseshoe. These high moors are ripe for exploring on foot, and a walk from the Kinder Reservoir will lead to the western edge of Kinder Scout. This whole area is really a series of plateaux, rather than mountains and valleys, with the highest point on Kinder Scout some 2,088 feet above sea level. In this remote and wild area the walker can feel a real sense of freedom - however, it is worth remembering that the moors, with their treacherous peat bogs and unpredictable mists which can rise quickly even in summer, should not be dismissed as places for a casual ramble.

Pavilion Gardens, Buxton

To the eastern side of this region are the three reservoirs created by flooding of the upper valley of the River Derwent. Howden, Derwent, and Ladybower provide water for the East Midlands but their remote location, along with the many recreational activities found there, make them popular places to visit. The Derwent dam is particularly famous as the site of practice exercises for the Dambusters of the Second World War. Even those who have not visited the area before will be familiar with some of the place names, as they feature heavily in winter weather reports. Snake Pass (the A57), one of the few roads that runs through this northern section of the National Park, is often closed during the winter; and even in spring, conditions can deteriorate quickly to make driving hazardous.

KINGS CROFT

10 Green Lane, Buxton, Derbyshire SK17 9DP
Tel: 01298 22757 Fax: 01298 27858
e-mail: kings_croft@btopenworld.com
website: kingscroft-buxton.co.uk

Kings Croft is an elegant late-Victorian Guest House located in a central yet quiet position in the popular town of Buxton. Lying in the heart of the Peak District, this would make an ideal base for exploring the countryside, visiting the many historic houses in the area, or perhaps enjoying the cultural offerings of the Buxton Opera House. Owned and personally run by David Sedgwick, with the assistance of manageress Baz Sitcheran, here you will find period décor and furnishings and comfortable, relaxed surroundings. There are eight superior en-suite rooms available, of varying sizes, all decorated and furnished to a high standard.

The rooms are also thoughtfully provided with a colour TV and video, tea and coffee making facilities and hairdryers. The elevated location means that the bedrooms enjoy some fine views over the town and surrounding countryside. In the morning you can sample the home-cooked breakfast with an option for a continental breakfast should you prefer. Vegetarians and other special dietary requirements can also be catered for on request. Kings Croft is licensed, so in the evening you can enjoy a drink in the lounge. Although evening meals are not served, there are a number of fine eating establishments in Buxton which can be recommended. Special rates for longer stays. Off-road car parking.

THE WHITE LION

Spring Gardens, Buxton, Derbyshire SK17 6BZ
Tel: 01298 23099

The White Lion public house is a distinguished establishment located in a traffic-free precinct in Buxton town centre close to all of the town's amenities, including the Opera House. The convenient location makes this an ideal place to enjoy a refreshing drink while sight-seeing or shopping and proves to be popular with locals and visitors alike. Occupying a listed building it dates back in parts to 1661 and was originally a coaching inn. Inside there is a traditional feel, with the deceptively spacious

interior divided into three bars, including one with pool tables and a football table.

The Tap Room is cosy, welcoming and furnished with an eye towards comfort - it is a relaxing place where guests can enjoy the many offerings of the bar. There are two real ales kept on tap – Marston's Pedigree and Bitter – together with a good selection of lagers and a variety of wines and spirits. Owner Ann Smith has run the pub for over 20 years – she brings a wealth of experience to the task and offers every visitor a genuinely warm welcome. Open all day every day.

BUXTON

Referred to as the heart of the Peak District, Buxton, like Bakewell, is right on the divide between the Dark Peak and White Peak areas of the National Park and a large part of the White Peak lies between the two towns. Buxton is England's highest market town at 1,000 feet above sea level and provides a wealth of things to do. The current popularity of the town can be attributed to the 5th Duke of Devonshire; however it was the Romans who first discovered the waters here and named the place *Aquae Arnemetiae* - The Spa of the Goddess of the Grove. With waters maintained at a constant temperature of 82 degrees F (28 degrees C), Buxton soon became a place of pilgrimage, particularly for sufferers of rheumatism. Among the pilgrims from all over Britain was Mary Queen of Scots, held at Chatsworth for many years. **St Anne's Well** still provides water and many people coming to the town make a point of trying the tepid waters. The people of Buxton also say that it makes the best cup of tea possible, and collect bottles of it to take home.

In the 18th century, the 5th Duke of Devonshire, with the intention that Buxton would rival Bath as a spa town, commissioned the building of The Crescent to ensure that visitors would flock here. Designed by John Carr of York, the building is similar to the architecture found in Bath and, after suffering from neglect, underwent a huge restoration programme. Next to The Crescent, the Thermal Baths are now the Tourist Information Centre, and the former town house of Bess of Hardwick and her husband the Earl of Shrewsbury, where Mary Queen of Scots stayed when she visited Buxton, is now the Old Hall Hotel.

As with many places, the coming of the railway to Buxton in 1863 marked the height of popularity of the town. Nothing,

Pavilion Gardens, Buxton

The Miltons Head

Spring Gardens, Buxton, Derbyshire SK17 6BJ
Tel/Fax: 01298 22041

The Miltons Head lies in the heart of Buxton Town in the pedestrianised Spring Gardens area. In premises that date back over 200 years, the pub can boast a varied history including in the last century having been a police station and a place where the Yeomanry enlisted new recruits. With there being plenty to see and do in the town this makes an ideal stop while shopping or sightseeing, especially as it's open all day, seven days a week.

Here, in the cosy, comfortable interior, customers can enjoy a refreshing drink from the well-stocked bar with a selection that

includes Caffreys, Stones, Boddingtons and Guinness. The pub is recommended for its food, but serving times can vary through the year so ring ahead to be sure it will be available at the time you visit. Meals can be taken in the intimate non-smoking restaurant, or in the lounge and tap room should you prefer. The chef offers a good range of home-made dishes, with a sizeable main menu supplemented by daily specials. It is advisable to book ahead for Saturday night, Sunday lunch and during the Buxton Festival. Children are welcome if they are eating.

The Robin Hood

131 London Road, Buxton, Derbyshire SK17 9NW
Tel/Fax: 01298 24335
e-mail: ben.markie@btinternet.com

Situated directly on the main Ashbourne road, just a short stroll from the centre of Buxton, you will find **The Robin Hood**. Popular with locals and visitors, a warm welcome is assured. Open all day every day, the bar stocks a choice of real ales and an excellent menu of food is available most lunchtimes and evenings, with all the dishes home-made and cooked to order. Bookings required for Sunday lunch. Live music Fridays and a quiz on Wednesday nights.

Café Nats and Bar Nats at The George

9/11 Market Street, Buxton, Derbyshire SK17 6JY
Tel: 01298 23969
The Square, Buxton, Derbyshire SK17 6AZ
Tel: 01298 24711

Café Nats is one of two fine establishments owned by Sue and Mike Jordan and can be found in the centre of Buxton. Open daily 10am to 9pm and 10am to 6pm Sundays, (closed Bank Holidays), here you can enjoy a drink, light snack or a full meal, from a superb menu. There are five en-suite letting rooms also available. Three years ago the couple created **Bar Nats at The George** and have restored it to its former glory. Open all year for fine ales and food.

however, could be done to alter the harsh climate, and the incessant rainfall meant that the Duke's dream of making Buxton the 'Bath of the North', was never truly realised.

Among the other notable architectural features of the town are **The Colonnade** and the Devonshire Royal Hospital. They were originally built as stables for hotel patrons of The Crescent and, after their conversion by the 6th Duke in 1858, the largest unsupported dome in the world was built to enclose the courtyard in 1880.

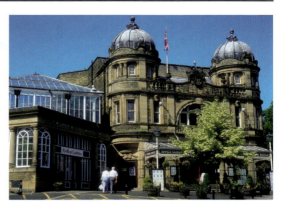

Buxton Opera House

The attractive **Buxton Opera House** was designed and built in 1903 by the renowned theatre architect, Frank Matcham. Gertrude Lawrence, Gracie Fields and Hermione Gingold all played here and on one memorable occasion, the famous Hollywood screen stars Douglas Fairbanks and Mary Pickford were in the audience to watch the Russian ballerina, Anna Pavlova. However in the 1930s it was the cinema, which virtually wiped out live performances for many years, apart from an annual pantomime and a handful of amateur performances. Restored in 1979, to its grand Edwardian style, it once again hosts live performances. The Buxton Opera Festival is one of Britain's best-known and largest opera-based festivals and, since 1994, the International Gilbert & Sullivan Festival has been held here. Throughout the rest of the year, its comprehensive and popular programme has won it a well deserved reputation nationally and internationally.

The Opera House stands in 23 acres of ornamental gardens in the heart of Buxton. The attractive **Pavilion Gardens** have a conservatory and octagon within the grounds - antique markets and arts shows are often held here, and it is a very pleasant place to walk at any time of year. Laid out in 1871 by Edward Milner, with money donated by the Dukes of Devonshire, the 23 acres include formal gardens, serpentine walks and decorative iron bridges across the River Wye. The conservatory was reopened in 1982 following extensive renovation; there is also a swimming pool filled with warm spa water.

St John the Baptist church was built in Italian style in 1811 by Sir Jeffrey Wyatville. That same year Wyatville laid out The Slopes, the area below the Market Place in Upper Buxton. The grand Town Hall was built 1887—1889 and dominates the Market Place. Further down Terrace Road is the **Buxton Museum** (see panel on page 8), which reveals the long and varied history of the town and its surrounding area. As well as housing an important local archaeology collection, the Museum also has a fine collection of Ashford Marble, Blue John ornaments, paintings, prints, pottery and glassware.

It is not known for certain whether well-dressing took place in Buxton before 1840, though there are stories that Henry VIII put a stop to the practice, but it has

Buxton Museum and Art Gallery

Terrace Road, Buxton, Derbyshire SK17 6DA
Tel: 01298 24658 Fax: 01298 79394
e-mail: buxton.museum@derbyshire.gov.uk
website: www.derbyshire.gov.uk/libraries

Explore the Wonders of the Peak through seven time zones. Discover when sharks swam in warm 'Derbyshire' seas; when lions and sabre tooth cats terrorised mastodons. Meet the Roman Legionaries, and the scientists unravelling the history of Earth. In 2003, you will be able to enjoy an audio visit of the gallery.

For art lovers, enjoy intricate Ashford Black Marble inlay and Blue John ornaments, and a regular programme of exhibitions, featuring work by national and local artists, photographers and craftworkers. 2003 highlights include the Derbyshire Open Exhibition and works by Peter Knight. Programmes of activities for all the family accompany the exhibitions. The museum welcomes visits from school parties. Accessible for disabled, local parking (pay & display), shop, toilets and nearby tearooms.

certainly been a part of Buxton's cultural calendar since the Duke of Devonshire provided the townsfolk with their first public water supply at **Market Place Fountain**. From then on, High Buxton Well (as the fountain came to be called) and St Anne's Well were decorated sporadically. In 1923, the Town Council set about organising a well-dressing festival and carnival that continues to this day. Every year on the second Wednesday in July, this delightful tradition is enacted.

St Anne's Church, built in 1625, reflects the building work here before Buxton's 18th century heyday when limestone was the most common construction material rather than the mellow sandstone that dominates today.

Buxton is surrounded by some of the most glorious of the Peak District countryside. These moorlands also provide one of the town's specialities - heather honey. Several varieties of heather grow on the moors: there is ling, or common heather which turns the land purple in late summer; there is bell-heather which grows on dry rocky slopes; and there is cross-leaved heather which can be found on wet, boggy ground.

The town is also the starting point for both the Brindley Trail and the Monsal Trail. Covering some 61 miles, the Brindley Trail, which takes its name from the famous canal engineer, leads southwest to Stoke-on-Trent, while the Monsal Trail, beginning just outside Buxton at Blackwell Mill Junction, finishes at Coombs Viaduct near Bakewell, some 8 miles away.

AROUND BUXTON

To the west of Buxton lies **Axe Edge**, the highest point of which rises to 1,807 feet above sea level. From this spot on a clear day (and the weather here is notoriously changeable) the panoramic views of Derbyshire are overwhelming. Just beyond, at 1,690 feet above sea level, the **Cat and Fiddle Inn** is the second highest pub in England. Axe Edge Moor, which receives an average annual rainfall of over 4 feet, is strictly for hardened walkers. It should come as no surprise that this Moor is the source of several rivers which play important roles in the life of the Peak District. The River Dove and the River Manifold, which join at Ilam, rise not far from one another; the River Wye rises above Buxton to join the Derwent further south; the River Goyt, a major source of the Mersey, rises to the west of Axe Edge.

The entire length of the River Goyt can be walked, from its source to its confluence with the River Etherow to the north and just outside the boundaries of the National Park. Once marking the boundary between Derbyshire and Cheshire (which now lies just to the west), a walk along the Goyt takes in sections of the riverbank as well as the Errwood and Fernilee reservoirs before leaving Derbyshire just north of New Mills. Although the two reservoirs look well established and very much part of the landscape, they are relatively recent additions: the Fernilee was opened in 1938 while the Errwood was flooded in 1967.

Those who venture to Errwood Reservoir will be surprised to see rhododendrons growing near the banks of a man-made lake. They once stood in the grounds of Errwood Hall, which was built in the 1830s for the Grimshawe family. The house was demolished before the Reservoir was flooded, but the gardens were left to grow wild. Not far away can be seen the strange-looking **Spanish Shrine**. Built by the Grimshawes in memory of their Spanish governess, it is a small stone building with an unusual beehive roof.

The highest point in this area is Shining Tor, overlooking Errwood Reservoir and standing some 1,834 feet above sea level. To the north is **Pym Chair**, the point at which an old packhorse road running east to west crosses this gritstone ridge. An old salters' route, it was used for transporting salt from the Cheshire plains across the Peak District moorlands to the industrial and well-populated areas of south and west Yorkshire.

During the 19th century, the Goyt valley with its natural resources of both coal and water developed rapidly into one of the nation's major textile production centres. In order to service this growth, the valley also developed an intense system of transport including canals and railways. The rugged terrain that had to be negotiated has made for some spectacular solutions to major engineering difficulties.

Also to the west of town on Green Lane is **Poole's Cavern**, so called for 'The robber Poole', who supposedly lived in the cave in the 15th century. It is a natural limestone cave, which was used by tribes from the Neolithic period onwards. Archaeological digs have discovered Stone Age, Bronze Age and Roman artifacts near the cave entrance. Mary, Queen of Scots visited and the 'chair' she used is still in evidence, and pointed out during the regular tours of the cave on offer. The spectacular natural formations in the cavern include a large stalactite called the 'Flitch of Bacon' and the 'Poached Egg Chamber', with blue grey and orange formations, coloured by manganese and iron soaking down from the lime-tips above.

Poole's Cavern

Above the cavern and about 20 minutes' walk away is Grin Low Wood which is part of **Buxton Country Park** and the prominent folly and scenic viewpoint, built by public subscription in 1895, known as Solomon's Temple.

NORTH OF BUXTON

TAXAL
5 miles NW of Buxton off the A5004

Overlooking the Goyt Valley, Taxal is home to the church of **St James**, in which can be found a series of fascinating memorials - the earliest to William Jaudrell, who died in 1375, and Roger Jaudrell, a soldier at Agincourt.

West of Taxal are **Windgather Rocks**, a gritstone outcrop popular with trainee rock-climbers. East of the village is the elegant and gracious **Shallcross Hall**, dating back to the 18th century.

COMBS
3 miles N of Buxton off the A6

Combs Reservoir southwest of Chapel-en-le-Frith is crossed at one end by Dickie's Bridge. 'Dickie' is said to have resided at a farm in Tunstead where he was known as Ned Dixon. Apparently murdered by his cousin, he nevertheless continued his 'working life' as a sort of guard-skull, alerting the household whenever strangers drew near. Various strange occurrences are said to have ensued when attempts were made to move the skull.

The new road from Combs to Chapel was created because the railway bridge would not stand over the Dane Hey Road on account of 'Dickie's Skull', or more likely because of soft foundations. The Bridge was completed, but one night it collapsed, burying the workmen's tools. Local superstition has it that it was because Dickie was annoyed at the railway crossing Tunstead land.

Samuel Bagshaw's Directory for Derbyshire mentions that there were two beer houses and one public house in the village of Combs. One beer house was kept by John Lake at Dove Cottages, on the old road to Chapel, which was then called Dove Lane. A second beer house was kept by Isaac Lomas. It is said that this latter was once called the Robin Hood, while the one at Dove Cottages was known as the Little John.

The Beehive Inn public house began life in the 1860s - purportedly from profits made from the construction of the railway and the then 'new' road to Chapel - from stone out of Spire Hollin's Quarry, near the village. The cottage at the side of the Beehive was part of the old inn, and was enlarged with stone from the Combs Mill in about 1914. The landlord at the time, W Newlands, had his portrait painted by the famous artist Dugdale, who was then living in the cottage adjacent to the inn. This portrait was exhibited at the Royal Academy.

On Castleton Road just a few miles northeast of the town, the **Chestnut Centre** is a fascinating wildlife conservation centre, popular with children and adults alike. It is famed for its otters, with award-winning otter and owl enclosures set along an extensive circular nature trail, which meanders through some historic wooded parkland.

CHAPEL-EN-LE-FRITH
4 miles N of Buxton off the A6

This charming town is often overlooked by travellers on the bypass between Buxton and Stockport, but it repays a closer look.

In 1225 the guardians of the High Peak's Royal Forest purchased land from the Crown and built a chapel here, dedicating it to St Thomas à Becket of Canterbury. A century later the chapel was replaced with a more substantial building; further modernisation took place in the early 1700s. The building of the original chapel led to the foundation of the town and also its name, which is Norman French for 'chapel in the forest'. Although the term 'forest' suggests a wooded area, the frith or forest never really existed, but referred to the Royal Forest of the Peak, hunting grounds which extended over much of north Derbyshire during the Middle Ages.

A curious legacy has been passed down allowing owners of freehold land in the district the right to choose their vicar. The interior of the church boasts 19th century box pews and a monument to 'the Apostle of the Peak', William Bagshawe of nearby Ford Hall, a Non-Conformist minister of the late 17th century, who was forced to resign his ministry for refusing to accept the Book of Common Prayer.

In 1648 the church was used as a gaol for 1,500 Scottish prisoners and the dreadful conditions arising from such close confinement caused unimaginable suffering. Their ordeal lasted for 16 days and a total of 44 men died.

Chapel Brow is a steep and cobbled street lined with pictuesque little cottages leading down from the church to Market Street. An ancient market town, the cross still stands in Market Square, as do the town's stocks. This is the true centre of Chapel, surrounded by a variety of old inns and buildings.

CHINLEY
6 miles N of Buxton off the B6062

This small north Derbyshire village lays claim to the superb **Chinley Viaducts**, a masterpiece of Victorian engineering. Chinley Station was once an important railway junction, as the railway lines from Derby to Manchester and Sheffield linked up here. Chinley Chapel dates back to the late 17th century, looking deceptively like an ordinary house from the outside.

BUXWORTH
6½ miles N of Buxton off the B6062

Once known as Bugsworth, before the villagers got tired of the jokes and changed the village's name in 1929, Buxworth is the site of the terminal basin for the **Peak Forest Canal**, finished in 1800. The village is popular with visitors attracted by the historic Bugsworth Basin, where limestone and lime were brought down from the works up at Dove Holes to be transported by canal barge. The limestone was carried in small horse drawn wagons on the Peak Forest Tramway, which was operated in part by the force of gravity. The wagons were rolled down the track to the Basin full and then pulled back up empty by horses. The basin was not used after 1926 but re-opened in 1999 thanks to the efforts of the Inland Waterways Preservation society.

Buxworth used to have several public houses. Nowadays there is one Inn, the Navigation, and a war memorial club known as 'Buggy Club', where sixteen year old members are allowed with parental permission to buy alcohol at the bar.

WHALEY BRIDGE
6 miles N of Buxton off the A5004

This small industrial town at the gateway to the **Goyt Valley** grew up around the coal-mining and textile industries. Both have now gone, but the Peak Forest Canal flowing through the town remains very much the centre of activity.

The 'bridge' of the village's name crosses the River Goyt, on the site of what may once have been a Roman crossing.

Many of the old warehouses in Whaley Bridge have been restored and converted to meet the needs of the late 20th century and, where once narrow boats transported goods and raw materials to and from the town, boats can be hired to those who want to explore the delights of the waterways in the area.

The **Toddbrook Reservoir** was built in 1831 to be a feeder for the Peak Forest Canal. The wharf here is dotted with picturesque narrowboats.

Just outside Whaley Bridge is the curiously shaped ridge known as **Roosdyche**, a natural feature running up towards Eccles Pike. The great scoop taken out of the hillside was the result of glacier erosion, though its distinctive shape gave rise to the theory that it was once a racecourse for Roman chariots.

Above Roosdyche is **Bing Wood**, a charming name until the true meaning of Bing is revealed - it means 'slag heap' - a name that hearkens back to the locality's prominence during the 19th century in the coal industry.

Goyt Valley

LYME PARK
8 miles NW of Buxton off the A6

Lyme Park is an ancient estate, now in the hands of the National Trust, was given to Sir Thomas Danyers in 1346 by a grateful King Edward III after a battle at Caen. Danyers then passed the estate to his son-in-law, Sir Piers Legh, in 1388. It remained in the family until 1946, when it was given to the Trust. Not much remains of the original Elizabethan manor house; today's visitors are instead treated to the sight of a fantastic Palladian mansion, the work of Venetian architect Giacomo Leoni. Not daunted by the bleak landscape and climate of the surrounding Peak District, Leoni built a corner of Italy here in this much harsher countryside. Inside the mansion there is a mixture of styles: the elegant Leoni-designed rooms with rich rococo ceilings, the panelled Tudor drawing room, and two surviving Elizabethan rooms. Much of the three-dimensional internal carving is attributed to Grinling Gibbons, though a lot of the work was also undertaken by local craftsmen.

As well as the fantastic splendour of the mansion, the estate includes a late 19th century formal garden. The 17-acre Victorian garden is laid out with impressive bedding schemes, a sunken parterre, an Edwardian rose garden, Jekyll-style herbaceous borders, a reflection lake, a ravine garden and Wyatt conservatory. The garden is surrounded by 1400 acres of medieval deer park of moorland, woodland and parkland, including an early 18th-century hunting tower. Lyme featured as 'Pemberley' in the 1995 BBC film of Jane Austen's novel *Pride and Prejudice*.

The grounds now form a country park owned and managed by the National Trust and supported by Stockport Metropolitan Borough

Council. Though close to the Manchester suburb of Stockport, the estate lies wholly within the Peak District National Park.

NEW MILLS
9 miles N of Buxton off the A6015

Situated by the River Sett, New Mills takes its name from the Tudor corn mills that once stood on the riverbanks. Later, in the 18th and 19th centuries water power was used to drive several cotton-spinning mills in the town and, as New Mills grew, the textile industry was joined by engineering industries and the confectionery trade. There is a still a rich legacy of this industrial heritage to be found in the town. The Torr Mills featured on the millennium series of postage stamps issued by the Post Office. The elevated **New Mills Millennium Walkway**, built on stilts rising from the River Goyt, sits directly opposite the Torrs Mill. The walkway answered public demand for a route through the impassable gritstone **Torrs Gorge**. The gorge is an area of exceptional natural beauty and unique industrial archaeological heritage. The 175 yard long steel walkway is fixed to the rock face and adjoining railway retaining wall at a height of about 20 feet from the base of the 100 foot-deep gorge.

The Little Mill at Rowarth still retains a working water wheel, although the mill building is now a well-known public house. Opposite the library is the Police Station, where the ringleaders of the 'Kinder Trespassers' were kept in the cells, following their arrest in 1932, after the mass public trespass on Kinder Scout. Although it is now a private house, the site is identified by a plaque on the wall. The trespass was a significant factor in the creation of National Parks, to allow public access to the countryside.

The serious walker or the stroller can use New Mills as a starting point for various way-marked walks. The Goyt Valley Way leads south to Buxton via Whaley Bridge and the Goyt Valley north to Marple. There are local signposted walks below the Heritage Centre and the **Sett Valley Trail** follows the line of the old branch railway to Hayfield and then on to Kinder Scout. Opened in 1868, the single track line carried passengers and freight for over 100 years. However, by the late 1960s much of the trade had ceased and the line closed soon afterwards. In 1973, the line was reopened as a trail and is still well used by walkers, cyclists and horse riders and it takes in the remains of buildings that were once part of the prosperous textile industry. Kinder Scout is a high gritstone plateau, rising steeply from the surrounding ground to a height of around 600 metres. The edges are studded with rocky outcrops and crags and the highest point at 631 metres is Crowden Head. This is also the highest point in the Peak District.

HAYFIELD
9½ miles N of Buxton off the A624

This old village below the exposed moorland of Kinder Scout was once a staging post on the pack-horse route across the Pennines. The old pack-horse route went up the Sett valley and by Edale Cross, where the remains of an old cross can still be seen, down to Edale by Jacob's Ladder. Some ancient cottages still survive around the centre of the old village, and some local farmhouses date from the 17th century.

Hayfield is a popular centre for exploring the area and offers many amenities for hillwalkers. Like its neighbour New Mills, Hayfield grew up around the textile industry, in this case wool weaving and calico printing. Many of the houses were originally weavers' cottages. A curious building can be found in Market Street on the left of a small square known as Dungeon Brow. Built in 1799, this was the town's lock-up and was referred to as the New Prison. However, the stocks in front of the building appear to be somewhat newer than the prison itself.

At the other end of the Sett Valley Trail, the old station site has been turned into a picnic area and information centre. The elegant Georgian parish **Church of St Matthew** is a reminder of this Pennine town's former prosperity. **Bowden Bridge Quarry** was the starting point for the famous 'Mass Trespass' on Kinder Scout and is now a car park with public toilets and a Peak Park camp site opposite.

Three miles northeast of the town is **Kinder Downfall**, the highest waterfall in the county, where the River Kinder flows off the edge of Kinder Scout. In low temperatures the fall freezes solid - a sight to be seen. It is also renowned for its blow-back effect: when the wind blows, the fall's water is forced back against the rock and the water appears to run uphill! There are not many natural waterfalls in Derbyshire, so Kinder Downfall appears on most visitors' itineraries. Not far from the bottom of the fall is a small lake known as **Mermaid's Pool**. Legend has it that those who go to the pool at midnight on the night before Easter Sunday will see a mermaid swimming in the dark waters.

CHARLESWORTH
12 miles N of Buxton on the A626

On the western edge of the Pennines, Charlesworth has many old and typically Pennine cottages. Three storeys tall, they were built as weavers' cottages. Apart from the 1849 mock-Gothic parish church of St John the Baptist there is also a Catholic church built primarily for the Irish

LITTLE MILL INN
Rowarth, Via Marple Bridge, Nr. Stockport, Cheshire SK12 5EB
Tel: 01663 743178
website: www.thelittlemillinn.fsnet.co.uk

The **Little Mill Inn** can be found in the tiny hamlet of Rowarth and has such a lot to offer the customer that it is well worth a visit. Family-run, the inn is open all day every day serving a wide range of ales and food. Meals can be taken in the upstairs restaurant, in the bar or outside. The pretty surroundings include a fully working waterwheel, bed and breakfast accommodation in a restored Pullman railway carriage and separate self-catering holiday cottages.

SPINNEY COTTAGE
Spinnerbottom, Birch Vale, High Peak, Derbyshire SK22 1BL
Tel: 01663 743230

Spinney Cottage is the country home of Jackie and David Waterhouse - situated just a mile from Hayfield, an excellent area for walkers with a bridleway adjacent to the cottage leading onto Lantern Pike with its panoramic views of surrounding Peak District. Bed and breakfast accommodation can be found here with three cosy bedrooms, all having en-suite or private facilities. The house dates back to the 18th century and a traditional atmosphere has been retained throughout. The breakfasts are superb with plenty of choice and packed lunches can be provided on request – ideal for a day's walking or sight-seeing.

BUXTON AND THE DARK PEAK **15**

immigrants working in the nearby mills, which stands at the edge of the village in a lovely position near the banks of the River Etherow.

GLOSSOP
13 miles N of Buxton off the A624

At the foot of the Snake Pass, Glossop is an interesting mix of styles: the industrial town of the 19th century with its towering Victorian mills and the 17th century village with its charming old cottages standing in the cobble streets. Further back in time, the Romans came here and established a fort now known as **Melandra Castle**, but probably then called Ardotalia. Built to guard the entrance to Longdendale, little survives today but the stone foundations. The settlement developed further, as part of the monastic estates of Basingwerk Abbey in north Wales and the village received its market

GLOSSOP HERITAGE CENTRE
Bank House, Henry Street, Norfolk Square, Glossop, Derbyshire SK13 8BW
Tel: 01457 869176

Nestling at the bottom of the spectacular Snake Pass is the market town of Glossop in North West Derbyshire. **The Heritage Centre** is in the Town's central square, housing changing exhibitions, illustrating the rich history of Glossop. It has an authentic Victorian Kitchen and an Art Gallery. On the ground floor is an old cotton loom to illustrate that Glossop was a Cotton town, but today the Mills have gone and Glossop is now a Commuter town for Manchester, 12 miles away. Open Mon - Sat 10.30 - 4.30.

THE RAINBOW BISTRO
The Basement, 14 High Street East, Glossop, Derbyshire SK13 8DA
Tel: 01457 865990

Tucked away in a quiet corner of Glossop is the outstanding **Rainbow Bistro** owned and run by Sarah Jane Manwaring. Having previously managed a pub in Rome this is her first solo venture and the result is a popular, high class establishment. Here, in the cosy, intimate surroundings, you can enjoy superb food from a wide-ranging menu of freshly prepared dishes which use mainly locally-sourced produce and display a strong Continental influence. Open Tuesday to Saturday lunchtimes and Wednesday to Saturday evenings.

WINDY HARBOUR FARM HOTEL
Woodhead Road, Glossop, Derbyshire SK13 7QE
Tel/Fax: 01457 853107
e-mail: graham@windyharbourfarm.fsnet.co.uk
website: www.peakdistrict-hotel.co.uk

Enjoying a countryside location, just a short drive from Glossop, **Windy Harbour Farm Hotel** has been owned and run by Graham and Julie Caesar for four years. Here you will find comfortable hotel accommodation with nine guest rooms of various sizes. The farmhouse restaurant is open all day serving a wide variety of meals, snacks and cream teas to non-residents, and there is also a licensed bar. Small caravan and camp site nearby.

THE QUEENS HOTEL

Shepley Street, Old Glossop, Derbyshire SK13 7RZ
Tel: 01457 862451

Tucked away in Old Glossop, **The Queens Hotel** is a popular pub both with locals and visitors to the area. An historic establishment, dating back to the early 19th century, it has recently benefited from a complete refurbishment enhancing the characterful, cosy surroundings. Open all day every day, here you can sample some fine ales from the well-stocked bar and tasty home-made food, which is served all day and features mainly local produce. Also three, spacious, en-suite guest rooms available for bed and breakfast and short breaks.

BARISTA COFFEE AND PATISSERIE

7 Jackson Buildings, Victoria Street, Glossop,
Derbyshire SK13 8AQ
Tel: 01457 866707 Fax: 01457 891454

In the heart of Glossop, just off the main street, you will find **Barista**. Opened in 2001 by Anne and Brian Coll, this is a Continental-style café where you can enjoy hot and cold drinks, sandwiches made with baguettes freshly-baked on the premises each day, superb patisserie and much, much more. Open Monday to Saturday from 9.30am-4.30pm (9.30am-5pm on Saturday), the superb menu also includes Continental breakfasts, jacket potatoes, salads and wicked desserts. Most of the menu, including speciality coffee, is available to take away. Non-smoking throughout.

charter in 1290 but subsequently there was a decline in its importance. Little remains of Old Glossop except the medieval parish **Church of All Saints**.

Planned as a new town in the 19th century by the Duke of Norfolk, the original village stood on the banks of the Glossop Brook at the crossing point of three turnpike roads. The brook had already been harnessed to provide power for the cotton mills, as this was one of the most easterly towns of the booming Lancashire cotton industry. Many still refer to the older Glossop as Old Glossop and the Victorian settlement as Howard Town, named after the Duke, Bernard Edward Howard.

DINTING
13 miles N of Buxton off the A624

The impressive **Dinting Viaduct**, built to carry the main Sheffield to Manchester railway line, stands 120 feet high. The village church of the Holy Trinity was built in 1875 in Victorian Gothic style and has a tall and elegant spire.

HADFIELD
14 miles N of Buxton off the A624

The small village of Hadfield is the terminus of the **Longdendale Trail**, which follows the line of the former Manchester to Sheffield railway line and is part of the Trans-Pennine Trail. It is now a safe, traffic-free trail for biking and walking. Its level sandy surface makes it suitable for wheelchair users and less agile people, as well as for families with small children and pushchairs.

It runs for nearly 7 miles from Hadfield to the Woodhead Tunnels before crossing the A628 and up a steep moorland track towards the Yorkshire border at Salter's Brook. Longdendale itself is the valley of the River Etherow, and is a favourite place for day-trippers. Along the footpath through this wild and desolate valley there are many reminders of the past, including **Woodhead Chapel**, the graveyard of which has numerous memorials to the navvies, and their families, who died in an outbreak of cholera in 1849 while working on the Sheffield to Manchester railway line.

Old Hall in The Square is the oldest building in the village, built in 1646. The Roman Catholic Church of St Charles was built in 1868 by Baron Howard of Glossop; members of the Howard family are buried here.

Rushup Edge, High Peak

NORTH EAST OF BUXTON

From Glossop, the A57 East is an exhilarating stretch of road, with hair-pin bends, known as the Snake Pass. The road is frequently made impassable by landslides, heavy mist and massive snowfalls in winter but, weather permitting, it is an experience not to be missed. For much of the length of the turnpike road that Thomas Telford built across Snake Pass in 1821, the route follows the line of an ancient Roman road, known as Doctor's Gate, which ran between Glossop and a fort at Brough. The route was so named after it was rediscovered, in the 16th century, by Dr Talbot, a vicar from Glossop. The illegitimate son of the Earl of Shrewsbury, Talbot used the road with great frequency as he travelled from Glossop to his father's castle at Sheffield.

EDALE
8 miles NE of Buxton off the A625

In the valley of the River Noe, Edale marks the start of the **Pennine Way**. Opened in 1965, this long-distance footpath follows the line of the backbone of Britain for some 270 miles from here to Kirk Yetholm, just over the Scottish border. Though the footpath begins in the lush meadows of this secluded valley, it is not long before walkers find themselves crossing the wild and bleak moorland of featherbed Moss before heading further north to Bleaklow. Many travellers have spoken of Derbyshire as a county of contrasts, and nowhere is this more apparent than at Edale. Not only does the landscape change dramatically within a short

Pennine Way, Edale

The Rambler Country House

Edale, Hope Valley, Derbyshire S33 7ZA
Tel: 01433 670268 Fax: 01433 670106
e-mail: carolemikepowell@aol.com
website: www.theramblerinn.co.uk

The Rambler Country House can be found in the heart of the village of Edale, surrounded by the delightful countryside that is the Peak District. The village also lends its name to the valley which lies between Mam Tor, Lose Hill and Kinder Scout – all well known names to keen walkers – and is at one end of England's most famous long-distance footpath, the Pennine Way. Located close to the railway station, which lies on the scenic Manchester to Sheffield line, the house was built around 125 years ago and originally called The Railway. Around this time it would have been an inn with accommodation, catering to the railway workers and visitors to the area. Situated in the heart of this pretty village, the location makes this a perfect base for sightseeing and exploring.

On arriving at the Rambler Country House Hotel you cannot fail to be aware of the warm welcome from the friendly staff and the inviting décor of a traditional country inn. Whether you want a drink, a snack, or simply need an up-to-date weather forecast, the staff will go out of their way to ensure your every need is catered for. Open all day, the bar stocks a choice of four real ales with Grays, Bass and Theakstons being permanent features together with a rotating guest ale. You will also find Carling, Fosters, Woodpecker Cider, Strongbow and Guiness on tap.

Excellent food is served from midday until nine in the evening (until eight on Sundays) with plenty of seating throughout the bar and dining areas, accommodating up to 100 diners. The Rambler has established a far-reaching reputation for fresh, tasty and good value meals, served in a convivial atmosphere, with a number of regular customers coming here for dinner in the evenings. The chefs have created a tantalising menu ranging from vegetarian and fish dishes to the popular Lamb Henry, supplemented by a daily specials board. There is plenty of choice, including some lighter meal options, and a special children's selection too. The Sunday roasts are also exceedingly popular, and reservations are advised for these, Friday evenings, and throughout the weekend.

If you want a relaxing break, or a convenient base for a more active holiday, then The Rambler Country House Hotel also offers superb accommodation. There are nine, en-suite guest rooms, all comfortably furnished and thoughtfully provided with a courtesy welcome tray, colour satellite TV and direct dial telephone. The rooms are available in a variety of sizes and you can be sure of enjoying a peaceful nights sleep. Not far from the main building there is also a self-contained, self-catering holiday cottage which sleeps up to four adults. Ring for full details.

distance from the heart of the village, but the weather - as all serious walkers will know - can alter from brilliant sunshine to snowstorms in the space of a couple of hours.

The village, in the heart of dairy-farming and stock-rearing country, began as a series of scattered settlements that had grown around the shepherds' shelters or bothies. The true name of the village is actually Grindsbrook Booth, but it is commonly known by the name of the valley. Tourism first came to Edale with the completion of the Manchester to Sheffield railway in 1894, though at that time there was little in the way of hospitality for visitors. Today there are several hotels, camping sites, a large Youth Hostel and adventure and walking centres.

Castleton Village

Not far from the village is the famous **Jacob's Ladder**, overlooking the River Noe. Nearby is the tumbledown remains of a hill farmer's cottage; this was the home of Jacob Marshall, who some 200 years ago cut the steps into the hillside leading up to Edale Cross.

CASTLETON
8 miles NE of Buxton off the A625

Situated at the head of the Hope Valley, Castleton is sheltered by the Norman ruin of **Peveril Castle** (built by Henry II in the 1170s) and is overlooked by Mam Tor. Approaching Castleton from the west along the A625, the road runs through the **Winnats Pass**, a narrow limestone gorge. Thought to have been formed under the sea, from currents eroding the seabed, the gorge has been used as a road for centuries and is still the only direct route to the village from the west.

Originally laid out as a planned town below its castle, the shape of the village has changed little over the years and it has become a popular tourist centre. The mainly 17th century church of St Edmund was heavily restored in 1837, but retains its box pews and a fine Norman arch, as well as a Breechers Bible dated 1611.

On Oak Apple Day 29th May the ancient ceremony of Garlanding takes place and after the Garland has been paraded though the streets, it is hoisted to the top of Saint Edmund's Church tower. The ceremony celebrates the ending of winter, and the restoration of Charles II to the throne in 1660 after the rule by the parliamentarians.

The Garland is a wooden frame, with bunches of wild flowers attached and a small 'Queen's' wreath of garden flowers on top. The 'King', dressed in Stuart costume, with the garland on his shoulders tours the village on horseback followed by a procession and a band. At the end of the ceremony the garland is left

Eastry Cottage and Hillside House

Pindale Road, Castleton, Derbyshire S33 8WV
Tel/Fax: 01433 620312

Eastry Cottage can be found just off the Market Place in the picturesque village of Castleton at the very heart of the Peak District. The 300-year old cottage was once a tea shop and has recently been renovated and converted into comfortable self-catering accommodation for four people. A high standard of decoration and furnishings can be seen throughout, with the double and twin bedrooms enjoying views towards Mam Tor. A bathroom is provided with a shower over the bath while downstairs there is a spacious lounge/dining area and a fully fitted kitchen. The cottage is cleaned and maintained to an exceedingly high standard, and there are always a few little extras supplied, such as fresh flowers, toiletries and a pint of milk, to get your holiday off to a flying start.

Owner, Jayne Webster, lives on the outskirts of Castleton at **Hillside House**, just a short walk from Eastry Cottage. Her large country house is set in attractive gardens and she provides bed and breakfast with many of the guest rooms having panoramic views over the Hope Valley and beyond. There are two comfortable guest rooms providing clean, home-from-home accommodation. There is a double and a king-size room, both with en-suite facilities and provided with colour TV and hot drinks tray. A full English breakfast is served each morning and although evening meals are not served there are plenty of pubs and restaurants in the village.

Ye Olde Nags Head

Cross Street, Castleton, Derbyshire S33 8WH
Tel: 01433 620248   Fax: 01433 621501

In the heart of historic Castleton, **Ye Olde Nags Head** is a convenient and popular stopping place while visiting the many tourist attractions, exploring the town or shopping. The large public house enjoys a corner location and can be dated as far back as 1753. Enjoying a fine reputation throughout the area, it has recently been taken over by local couple Jenny and Richard Gill. Open all through the day, most days, the bar serves a good selection of ales, with the permanent real ale being Black Sheep with a second guest ale also kept on tap. The premises incorporate a delightful tearooms, which open from 9.30am until 5.30pm each day with seating for up to 50 customers. Each night a menu of meals and snacks is available in the bar areas, while on Friday and Saturday evenings the tearooms are transformed into an intimate restaurant. Each Friday a selection of at least eleven fish dishes are served alongside the main menu and to avoid disappointment, bookings for the restaurant are essential.

There is bed and breakfast accommodation available with ten en-suite guest rooms on offer. The rooms are of varying sizes, all are non-smoking, and children are welcome.

on the top of the tower of St Edmunds Church to wither and the Queen's wreath is placed on the war memorial. **Castleton Village Museum** in the Methodist Church School Room has a collection of Garland memorabilia, including a King's costume worn 200 years ago.

The hills to the west of Castleton are famous for their caves. The **Blue John Mine and Caverns**, which have been in the hands of the Ollerenshaw family for many years, are probably one of Derbyshire's most popular attractions. Amazing trips down into the caves themselves can be made. During these trips, as well as seeing the incredible natural beauty of the caverns and the unique rock formations, there are collections of original 19th century mining tools. Above ground, in the gift shops various items can be bought made with the distinctive Blue John fluorspar with its attractive purplish veining. The village's **Ollerenshaw Collection** of huge vases and urns made with the same unique stone is open to the public. Once prized by the Romans, it is said that Petronius paid the equivalent of around £40,000 for a wonderfully ornate vase carved from the stone. It is said that in a fit of petty-mindedness he preferred to smash the vase rather than relinquish it to the Emperor Nero.

Blue John Mine and Caverns

At the bottom of Winnats Pass only 1000 metres (0.6 miles) from the centre of the village, lies **Speedwell Cavern.** It is a very gentle walk along the road to this former lead mine, which used boats on an underground canal to ferry the miners and iron ore to and from the rockface. The mine had a short life: it started up in 1771 and, following an investment of £14,000, closed in 1790 after only £3,000 worth of iron ore had been extracted. The cave can only be explored by underground boat and

ROSE COTTAGE CAFÉ

Castleton, Hope Valley, Derbyshire S33 8WH
Tel: 01433 620472

Rose Cottage Café is a charming, family-run café and tea rooms, located on the main road running through the heart of Castleton. Alma Parkinson has been running the place for over 35 years and has now been joined by daughter Elizabeth. Open 10am until 5pm each day, except Friday, you can choose from a wide-ranging menu of light meals, snacks and drinks. Everything is home-made, from the cakes to the quiches, and freshly prepared to order. Seating for 50, with room for a further 24 on the patio.

visitors can follow the same boat journey as the miners underground in the company of a guide. This underground canal is about 800 metres long finally reaching a glorious cavern with a huge subterranean lake known as the Bottomless Pit.

Peak Cavern, reached by a delightful riverside walk, has the widest opening of any cave in Europe. Up until the 17th century, little cottages used to stand within the entrance. The ropemakers who lived in these tiny dwellings used the cave entrance for making rope, the damp atmosphere being a favourable environment for rope making. Bert Marrison, the last rope maker in Castleton, worked here. His ashes, along with some of his tools, are buried here. The ropewalk, which dates back some 400 years, can still be seen and guides re-enact the process of making rope. One ropemaker's cottage still exists. Recently the cave was used by the BBC, who filmed an episode of *The Chronicles of Narnia* series here. Over the years successive Kings and Queens would entertain deep within the belly of the cave, which would be festooned with candles and other open flames - visitors can see the ledge on which the Royal musicians would perch. Peak Cavern was originally known as The Devil's Arse, though the Victorians - ever fastidious - felt this was 'inappropriate' and changed it to the name it carries today.

Peveril Castle

Above Peak Cavern is **Peveril Castle** with its spectacular views over Castleton and the surrounding countryside. The Castle, originally called Castle of the Peak, was built as a wooden stockade in 1080 by William Peveril, illegitimate son of William the Conqueror. Later rebuilt in stone, the keep was added by Henry I in 1176. It was originally about 60 feet high and faced with gritstone blocks, which still remain

---

CAUSEWAY HOUSE

Back Street, Castleton, Hope Valley, Derbyshire S33 8WE
Tel: 01433 623291   Fax: 01142 360675
website: www.causewayhouse.co.uk

Conveniently situated in the heart of Castleton, **Causeway House** Bed and Breakfast makes an ideal overnight stop or a base for exploring the area. The quaint, stone-built 16th-century cottage is home to Christopher and Susan Lomas and they offer six comfortable en-suite guest rooms of varying sizes. They serve superb cooked or Continental breakfasts in the morning which are sure to set you up well for a day's sight-seeing or walking. Midweek breaks and discounts for longer stays. Non-smoking throughout. Children welcome.

on the east and south sides and still dominates the view across Castleton. The foundations of the Great Hall and kitchens can be seen inside the courtyard. It remains the only surviving example of a Norman castle in Derbyshire, and is among the best preserved and most complete ruins in Britain.

No description of Castleton would be complete without a mention of **Mam Tor**. The name means 'Mother Hill', and locally the Tor is referred to as Shivering Mountain, because the immense cliff face near the summit is constantly on the move owing to water seepage. It was used as a hill fort in the late Bronze Age or early Iron Age and a climb to the top of the ridge shows what a splendid vantage point it provides over the surrounding landscape, in particular of the two diverse rock formations, which differentiate the White (limestone) Peak from the northern Dark (gritstone) Peak.

Halfway up Losehill, midway between Castleton and Hope, visitors can find the 300 year old gritstone-built Losehill Farm, nicknamed **Crimea Farm** during the Crimean War, and still known as such locally. It is a traditional working farm, which combines agriculture with education, conservation, recreation and traditional rural crafts. The Weaving Shed houses displays of fleeces from rare breed sheep and goats. There is spinning and other craft work in progress such as paper-making and natural dyeing. There is a farm trail, which takes in bottle-fed lambs, kids and calves, free-ranging hens, ducks and geese, playful Pygmy goats, rare breed Golden Guernseys and angora goats.

HOPE
9 miles NE of Buxton off the A625

Hope gets its first mention in 926 as the site of a battle won by King Athelstan. By the time of the Domesday survey of 1086, the parish of Hope had extended to embrace much of the High Peak area and included places such as Buxton, Chapel-en-le-Frith and Tideswell. It remained one of the largest parishes in the country until the 19th century, though a market charter was not granted it until 1715. Hope lies at the point where the River Noe meets Peakshole Water, which takes its name from its source in **Peak's Hole**, better known as Peak Cavern.

The parish **Church of St Peter** was built at the beginning of the 13th century; the only part remaining from the original church is the Norman font. The Latin inscription on a chair in the north aisle reads (in translation) 'You cannot make a scholar out of a block of wood' and is said to have been carved for Thomas Bocking, the vicar and schoolmaster here during the 17th century. His name also appears on the fine pulpit; his Breechers Bible is displayed nearby. From the outside, the squat 14th century spire gives the church a rather curious shape; in the churchyard can

Mam Tor

UNDERLEIGH HOUSE

off Edale Road, Hope, Hope Valley, Derbyshire S33 6RF
Tel: 01433 621372   Fax: 01433 621324
e-mail: underleigh.house@btinternet.com
website: www.underleighhouse.co.uk

Philip and Vivienne Taylor extend a warm welcome to all visitors to their charming home, **Underleigh House**. The extended barn and cottage conversion dates from 1873 and the cosy, traditional interior provides comfortable accommodation. The location, at the foot of Lose Hill and overlooking the Noe Valley, is as tranquil as it is stunning, and makes an ideal base for exploring the Peak District.

Underleigh has a superb reputation both with previous guests and all the major tourist guides, and has been awarded both a five diamond grading and a silver award from the English Tourism Council. There are six delightful bedrooms, all twins or doubles, with two on the ground floor. The Thornhill Suite has an adjoining lounge, corner bath, and its own direct access from the outside. The delicious breakfasts start any day in style and have received an award of their own – the AA's 'Egg Cup'

accolade for memorable breakfasts! They certainly are excellent, featuring Philip's home-made muesli, Aga-cooked porridge, local Derbyshire oatcakes, home-baked croissants, and much more. Among the home-made jams, three-fruit marmalade and Derbyshire honey, the Underleigh Breakfast Preserve comes highly recommended. Philip and Vivienne are only too happy to advise on your day's activities and can supply maps and a packed lunch if required. In the evening you can enjoy a drink on the terrace, or in front of a log fire in the lounge, and although evening meals are not served there are several fine eating establishments within a short drive.

THE LADYBOWER INN

Bamford (A57), Hope Valley, Derbyshire S33 0AX
Tel/Fax: 01433 651241
website: www.ladybower-inn.co.uk

The well-known **Ladybower Inn** can be found on the main A57 road and enjoys a prime location overlooking Ladybower Reservoir. The reservoir has an interesting history of its own having been constructed during the Second World War and flooding the villages of Derwent and Ashopton in the process. In 1943 it was also used as a practise site for the bouncing bomb by the famous Dambusters, immortalised

in the film of the same name. It is inevitable that the inn itself has an equally varied history and a detailed account can be found on its walls.

The current licensees are Deborah and Stephen, and they have been running the free house since August 2001. They open all day every day for a range of drinks, with two real ales on tap, and a varied selection of other lagers and beers. Deborah is an experienced chef and prepares an excellent menu of

dishes using locally sourced produce, with the speciality being game (when in season). The ever-changing menu of home-made dishes can be enjoyed in the non-smoking, 34-seater restaurant, for which bookings are essential, or alternatively meals can be taken in the bar, or outside. Food is served each lunchtime and evening and all day Friday to Sunday.

Bed and breakfast accommodation will shortly be available with seven en-suite guest rooms planned, including one on the ground floor and suitable for disabled guests. Ring for full details.

Ladybower Reservoir

be found the shaft of a Saxon cross.

The **Hope Agricultural Show** is held every year on August Bank Holiday Monday.

BROUGH
9 miles NE of Buxton off the A6187

At the village of Brough can be seen remains of the earthworks of the Roman fort of Navio. At the confluence of the River Noe and Bradwell Brook, this small, rectangular fort was built in AD158 to control the Romans' lead mining interests in the area. The site was excavated in the early 20th century.

BAMFORD
11 miles NE of Buxton off the A6187

This charming village situated between the Hope Valley and Ladybower Reservoir, stands at the heart of the Dark Peak below Bamford Edge and close to the Upper Derwent Valley Dams. When the Derwent and Howden Dams were built in the early years of the 20th century, the valley of the Upper Derwent was flooded, submerging many farms under the rising waters. The 1,000 or so navvies and their families were housed at Birchinlee, a temporary village which came to be known locally as 'Tin Town', for its plethora of corrugated iron shacks. During the Second World War the third and largest reservoir, the **Ladybower**, was built. This involved the inundating of two villages — Derwent and Ashopton. Many buildings were lost including ancient farms and Derwent Hall dating from 1672 and made into a youth hostel in 1931. The spire of the Parish church was visible at first, but was demolished in 1947. The dead from Derwent's church were re-interred in the churchyard of St John the Baptist in Bamford. The living were re-housed in Yorkshire Bridge, a purpose-built hamlet located below the embankment of the Ladybower Dam. A viaduct was built to carry the Snake Road over the reservoir at

YORKSHIRE BRIDGE INN
Ashopton Road, Bamford in the High Peak, Hope Valley, Derbyshire S33 0AZ
Tel/Fax: 01433 651361   e-mail: mr@ybridge.force9.co.uk
website: www.yorkshire-bridge.co.uk

For a friendly welcome, it would be difficult to beat the **Yorkshire Bridge Inn**, prettily located just a short stroll from Ladybower Reservoir. Privately owned and run by the Illingworth family this award-winning free house serves fine ales from a well-stocked bar. Tasty food, reasonably priced, is served each lunchtime and evening and all day Sunday from a wide-ranging menu. There are fourteen beautiful en-suite bedrooms available for bed and breakfast or short breaks all year round. Awarded ETC 2 stars Silver Award and AA 2 stars as well as being a finalist for Freehouse of the Year 2000 & 2001.

The Rising Sun Hotel

Castleton Road, Thornhill Moor, Bamford,
Hope Valley S33 0AL
Tel: 01433 651323 Fax: 01433 651601
e-mail: info@the-rising-sun.org
website: www.the-rising-sun.org

The elegant and charming **Rising Sun Hotel** can be found on the A625 Castleton to Hathersage road, in the ancient township of Thornhill. Located within the Hope valley, in the heart of the Peak District, this has inevitably become a popular stop for visitors to the area as well as attracting custom from the surrounding area. It is hard to believe that just two years ago, when the establishment was purchased by Carole and Graham Walker, that the property had been sadly neglected and was in a poor condition. The couple, with the help of daughter Helen, who is also the general manager, have completely refurbished the premises bringing them up to the very highest standards throughout and making this one of the most sought-after hotels in the area.

The inn dates back to 1795 when it was built by a local farmer to cater to the number of travellers using the coaching route between Manchester and Sheffield. By 1871 the area had become popular with Victorian tourists, who came to enjoy the picturesque surroundings, and it was around this time that the name was changed to the Rising Sun. Major additions were made to the structure in the 1920s and 30s, and this was when the former farmhouse became a hotel.

The Rising Sun is renowned for the quality of its food and its innovative menus. Graham is a chef and together with Carole oversees all the cooking. The elegant restaurant can seat up to 90 diners and presents an a la carte menu of tantalising dishes ranging from fresh Cromer Crab to Fillet of Venison. The menu is described as the very best of traditional British food with modern European and Oriental influences, all prepared using the freshest produce, so everyone is sure to find something to suit their taste and appetite. At lunchtimes (except Sunday) there is also a selection of light meals and sandwiches. Reservations are advisable for Thursday and Friday evenings and all weekend. The bar is open all day too, serving a good range of real ales, fine wines and other liquid refreshment. You can also enjoy a cup of coffee at any time of the day. Children are welcome and there are some non-smoking areas.

The superb accommodation comprises 12 individual bedrooms, ranging from singles and doubles to family rooms and suites. Like the rest of the property, they have recently been refurbished and redecorated, to provide comfortable surroundings in which to relax. The rates are extremely reasonable, and range from room only, bed and breakfast or an all inclusive dinner, bed and breakfast rate. The family pride themselves on their friendly, traditional service and look forward to welcoming you soon. This is not just another hotel - this is an experience.

Ashopton and another for the road to Yorkshire Bridge. The packhorse bridge at Derwent, which had a preservation on it, was moved stone by stone and rebuilt at Slippery Stones at the head of the Howden Reservoir. There is a Visitor Centre at **Fairholmes** (in the Upper Derwent Valley), which tells the story of these 'drowned villages'.

The **Derwent Dam**, built in 1935, was the practice site for the Dambusters, who tested dropping their bouncing bombs here.

Bamford's **Church of St John the Baptist** is unlike any other in Derbyshire. Designed in 1861 by famous church architect William Butterfield, it has a slender tower and an extra-sharp spire. Also worthy of note, particularly to lovers of industrial architecture, is **Bamford Mill**, just across the road by the river. This cotton mill, built in 1820, retains its huge waterwheel and also has a 1907 tandem-compound steam engine. Like many cotton mills of its time, the original mill burnt to the ground just 10 years after it was erected. The mill standing today was its replacement. It ceased to operate as a cotton mill in 1965 and was used by an electric furnace manufacturer until a few years ago. It has now been converted into flats. The village lies in the heart of hill-farming country, and each Spring Bank Holiday Bamford plays host to one of the most famous of the Peak District Sheepdog Trials, which draws competition from all over the country.

Along the A57 towards Sheffield, the road dips and crosses the gory-sounding **Cutthroat Bridge**. The present bridge dates back to 1830, but its name comes from the late 16th century, when the body of a man with his throat cut was discovered under the bridge which then stood here.

Derwent Valley

HATHERSAGE
12 miles NE of Buxton off the A625

The name Hathersage comes from the Old English for 'Haefer's ridge' - probably a reference to the line of gritstone edges of which the moorland slopes of **Stanage Edge**, overlooking the town to the east, is the largest. It is surrounded by spectacular tors, such as Higgar Tor, and the ancient fortress at Carl Wark. Several of the edges were quarried for millstones for grinding corn and metals.

It is difficult to know whether to classify Hathersage as a large village or a small town. In either event, it is a pleasant place with interesting literary connections. Charlotte Bronte stayed at Hathersage vicarage in 1845, and the village itself appears as 'Morton' in her novel *Jane Eyre*. The name Eyre was probably gleaned from the monuments to the prominent local landowners with this surname, which can be seen in the village church of St Michael and its churchyard.

The Eyre family has been associated with this area for over 800 years. Legend has it

Stanage Edge

that the family were given their name by William the Conqueror. During the Battle of Hastings, so it is said, William was knocked from his horse and, wearing his now battered helmet, found it difficult to breathe. A Norman, Truelove, saw the King's distress and helped him take the helmet off and get back on his horse. In gratitude the King said that from thenceforth Truelove would be known as 'Air' for helping the King to breathe. Later the King learned that Air had lost most of a leg in the battle, and made arrangements that Air and his family were cared for and would be granted land in this part of Derbyshire. The name became corrupted to Eyre over the years, and the family's coat of arms shows a shield on top of which is a single armoured leg. The 15th century head of the family, Robert Eyre, lived at Highlow Hall. Within sight of this Hall he built seven houses, one for each of his seven sons. **North Lees** was one, which Charlotte Bronte took as a model for Rochester's house, Thornfield Hall. It is one of the finest Elizabethan buildings in the region - a tall square tower with a long wing adjoining and the grounds are open to the public. Another was **Moorseats**, where Charlotte Bronte stayed on holiday and used as the inspiration for Moor House in *Jane Eyre*.

In Hathersage churchyard lie the reputed remains of Little John, Robin Hood's renowned companion. Whether or not the legend is to be believed, it is worth mentioning that when the grave was opened in the 1780s, a 32-inch thighbone was discovered. This would certainly indicate that the owner was well over seven feet tall.

Until the late 18th century Hathersage was a small agricultural village with cottage industries making brass buttons and wire, until in 1750 a Henry Cocker started the Atlas Works, a mill for making

ODDFELLOWS POOL CAFÉ AND TEA ROOMS

Oddfellows Road, Hathersage, Hope Valley, Derbyshire S32 1AC
Tel/Fax: 01433 651159

Oddfellows Pool Café and Tea Rooms can be found beside Hathersage Swimming Pool where the two have stood since they were established by local benefactor Mr Oddfellow in the 1930s. The café is open each day from 10am to around 8pm serving a varied menu of meals, snacks and drinks, together with a poolside and takeaway menu too. Traditional Sunday lunches are served and the home-made cake selection is tempting at any time. Friendly, helpful service.

wire. By the early 19th century it had become a centre for the manufacture of needles and pins. Though water power was used initially for the mills, by the mid 19th century smoke from the industrial steam engines enveloped the village. The fragments of dust and steel dispersed in the process of sharpening the needles destroyed the lungs of the workers, reducing their life expectancy to 30 years. The last mill here closed in 1902, as needle making moved to Sheffield but several of the mills still stand, including the Atlas Works.

Longshaw Country Park

Hathersage has a superb outdoor swimming pool, open to the public at certain times throughout the summer holidays.

EAST EDGES OF THE DARK PEAK

GRINDLEFORD
6 miles N of Bakewell off the B6521/B6001

This is one of the smallest Peak District villages and from here, each year in July, there is a pilgrimage to **Padley Chapel** to commemorate two Catholic martyrs of 1588. The ruins of ancient Padley Manor House, found alongside the track bed of the old railway line, are all that remain of the home of two devout Roman Catholic families. It was from here that two priests, Robert Ludlam and Nicholas Garlick were taken, in the 16th century, and sentenced to death, in Derby, by hanging, drawing and quartering. The then owner of the house, Thomas Fitzherbert, died in the Tower of London three years later whilst his brother died at Fleet Prison in 1598. In 1933, the charming chapel seen today was converted from the still standing farm buildings.

To the northwest of the village is the **Longshaw Country Park**, some 1,500 acres of open moorland, woodland and

SIR WILLIAM HOTEL
Grindleford, Hope Valley, Derbyshire S32 2HS
Tel: 01433 630303
e-mail: sirwilliamhotel@btinternet.com
website: www.sirwilliamhotel.com

The Sir William is a friendly, family-owned hotel and village pub dating back to the early 19th century. It is a welcoming establishment run by Philip and Diane Cone who have created a lovely place to stay with a special family atmosphere. In the relaxed setting of the bar customers can enjoy home-cooked dishes, choosing from a varied menu guaranteed to appeal to every taste. There are also seven comfortable en-suite guest rooms furnished to a high standard of comfort.

the impressive Padley Gorge. Originally the Longshaw estate of the Dukes of Rutland, the land was acquired by the National Trust by the 1970s. At the heart of the country park, is the Duke's former shooting lodge.

FROGGATT
5 miles N of Bakewell off the B6054

Nearby **Stoke Hall**, situated high above the Derwent Valley, was built in 1755 for Lord Bradford and was later leased to Robert Arkwright, son of Sir Richard Arkwright, who lived here while he managed the Lumsford Mill at Bakewell. The Hall is now a hotel and restaurant, but remains home to a ghost, said to have been haunting the building for well over 100 years. The ghost is claimed to be that of a maid at the Hall who, while pining for a soldier fighting overseas, was brutally murdered. Her employers at the Hall were so shocked by this that they built a memorial to her in the front garden. However, the memorial was seen to move not long after it had been erected, and so it was rebuilt in a quiet corner of the estate, where it remains undisturbed.

CURBAR
5 miles NE of Bakewell off the A623

Curbar is a hillside village very close to Calver. It grew up up around the crossing point of the River Derwent on the old turnpike road.

Although it is Eyam that is famous as the Plague Village, many communities suffered greatly at the hands of this terrible disease. During the height of the infection bodies were interred away from the centre of the village, and usually as quickly as possible, to prevent the spread of the disease. Many of the graves were left unmarked, but at Curbar the **Cundy Graves** (dating from 1632) can be seen on the moors above the village and below the Wesleyan Reform Church.

Missionaries used to be trained at Cliffe college, Curbar in the 19th century. It is now a college of Sheffield University, sponsored by the Methodist Church and operates as a training centre and a conference centre. Interesting older features of the village include a circular pinfold or stock compound on top of Pinfold Hill, where stray animals were kept until claimed by their owners, a covered well and circular trough, and an unusual village lock-up with a conical roof. The coarse gritstone ridge of **Curbar Edge**, which shelters the village, is popular with rock climbers.

Froggatt Edge

CALVER
4 miles NE of Bakewell off the A623

Recorded as Calvoure in the *Domesday Book*, evidence of an early Anglo Saxon settlement was found when skeletons were discovered in limestone rock in 1860. It is a pleasant stone-built village, situated by the River Derwent, with a pleasing 18th century bridge, which no longer carries the main road over the river. Calver is home to one of the most sinister buildings known to television viewers with long memories. The handsome, though austere, **Georgian Cotton Mill**, which is now converted into luxury flats, was the infamous Colditz Castle of the television series of that name.

BASLOW
4 miles NE of Bakewell off the A619

Standing at the northern gates to Chatsworth, Baslow has for centuries been closely linked with the affairs of the Cavendish family. The village has three distinct parts – Bridge End the oldest part around the church, Over End, a residential area to the north of the village and Nether End next to the Chatsworth Estate. The village is unusual in having thatched cottages rather than the more traditionally tiled, slate or gritstone shingled roofs. Though more houses in the area were thatched they are much less common today and give the village a very distinctive air. The village **Church of St Anne**, beautifully situated by the River Derwent, has a squat broach spire that dominates the village. The church has an unusual clock face, added to commemorate Queen Victoria's Diamond Jubilee in 1887, that is well worth a second glance. The idea of a local man, Dr Wrench, instead of the usual numerals the clock face has "Victoria" and "1897" around the edge. An ancient Saxon cross

GARDEN CAFÉ
Church Street, Baslow, Derbyshire DE45 1RY
Tel: 01246 582619 Fax: 01246 583888

In the centre of Baslow, lying on the A623 through road, you will find the charming **Garden Café**. This is a real gem, created by Linda and John Lowen just two years ago, and in just a short time it has become a highly popular eating place attracting regular customers from the surrounding area.

Open daily from 9am until 5pm, the regular menu offers a fine selection of home-made dishes. The range includes breakfasts, light meals, sandwiches, salads, drinks, cakes, and much more. The surroundings are charming and the service is excellent, all resulting in the Garden Café having been awarded Best Tea and Coffee House of 2001/2 by both Derbyshire Country Council and the English Tourist Board. On Friday and Saturday evenings, the café opens as a restaurant, serving a seasonal menu of delicious dishes which are sure to tempt any palate. It is essential to book for this in advance.

Adjacent to the Garden Café, Linda and John also own and run Avant Garde, where they sell a range of stylish items for the home and garden. Here you will find all sorts of things, ranging from furniture and wicker baskets, to vases and artificial flowers, books and giftwrap. Well worth a visit either for a gift for a friend, or a treat for yourself.

can also be found in the churchyard. Inside the church another unusual feature is preserved: the whip that was used to drive stray dogs out of the church during services.

The key building in the village is the Cavendish Hotel, which was originally known as the Peacock Hotel when it was in the ownership of the Duke of Rutland. The Hotel passed into the hands of the Duke of Devonshire in the 1830s and also changed its name to reflect its new owner. Extensively restored in the 1970s, the Hotel is famous for the 10 miles of trout fishing it offers along the banks of the Derwent and Wye rivers.

Baslow sits beneath its own Peakland "edge", which provides fine views across the Derwent Valley towards Chatsworth House. From the **Eagle Rock,** a 6 metre high block of gritstone on Baslow Edge, to the north of the village, there are wonderful views. Climbing to the top of this isolated rock was a test for every young Baslow man before he married. It is here that Dr Wrench, in 1866, erected the Wellington Monument to celebrate the Duke's victory at Waterloo and to counterbalance the monument to Nelson on Birchen Edge not far away.

Baslow has two very fine bridges over the Derwent. The **Bridge End Bridge**, which is near the church, was built in 1603 and features a tiny tollhouse with an entrance only 3½ feet high. It is the only bridge across the Derwent, which has never been destroyed by floods. The bridge at Nether End is a neighbour of one of the few thatched cottages in the Peak District.

2 Bakewell, Matlock and The White Peak

This region of the Derbyshire Dales, sometimes also known as the Central Peaks and occupying the central area of the Peak District National Park between the two major towns of Bakewell and Buxton, is less wild and isolated than the remote High Peak area. The limestone plateau of the White Peak was laid down in a tropical sea over 300 million years ago, along with the fossilized remains of countless tiny sea creatures. The two main rivers, the Wye and the Derwent, which both have their source further north, are, in this region, at a more gentle stage of their course. Over the centuries, the fast-flowing waters were harnessed to provide power to drive the mills situated on the riverbanks; any walk taken along these riverbanks will not only give the opportunity to discover a wide range of plant and animal life, but also provide the opportunity to see the remains of buildings that once played an important part in the economy of north Derbyshire. The landscape of the White Peak is gentler than the dark brooding peat moors and sharp gritstone edges of the Dark Peak. Sheep graze on rolling pasture land criss-crossed by miles of dry stone walls.

Wye Valley

Rolling hills, Peak District

The town of Bakewell lies on the edge of the White Peak and, although to the northeast of the town lie the eastern edges of the Dark Peak, most of its surrounding villages are in the White Peak. It is the only sizeable town in the Peak District National Park and is often called the 'Gateway to the Peak'.

34 THE HIDDEN PLACES OF DERBYSHIRE

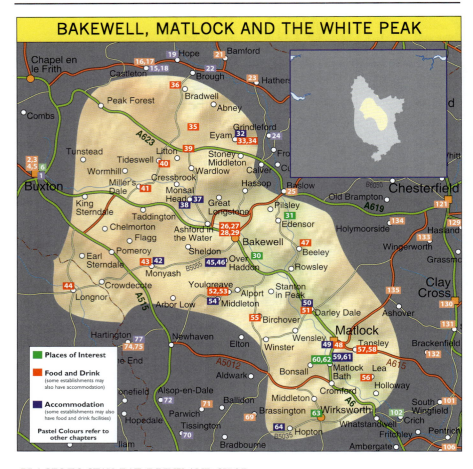

PLACES TO STAY, EAT, DRINK AND SHOP

26	Treeline, Bakewell	Craft Shop, Gallery and Food	Page 36
27	The Castle Inn, Bakewell	Pub, Food and Accommodation	Page 36
28	Upstairs Café and Gift Store, Bakewell	Coffee Shop and Gift Shop	Page 36
29	The Australian Bar Diner, Bakewell	Bar and Food	Page 36
30	Haddon Hall, Bakewell	Manor House	Page 39
31	Chatsworth House, Edensor	Stately Home and Gardens	Page 41
32	Crown Cottage, Eyam	Bed & Breakfast	Page 42
33	Eyam Tea Rooms, Eyam	Tea Rooms, Bistro and Accommodation	Page 43
34	Miners Arms, Eyam	Pub, Restaurant and Accommodation	Page 44
35	The Queen Anne, Great Hucklow, Nr Tideswell	Pub, Food and Accommodation	Page 44
36	Ye Old Bowling Green Inn, Smalldale	Pub, Restaurant and Accommodation	Page 45
37	Castle Cliffe, Monsal Head, Nr Bakewell	Guest House	Page 47
38	Riversdale Farm, Monsal Dale, Nr Buxton	Self Catering	Page 48
39	The Mires Café, Wardlow Mires, Nr Tideswell	Café	Page 48
40	The George Hotel, Tideswell	Pub, Food and Accommodation	Page 49

BAKEWELL, MATLOCK AND THE WHITE PEAK 35

PLACES TO STAY, EAT, DRINK AND SHOP

41	The Anglers Rest, Millers Dale, Nr Buxton	Pub with Food	Page 52
42	Sheldon House, Monyash, Nr Bakewell	Self Catering and Bed & Breakfast	Page 54
43	The Old Smithy Tea Rooms, Monyash	Tea Rooms	Page 54
44	The Crewe and Harpur Arms Hotel, Longnor	Pub, Food and Accommodation	Page 56
45	The Lathkil Hotel, Over Haddon, Nr Bakewell	Hotel	Page 57
46	Burton Manor Farm Cottages, Over Haddon	Self Catering	Page 58
47	The Devonshire Arms, Beeley, Nr Matlock	Pub with Food	Page 60
48	The Duke William, Matlock	Pub with Restaurant	Page 60
49	Riverbank Guest House, Matlock	Guest House	Page 62
50	The Red House Country Hotel, Darley Dale	Hotel	Page 64
51	The Grouse Inn, Darley Dale, Nr Matlock	Pub with Food	Page 64
52	The George Hotel, Youlgreave, Nr Bakewell	Pub, Food and Accommodation	Page 66
53	The Farmyard Inn, Youlgrave, Nr Bakewell	Pub, Restaurant and Accommodation	Page 66
54	Eastas Gate, Middleton, Nr Matlock	Bed & Breakfast	Page 68
55	The Red Lion Inn, Birchover, Nr Matlock	Pub with Food	Page 69
56	The Jug and Glass, Lea, Nr Matlock	Pub, Food and Accommodation	Page 71
57	The Gate, Tansley, Nr Matlock	Pub with Restaurant	Page 71
58	Scotland Nurseries Garden Centre, Tansley	Garden Centre and Coffee Shop	Page 72
59	Hodgkinson's Hotel/Restaurant, Matlock Bath	Hotel and Restaurant	Page 74
60	Matlock Bath Aquarium, Matlock Bath	Aquarium	Page 75
61	Ashdale Guest House, Matlock Bath	Guest House	Page 75
62	Heights of Abraham, Matlock Bath	Country Park	Page 76
63	Wirksworth Heritage Centre, Wirksworth	Heritage Centre	Page 79
64	Carsington Cottages, Carsington	Self Catering	Page 80

BAKEWELL

Bakewell, the largest town in the Peak District, dominates the area and close to it are two of the most magnificent stately homes in Britain, Chatsworth House and Haddon Hall. The vast Chatsworth estate straddles the River Derwent east of Bakewell, but the influence of the Cavendish family extends much further and few villages in the surrounding area have escaped.

The only true town in the Peak District National Park, Bakewell attracts many day-trippers, walkers and campers as well as locals who come to take advantage of its many amenities. The beautiful medieval five-arched bridge spanning the River Wye is still in use today as the main crossing point for traffic. A stone built town set along the banks of the River Wye, Bakewell enjoys a picturesque setting among well-wooded hills. With only 4,000 inhabitants it is nevertheless generally

River Wye, Bakewell

Treeline

Diamond Court, Water Street, Bakewell,
Derbyshire DE45 1EW
Tel: 01629 813749

Treeline is a multi-faceted establishment, with a gallery, craft shop and eatery. The food outlet is open daily serving a superb selection of home-baked meals, snacks and cakes, all created on the premises using free-range and organic produce, and the specialities are the hot Italian-style panninis. The craft shop sells a wide variety of unique items ranging from ceramics and jewellery to textiles and hand-made cards. Upstairs there is a gallery used for exhibitions by local artists and a display of wooden furniture and crafts, some created by the co-owner, Chris Low.

The Castle Inn

Castle Street, Bakewell, Derbyshire DE45 1DU
Tel: 01629 812103   Fax: 01629 814726

In the heart of popular Bakewell you will find the traditional 16th century **Castle Inn**. Open all day every day, here you are invited to enjoy a pint of refreshing ale from the selection that is offered from the well-stocked bar. The superb food is well recommended and served each lunchtime and evening from an extensive menu of classic favourites, all home-made and reasonably priced. On Sundays a popular roast is served. Four guest rooms of varying sizes available for bed and breakfast.

Upstairs Café and Gift Store

3 Market Street, Bakewell, Derbyshire DE45 1HG
Tel: 01629 815567

In the heart of Bakewell, built on the site of the former auction house, you will find the **Upstairs Café and Gift Store**; as its name suggests it is on the first floor. This is a modern coffee shop serving delicious food with friendly and

speedy service. There is plenty of choice and all the dishes are reasonably priced. Adjacent to the dining area is the superb gift shop with something to suit all ages, tastes and pockets. Many of the items are locally made.

The Australian Bar Diner

Granby Road, Bakewell, Derbyshire DE45 1ES
Tel: 01629 814909   Fax: 01629 812727

Centrally located within the town of Bakewell, **The Australian Bar Diner** is a family-run eating-place, established in 1992. Open daily (from 8am on market days) for drinks and traditional menus with plenty of choices and an Australian twist. The evening offers a more extensive menu, with unusual choices, Ostrich and Kangaroo steaks, chargrilled steaks, pasta and a Mexican selection, everyone is sure to find something to appeal. Seating for up to 100 diners.

acknowledged as the capital of the Peak District National Park.

However, for most people it is a dessert that has made the name of Bakewell so famous, but please remember it is referred to locally as a *pudding* and most definitely not as a tart! Its invention is said to have been an accident when what was supposed to have been a strawberry tart turned into something altogether different. The cooking mishap took place in the kitchens of the Rutland Arms Hotel, which was built in 1804 on the site of an old coaching inn. Mrs Greaves the mistress instructed the cook to prepare strawberry tart and the cook, instead of stirring the egg mixture into the pastry, spread it on top of the jam. The result was so successful that a Mrs Wilson, wife of a Tallow Chandler, where candles were made, saw the possibility of making the puddings for sale and obtained the so-called recipe and commenced in a business of her own. Several businesses in the town claim to have the original recipe. Although it's a delightful tale, a more likely explanation is that Bakewell pudding originated as a type of 'transparent' pudding, popular in the eighteenth century, in which a layer of fruit or jam was covered with a mixture of sugar, butter and eggs and then baked. These puddings were usually baked in a dish without pastry. Eliza Acton's recipe for Bakewell pudding without pastry first appeared in 1845 in 'Modern Cookery'. By 1861 Mrs Beeton's recipe had a puff pastry case. Almonds weren't used either in the original Bakewell pudding, although either almond essence or ground almonds feature in most modern recipes.

The novelist Jane Austen stayed at the Rutland Arms in 1811 and it featured in her book *Pride and Prejudice*, while Bakewell itself appears as the town of Lambton.

Bakewell's situation has always made it the ideal place for a settlement and, as well as being home to the Romans, an Iron Age fort has been discovered close by. Another reason for the popularity of the town was the existence of 12 fresh water springs which gave the town its name - Bad kwell means bath spring. This Old English name means "Badeca's spring" or "well", and is a reference to the warm, iron-bearing springs which rise in and around the town.

The market town for this whole central area of the Peak District, markets were held here well before the granting of a charter in 1330. In fact, its importance during the 11th century was such that, as recorded in the *Domesday Book* of 1086, Bakewell had two priests. Monday is now Bakewell's market day and the cattle market, one of the largest in Derbyshire, is an important part of the area's farming life. The annual Bakewell Show, held every summer, started in 1819 and has gone on to become one of the foremost agricultural shows in the country. Across the River Wye stands the enormous, new Agricultural and Business Centre, where the livestock market takes place.

The large parish **Church of All Saints** was founded in Saxon times, as revealed by the ancient preaching crosses and stonework. Its graceful spire, with its octagonal tower, can be seen for miles around. One of the few places in Derbyshire in the *Domesday Book* to record two priests and a church, the churchyard and church itself contain a wonderful variety of headstones and coffin slabs and, near the porch, a most unusual cross. Over 1,200 years old, it stands an impressive 8 feet high. On one side it depicts the Crucifixion, on the other are the Norse gods Odin and Loki. The west front is still essentially Norman. Most of the eastern end of the church, the south transept, and the chancel date from the 13th century. The decorative font is early 14th century, as are the chancel stalls, which have

Bakewell Parish Church

Historical Society and now displays its original wattle and daub interior walls. It was extended during the early 17th century and, at one time, the building was converted into tenements by the industrialist Richard Arkwright for his mill-workers. Now established as a folk museum, it houses a fascinating collection of rural bygones.

The town is full of delightful, mellow stone buildings, many of which date from the early 17th century and are still in use today. The **Old Town Hall**, famous as the scene of the Bakewell riots, is now the Tourist Information Centre of the Peak District. Few buildings remain from the days when Bakewell was a minor spa town, but the **Bath House**, on Bath Street, is one such building. Built in 1697 for the Duke of Rutland, it contained a large bath which was filled with the spa water and kept at a constant temperature of 59 degrees Fahrenheit. At the nearby Bath Gardens a Roman bath was discovered near the British Legion's Garden of Remembrance.

interesting misericords. The Vernon Chapel in the south aisle has impressive monuments to "The King of the Peak", Sir George Vernon of Haddon Hall, who died in 1567, and also to Sir John Manners, who died in 1584, and his wife Dorothy Vernon - these latter two feature in one of the great romantic legends of the Peak District.

Behind the church is the lovely **Old House Museum**, housed in a building on Cunningham Place which dates back to 1534. It is thought to be the oldest house in Bakewell. This beautiful building escaped demolition and has been lovingly restored by the Bakewell

Traditionally well-dressing flourished in the town in the 18th century, when

River Wye, Bakewell

Bakewell had aspirations to become a fashionable spa. However, the recent revival dates back only to the 1970s, when the British Legion - with the help of the well-dressers of Ashford in the Water - dressed the warm well at Bath House. Today, all five wells - all in the same room - are dressed on the last Saturday in June.

There is little evidence of industry in the town, which is not very surprising considering Bakewell is surrounded by farming country, but the remnants of **Lumsford Mill** can still be seen. Originally built in 1778 by Sir Richard Arkwright as a cotton spinning mill, over 300 hands, mainly women and children, were employed here. Badly damaged by fire in 1868, the Mill has been rebuilt and it is used as offices today. Here can also be found a very fine example of a low-parapeted packhorse bridge across the Wye, dating from 1664. Holme Hall to the

HADDON HALL

nr. Bakewell, Derbyshire DE45 1LA
Tel: 01629 812855 Fax: 01629 814379
e-mail: info@haddonhall.co.uk
website: www.haddonhall.co.uk

Only a mile to the south of Bakewell down the Matlock Road, on a bluff overlooking the Wye, the romantic **Haddon Hall** stands hidden from the road by a beech hedge. The Hall is thought by many to have been the first fortified house in the country, although the turrets and battlements were actually put on purely for show. The home of the Dukes of Rutland for over 800 years, the Hall has enjoyed a fairly peaceful existence, in part no doubt because it stood empty and neglected for nearly 300 years after 1640, when the family chose Belvoir Castle in Leicestershire as their main home. Examples of work from every century from the 12th to the 17th are here in this treasure trove. As with all good ancestral homes, it has a family legend. In this case the story dates from the 16th century when Lady Dorothy Vernon eloped with Sir John Manners. Many feel this legend was invented by the Victorians, partly because there is no historical evidence to back the claim that the two eloped together during a ball and also because neither the steps nor the pretty little packhorse bridge across the Wye, over which Dorothy is supposed to have escaped, existed during her time. However the small museum by the gatehouse tells of their romantic journey, as well as the history of the Hall.

Little construction work has been carried out on the Hall since the days of Henry VIII and it remains one of the best examples of a medieval and Tudor manor house. The 16th century terraced gardens are one of the chief delights of the Hall and are thought by many to be the most romantic in England. The Hall's splendour and charm have led it to be used as a backdrop to television and film productions including *Jane Eyre, Moll Flanders* and *The Prince and the Pauper*. Nikolaus Pevsner described the Hall as "The English castle par excellence, not the forbidding fortress on an unassailable crag, but the large, rambling, safe, grey, loveable house of knights and their ladies, the unreasonable dream-castle of those who think of the Middle Ages as a time of chivalry and valour and noble feelings. None other in England is so complete and convincing."

The Hall's chapel is adorned with medieval wall paintings. The kitchens are the oldest extant part of the house, and feature time-worn oak tables and dole cupboards. The oak-panelled Long Gallery features boars' heads (to represent Vernon) and peacocks (Manners) in the panelling.

north of town dates from 1626. This Jacobean hall faces the water-meadows of the Wye.

Only a mile to the south of Bakewell down the Matlock Road, on a bluff overlooking the Wye, the romantic **Haddon Hall** stands hidden from the road by a beech hedge (see panel on page 39).

NORTH OF BAKEWELL

EDENSOR
2 miles E of Bakewell off the B6012

This model village (the name is pronouced Ensor) was built by the 6th Duke of Devonshire between 1838 and 1842 after the original village had been demolished because it spoilt the view from Chatsworth House. Unable to decide on a specific design for the buildings, as suggested by his architect Paxton, the Duke had the cottages and houses in the new village built in a fascinating variety of styles. The village church was built by Sir George Gilbert Scott; in the churchyard is buried the late President Kennedy's sister Kathleen, who had married into the Cavendish family. Both she and her husband, the eldest son of the 10th Duke, were killed during the Second World War. The original village of Edensor lay nearer to the gates of Chatsworth House; only Park Cottage remains there now.

On the outskirts of the village lies **Chatsworth House**, known as the "Palace of the Peak". It is without doubt one of the finest of the great houses in Britain (see panel opposite).

PILSLEY
2 miles NE of Bakewell off the A619

This is a relatively new village created by the Duke of Devonshire after he had demolished Chatsworth village to make way for his mansion house and estate. It is now the estate workers who help the villagers dress four wells to coincide with the village fair in mid-July. Though the custom was only revived in 1968, the village wells were known to be dressed right up to the beginning of this century. The Shire Horse Stud Farm, built by the 9th Duke of Devonshire in 1910, has been converted into a variety of craft workshops.

HASSOP
3 miles N of Bakewell off the B6001

This little village is dominated by its fine Roman Catholic **Church of All Saints,** which dates from 1818. It was built by the Eyre family who, as well as being devout Catholics, also owned some 20 manors in the area. Hidden behind a high wall is one of the Eyre manor houses, **Hassop Hall**. Dating from the 17th century, the Hall was garrisoned for the King by Thomas Eyre during

Edensor Church

the Civil War and it remained in the family until the mid 19th century when there were a series of contested wills. The Hall is now a private hotel and restaurant and it contains a lead mine shaft in its cellars.

To the south of the village is Hassop Station, built in 1863, to serve the Duke of Devonshire at Chatsworth House and not for the convenience of the villagers. Now situated along the **Monsal Trail**, the station building is a bookshop.

GREAT LONGSTONE
3 miles NW of Bakewell off the B6465

An attractive stonebuilt Peak District village nestling below Longstone Edge, **Longstone Hall**, built in 1747 of red brick, was the home of the Wright family (who now live at Eyam Hall). The present Hall replaced a much larger Elizabethan building which is said to have been similar in style, but bigger, than the present Eyam Hall. The 13th century village church has a particularly fine roof, with moulded

CHATSWORTH HOUSE

nr Edensor, Derbyshire
Tel: 01246 565300 Fax: 01246 583536
e-mail: visit@chatsworth.org
website: www.chatsworth-house.co.uk

On the Outskirts of the village lies the home of the Dukes of Devonshire, **Chatsworth House**, known as the "Palace of the Peak", is without doubt one of the finest of the great houses in Britain. The origins of the House as a great showpiece must be attributable to the redoubtable Bess of Hardwick, whose marriage into the Cavendish family helped to secure the future of the palace.

Bess's husband, Sir William Cavendish, bought the estate for £600 in 1549. It was Bess who completed the new House after his death. Over the years, the Cavendish fortune continued to pour into Chatsworth, making it an almost unparalleled showcase for art treasures. Every aspect of the fine arts is here, ranging from old masterpieces, furniture, tapestries, porcelain and some magnificent alabaster carvings.

The gardens of this stately home also have

some marvellous features, including the Emperor Fountain, which dominates the Canal Pond and is said to reach a height of 290 feet. There is a maze and a Laburnum Tunnel and, behind the house, the famous Cascades. The overall appearance of the park as it is seen today is chiefly due to the talents of "Capability" Brown, who was first consulted in 1761. However, the name perhaps most strongly associated with Chatsworth is Joseph Paxton. His experiments in glasshouse design led him eventually to his masterpiece, the Crystal Palace, built to house the Great Exhibition of 1851.

beams, that dates from the 15th century. In the nave is a plaque placed to commemorate the work of Dr Edward Buxton when, in the 1820s and aged 73 years, he treated the whole village against an outbreak of typhus.

STONEY MIDDLETON
4½ miles N of Bakewell off the A623

This village, known simply as "Stoney" locally, is certainly well named as, particularly in this part of **Middleton Dale**, great walls of limestone rise up from the valley floor. Further up the Dale there are also many disused limestone quarries as well as the remains of some lead mines. Not all industry has vanished from the area, as this is the home of nearly three-quarters of the country's fluorspar industry. Another relic from the past also survives, a shoe and boot-making company operates from the village and is housed in a former corn mill.

An ancient village, the Romans built a bath here and the unusual octagonal village church was built by Joan Padley in thanksgiving for the safe return of her husband from the field of the Battle of Agincourt in the 15th century. The lantern storey was added to the Perpendicular

Maypole Dancing, Stoney Middleton

tower in 1759. Stoney Middleton has preserved its village identity and character and also partakes in the custom of well-dressing, when two wells around The Nook are dressed in late July/early August.

Higher up the dale from the village is the dramatically named **Lover's Leap**. In 1762, a jilted girl, Hannah Badderley, tried to jump to her death by leaping from a high rock. Her voluminous skirts, however, were caught on some brambles and she hung from the ledge before gently rolling down into a sawpit and escaping serious injury.

EYAM
5 miles N of Bakewell off the B6521

Pronounced "Eem", this village will forever be known as the **Plague Village**. In

---

CROWN COTTAGE
Main Road, Eyam, Hope Valley, Derbyshire S32 5QW
Tel: 01433 630858
e-mail: crown-cottage@amserve.com
website: www.crown-cottage.co.uk

Crown Cottage, home of Angela and Mike Driver, is an 18th century former village inn, which for the past four years has been run by the couple as a bed and breakfast. Here you will find four comfortable bedrooms, all with en-suite or private facilities, furnished in a cosy, cottage style, and guests are welcome to make use of the pretty garden in summer months. Superb cooked breakfasts featuring home-made traditional oatcakes. No smoking throughout; children and pets welcome.

1666, a local tailor received a bundle of plague-infected clothing from London. Within a short time the infection had spread and the terrified inhabitants prepared to flee the village. However, the local rector, William Mompesson, persuaded the villagers to stay put and, thanks to his intervention, most neighbouring villages escaped the disease. Eyam was quarantined for over a year, relying on outside help for supplies of food which were left on the village boundary. Out of a total of 350 inhabitants, only 83 survived.

Eyam Village

An open-air service is held each August at Cucklet Delf to commemorate the villagers' brave self-sacrifice, and the well-dressings are also a thanksgiving for the pureness of the water. Taking place on the last Sunday in August, known as Plague Sunday, this also commemorates the climax of the plague and the death of the rector's wife, Catherine Mompesson.

The village itself is quite large and self-contained, and typical of a mining and quarrying settlement. An interesting place to stroll around, there are many

EYAM TEA ROOMS

The Square, Eyam, Hope Valley, Derbyshire S32 5RB
Tel/Fax: 01433 631274

The highly popular **Eyam Tea Rooms** can be found in the very heart of this picturesque village. An historic property, it is thought to date back at least to the mid-17th century as it is known that the then owner died when the plague hit the town. Coming from many years working in the catering trade, throughout the world, this is a first venture for the present owners, David and John, and they have created a delightful establishment with an excellent reputation. The tea rooms open during the day, 10am to 5pm, seven days a week serving a wide range of hot and cold drinks, light meals and snacks. There is a regular printed menu and a specials board which offers at least four main courses. The specialities are the home-made cakes and cream teas. Wednesday to Saturday evenings, the place

opens as a bistro, serving meals from 7pm with last orders at 9pm. The superb evening menu offers an a la carte selection of freshly prepared dishes using the finest ingredients. The dishes are based on traditional British cuisine with an international flavour, inspired by John's world travels, and to accompany your meal there is an extensive wine list. Children are welcome and major credit cards are accepted.

If you need somewhere to stay the night, then there are two guest rooms available for bed and breakfast. Closed for two weeks in January. Ring for details.

Miners Arms

The Water Lane, Eyam, Hope Valley, Derbyshire S32 5RG
Tel: 01433 630853 Fax: 01433 639050
e-mail: minersarmseyam@aol.com

In the heart of the Peak District, within the historic village of Eyam, you will find the cosy, traditional **Miners Arms** inn. Enjoying a long history, and a popular local reputation, here you can enjoy a fine pint of ale and some tasty home-cooked food. There is a non-smoking restaurant for which bookings are advisable at weekends, though bar meals are also served at most sessions. Seven comfortable en-suite rooms available for bed and breakfast. Children and dogs welcome.

---

information plaques documenting events where they took place. The **Church of St Lawrence** houses an excellent exhibition of Eyam's history. Also inside the Church are two ancient coffin lids; the top of one of the lids is known as St Helen's Cross.

Born in Derbyshire, St Helen was the daughter of a Romano-British chief and the mother of Emperor Constantine. She is said to have found a fragment of the cross on which Jesus was crucified. In the churchyard is the best preserved Saxon cross to be found in the Peak District, along with an unusual sundial which dates from 1775.

The home of the Wright family for over 300 years, **Eyam Hall** is a wonderful, unspoilt 17th century manor house that is now open to the public. As well as touring the house and seeing the impressive stone-flagged hall, tapestry room and the magnificent tester bed, there is also a cafe and gift shop. The Eyam Hall Crafts Centre, housed in the farm building, contains several individual units which specialise in a variety of unusual and skilfully-fashioned crafts.

ABNEY
8 miles NW of Bakewell off the A625

Abney, and the neighbouring hamlet of **Abney Grange**, are isolated settlements guarding the upper reaches of the Highlow Brook on Abney Moor. First recorded as *Habenai* in the *Domesday Book*, Abney was at that time owned by William Peverel, William the Conqueror's illegitimate son and creator of Peveril Castle at Castleton.

Abney is very popular with walkers, and with the Derbyshire and Lancashire Gliding Club located at the ridge end at Camphill, overlooking Bradwell Dale.

To the east of the village, **Highlow Hall** is a fine, battlemented manor built in the 1500s by the Eyre family. It features an attractive gateway and a stone dovecote.

The Queen Anne

Great Hucklow, Nr. Tideswell, Derbyshire SK17 8RF
Tel: 01298 871246
e-mail: malcolm_hutton@bigfoot.com

Tucked away in the hamlet of Great Hucklow you will find the traditional 17th-century inn that is **The Queen Anne**. Owned and run by Malcolm and Stella Hutton this free house is open at every session serving real ales and tasty home-cooked food. There is a wide-ranging menu and meals can be enjoyed throughout the pub, with half of the seating being non-smoking. Former outbuildings have been converted to provide two comfortable en-suite guest rooms for bed and breakfast. Beer garden with superb views.

BRADWELL
9 miles NE of Buxton off the B6049

Usually abbreviated in the unique Peak District way to 'Bradder' - Bradwell is a charming little limestone village sheltered by Bradwell Edge. At one time this former lead-mining community was famous as the place where miners' hardhats - hard, black, brimmed hats in which candles were stuck to light the way underground - were made; thus these hardhats came to be known as Bradder Beavers. It owes its fortune to the lead mining industry of the 18th and 19th centuries, though among other items manufactured in Bradwell include coarse cotton goods, telescopes and opera glasses. It was also the birthplace of Samuel Fox, the 17th century inventor of the folding-frame umbrella. His house is marked with a plaque and lies just off the main street. The centre of the village, which lies above the stream south of the main road, is a maze of narrow lanes with tiny cottages.

Though most of the village dates from the lead-mining era, Bradwell has been occupied in Roman times. A narrow street called Smalldale follows the line of the Roman road between Brough and Buxton. Near the New Bath Hotel, where there is a thermal spring, the remains of a Roman Bath were found. Legend has it that Bradwell was also once a Roman slave camp, to serve the lead mines. During the period of struggle that followed the Roman's departure, the mysterious fortification to the north of the village, known as **Grey Ditch**, was built. It may have been constructed to defend Bradford Dale and the village against the Hope Valley. A different local legend speaks of Bradwell as the scene of the hanging of the Saxon King Edwin. The local name 'Eden Tree' is said to stem from this. Today it is more famous for producing the delicious Bradwell's Home-made Dairy Ice Cream.

A key attraction here is the massive

YE OLD BOWLING GREEN INN

Smalldale, Bradwell, Hope Valley S33 9JQ
Tel: 01433 620450 Fax: 01433 620280
e-mail: bowling.green@barbox.com
website: www.yeoldbowling-greeninn.co.uk

Tucked away on Smalldale, in the village of Bradwell, **Ye Olde Bowling Green Inn** is a delightful former coaching inn dating to the 16th century. Retaining the original bow windows the whitewashed exterior is set off with climbing roses, hanging baskets and shrub borders in a lovely show of colour. It is larger inside than might at first be expected and many of the rooms enjoy panoramic views in all directions.

The owners are Geoff Robins and his son Martin, and they have been here for just two years, continuing a long-established tradition of friendly service and a welcoming atmosphere. This is a free house, and the bar stocks a choice of three real ales with Timothy Taylor Landlord, Bass and Stones usually permanent features, together with a rotating guest ale. There are two super restaurants, one non-smoking, and both seat up to 32 diners. Meals can also be taken in the snug, the lounge and, weather permitting, on the patio. The variety of food available is impressive, with a printed menu and specials board on offer at lunchtimes and in the evening, seven days a week. The specialities are the fish dishes, with a delivery of fresh fish being made each day. Bookings are required for Friday and Saturday nights and Sunday lunch. In a newly refurbished barn there are six superb en-suite guest rooms available for bed and breakfast.

Bagshawe Cavern, a cave reached by a descending flight of 98 steps through an old lead mine. Along the half-mile walk to the main show cave there are wonderful rock formations and other interesting sights. For the more adventurous there are caving trips available.

A mile south of the village is the mid 16th century **Hazelbadge Hall**. One of several manors of the Vernon family, whose main seat was at Haddon Hall, their coat of arms can be seen above the upper mullioned windows. The house dates from 1549 and was part of Dorothy Vernon's dowry to her new husband, John Manners.

On the Saturday before the first Monday in August, four wells are dressed in the village. Although wells were dressed even at the turn of the 20th century, the present custom dates back only to 1949, when the Bowling Green Well was dressed during Small Dale Wakes. The village has its own particular method for making the colourful screens, section by section, so that the clay does not dry out.

ASHFORD IN THE WATER
1½ miles NW of Bakewell off the A6

Not exactly in the water, but certainly on the River Wye, Ashford is another candidate for Derbyshire's prettiest village. It developed around a ford that spanned the river and was once an important crossing place on the ancient Portway. Originally a medieval packhorse bridge, **Sheepwash Bridge** crosses the Wye, with overhanging willows framing its low arches. It is one of three bridges in the village, and a favourite with artists. There is a small enclosure to one side that provides a clue to its name, as this is still occasionally used for its original purpose - crowds gather to witness sheep being

Sheepwash Bridge, Ashford in the Water

washed in the river to clean their fleece before they are shorn. The lambs would be penned within the enclosure and the ewes, left on the other side of the river would conveniently swim across, getting a good wash in the process. Sheepwash Bridge is older than Mill Bridge which is dated 1664.

So-called Black Marble, actually a highly polished grey limestone from quarries and mines near the village, was mined nearby for some considerable time, and particularly during the Victorian era when it was fashionable to have decorative items and fire surrounds made from the stone. It was also exported all over the world. Once a thriving cottage industry, Ashford Marble, as it was known, was inlaid with coloured marbles, shells and glass.

The great limestone parish **Church of the Holy Trinity**, largely rebuilt in 1871 but retaining the base of a 13th century tower, has a fine Ashford marble table on show as well as a tablet to the memory of Henry Watson, the founder of the marble works who was also an authority on the geology of the area. Several of the pillars within the church are made of the rare Duke's Red marble, which is only found in the mine at Lathkill Dale owned by the Duke of Devonshire. The church also boasts a Norman tympanum, complete with Tree of Life, lion and hog, over the south door. Hanging from the roof of Ashford's church are the remains of four "virgin's crants" - paper garlands carried at the funerals of unmarried village girls.

Churchdale Hall, near the village, dates from the 18th century and is part of the vast Chatsworth estate. It was also the home of the 10th Duke of Devonshire, who never resided at Chatsworth, until his death in 1950. To the south of Ashford is another manor House, **Ashford Hall** overlooking a picturesque lake on the river Wye. Owned by the Dukes of Devonshire, it was built in 1785 to a design by Joseph Pickford of Derby. It was occupied by the family for a time, but was sold in the early 1950s. It now belongs to the Olivier family.

Ashford is perhaps most famous for its six beautifully executed well-dressings, which are held annually in early June.

After a break of many years the custom of well-dressing was briefly revived at Sheepwash Well in 1930, though this revival petered out until the arrival in the village of an enthusiastic vicar in the 1950s when the well dressings became an annual custom once more. Rather than adhering strictly to the custom of depicting scenes from the Bible, the well-dressers of Ashford have pictured such unusual themes as a willow pattern to celebrate the Chinese Year of the Dog, and have also paid tribute to the Land Girls of the First World War. The village also has a pleasant range of mainly 18th century cottages, and a former tithe barn which now serves as an art gallery.

MONSAL HEAD
3 miles NW of Bakewell off the B6465

Monsal Head is a renowned, and deservedly so, beauty spot from which

CASTLE CLIFFE

Monsal Head, Bakewell, Derbyshire DE45 1NL
Tel/Fax: 01629 640258
e-mail: relax@castle-cliffe.com
website: www.castle-cliffe.com

A warm welcome awaits all visitors to the family-run establishment of **Castle Cliffe**. Located in the heart of the Peak District National Park this guest house is an ideal place to base your holiday. Situated high up at the head of the beautiful Monsal Dale there are spectacular views into the valley and across the old Peak railway. Leave your car at the house and walk in almost any direction amidst magnificent Peak District scenery. The owners are Jackie and Neil Mantell who over the past two years have continued to enhance the fine reputation already enjoyed by Castle Cliffe. Open all year round, except over Christmas, they offer six comfortable en-suite guest rooms all looking out over the surrounding countryside or the gardens.

The emphasis is on ensuring that all guests have a relaxing and stress-free stay. You are invited to unwind in the garden with tea and home-baked cakes on sunny afternoons and to relax in the lounge in front of the open log fire on cold winter's days. Generous breakfasts are served each morning, and there are number of eating places which can be recommended in the evenings, all within easy reach. The relaxed atmosphere, together with a combination of twins, doubles and family rooms also makes Castle Cliffe a great place for group bookings or family reunions.

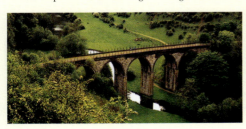

48 THE HIDDEN PLACES OF DERBYSHIRE

RIVERSDALE FARM

Monsal Dale, Buxton, Derbyshire SK17 8SZ
Tel: 01629 640500
e-mail: mick@riversdale-farm.freeserve.co.uk
website: www.riversdalefarm.co.uk

Riversdale Farm, home of Michael and Margaret Jackson, enjoys an unbeatably idyllic location within Monsal Dale and on the banks of the River Wye. Here you will find two charming holiday cottages, converted from former farm buildings, and comfortably furnished in a traditional, country style. The well-equipped properties sleep up to six adults and make an ideal base whether you are active hill walkers, or just want to gently explore the attractions in the area. Delightful gardens available to all residents.

there are tremendous views - particularly over **Monsal Dale**, through which the River Wye flows.

CRESSBROOK
5 miles NW of Bakewell off the B6465

Clinging to the slopes of the Wye Valley, the village cottages of Cressbrook are found in terraces amongst the ash woodland. The handsome **Cressbrook Mill**, built in 1815, is still partly in use; the apprentice house, used to house the pauper children from London and elsewhere who worked long hours in the mill, also exists. The owner of the Mill, William Newton, saw that the apprentices were treated well. The stretch of the River Wye between Cressbrook and Litton mills is known as Water-Cum-Jolly Dale. Cressbrook's well-dressing takes place during the first week in June.

Viaduct, Monsal Dale

WARDLOW
6 miles NW of Bakewell off the B6465

At a crossroads near Wardlow the

THE MIRES CAFÉ

Wardlow Mires, Nr. Tideswell, Nr. Buxton, Derbyshire SK17 8RU
Tel: 01298 872880

Situated on an area of reclaimed land, the **Mires Café** can be easily located on the A623 at Wardlow Mires. The low stone building had fallen into disrepair when it was taken over by Margaret Shear in 2000 but she has successfully created a friendly, family-run café which is well-liked by walkers, tourists and locals alike. Open daily, the wide ranging menu offers something for all, with all the home-made dishes being sensibly priced. Children's play area to the rear. Large car park.

BAKEWELL, MATLOCK AND THE WHITE PEAK   49

highwayman Anthony Lingard was hanged in 1812 for the murder of a local widow. He was the last felon to hang in the county, and his execution drew an enormous crowd - so much so that the local lay-preacher at Tideswell found himself preaching to virtually empty pews. Determined not to waste this opportunity to speak to so large a congregation, he relocated to the gibbet in order to give his sermon.

LITTON
6 miles NW of Bakewell off the A623

Situated in the Wye Valley, Litton is a typical example of a Peak District limestone village. Though the oldest house dates from 1639 - many of the buildings have date stones - most date from the mid 18th century, a time of prosperity for the area when the local lead mining industry was booming. As well as strolling around the village taking in the typical architecture of the Peak District found here, the ancient patterns of the small, stone-walled fields can also still be seen here.

The young apprentices at **Litton Mill**, unlike those at nearby Cressbrook Mill, experienced very harsh conditions. The Mill still stands, beside the Wye Mill stream, and is said to be haunted by the ghosts of the orphans who were exploited as cheap labour.

TIDESWELL
6 miles E of Buxton off the B6049

One of the largest villages in the area, Tideswell takes its name from the nearby ebbing and flowing well which can no longer be seen. Over 900 feet above sea level, the surrounding countryside offers many opportunities to wander, stroll, or take a leisurely (or energetic) hike through some varied and impressive scenery.

Known as the 'Cathedral of the Peak', the magnificent 14th century church of **St**

THE GEORGE HOTEL
Commercial Road, Tideswell, Derbyshire SK17 8NU
Tel/Fax: 01298 871382
e-mail: georgehoteltideswell@yahoo.co.uk

In the heart of the ancient market town of Tideswell, the historic **George Hotel** can be found lying in the shadow of the famous 'Cathedral of the Peak'. An 18th-century coaching inn dating back to 1730, this is a friendly pub offering a warm welcome to locals and visitors to the town. Under the management of local couple Phil and Tina, here you can enjoy a fine pint of ale, with three real ales usually available. The well-stocked bar also has a good selection of lager, beer and cider. A menu of home-cooked food is served each lunchtime and evening, except Sunday night, ranging from sandwiches to an extensive a la carte menu. There is also a blackboard of seasonal specials and the Sunday lunches, with a choice of roasts,

are very popular. It is advisable to book a table to eat at weekends. In fine weather meals and drinks can be taken outside to the attractively-styled beer garden, with patio heaters at most of the tables. Live entertainment is arranged each Friday night and there are occasional themed food nights.

Should you wish to linger in the area, Phil and Tina can offer bed and breakfast accommodation with five letting rooms. There is also a self-catering cottage sleeping six located nearby.

John the Baptist has a wealth of splendid features. The tower is impressive, the windows are beautiful, there is a fine collection of brasses inside and the 'Minstrel of the Peak', William Newton, is buried in the churchyard. Eccles Hall, overlooking the Market Place, was built in 1724 and became the home of the headmaster of the Grammar School in 1878.

Morris Dancing, Tideswell

The village received its market charter in 1250; by the 14th century it was a flourishing centre for the local wool trade. Today the village is home to a number of craftspeople working in buildings converted from other uses. The excellence of their work is apparent not only in the items they display but also in the splendid well-dressing they help to enact, annually on the Saturday nearest St John the Baptist's Day on 24th June.

PEAK FOREST
5 miles NE of Buxton off the A623

High on the White Peak plateau, the village of Peak Forest takes its name from the fact that it once stood at the centre of the Royal Forest of the Peak. The parish **Church of King Charles the Martyr** speaks of the fierce independence of the village inhabitants. It was built in 1657 by the wife of the 2nd Earl of Devonshire, during a time when there was a ban on building churches. The church that stands today on the site of the former chapel was built in 1878.

A quirk of ecclesiastical law ensured – up until early in the 19th century – that the village was outside the jurisdiction of the bishop. Thus it was not subject to the laws regarding posting the banns before marriage; hence it became known as 'the Gretna Green of the Peak'. If one or other of the couple has lived in the village for 15 days prior to the ceremony, to this day they can still be married in the church without banns being read.

At Chamber Farm, rebuilt in the 18th century, the Forest courts were held, attended by some 20 foresters whose job it was to maintain the special laws of the area. The **Peak Forest Canal**, completed in 1800, followed the valley of the River Goyt and had its terminal basin at Buxworth. At this time the whole area around the River Goyt was in the grip of the booming textile industry and, in 1831, the **Peak Forest Tramway** was built to join up with the canal.

Within walking distance of Peak Forest is the 'bottomless' pit of **Eldon Hole**. Once thought to be the Devil's own entrance to Hell, stories abound in which various people were lowered down on increasingly longer pieces of rope. They all returned, in differing states of mental anguish, but none ever reached the bottom! However, seasoned pot-holers, who view the hole as no more than a practice run, maintain that it is, in fact, 'only' 180 feet deep.

TADDINGTON
5 miles E of Buxton off the A6

Now lying just off the main Bakewell to Buxton road, Taddington was one of the first places to be bypassed. A small village and one of the highest in England, the cottages here are simple but the church is rather grand. Like many churches in the Peak District, it was rebuilt in the 14th century with money gained from the then-booming woollen and lead industries in the area.

Taddington Hall, one of the smaller of the Peak District manor houses, dates back to the 16th century though much of the building seen today was constructed in the 18th century. As with all good halls, Taddington has its share of ghost stories. One in particular concerns two brothers. The pair ran a hessian factory from the Hall and one day they quarreled. The next day one of the brothers, named Isaac, was found dead. The other brother was found guilty of the act. It is said that Isaac has been heard wandering around the passages of the Hall from time to time.

Up on Taddington Moor can be found **Five Wells** tumulus, at 1400 feet, the highest megalithic tomb in England. The harsh moorland weather has eroded the earth away to reveal two limestone slabs, the burial chambers of 12 people. Flint tools and scraps of pottery were also found in the chambers.

MILLER'S DALE
7 miles NE of Buxton off the B6049

The hamlet takes its name from one of several charming and compact dales that lie along the River Wye and provide excellent walking. The nearby nature reserve occupies land that was originally a limestone quarry, which was blown up in 1971. This tiny settlement, situated in the narrow valley of the River Wye, began life as late as the 1860s when it was built to provide housing for the workers building the London to Manchester railway. All this has now gone but the dramatic Monsal Dale Viaduct (built in the 1860s to carry the railway line) remains and is now crossed by walkers taking the Monsal Trail. The disused railway has been converted to a track for walkers, cyclists, horse riders and less active people, including wheelchair users. Between Blackwell and Monsal Head the trail follows the deep limestone valley of the River Wye for

Taddington Village

The Anglers Rest

Millers Dale, Buxton, Derbyshire SK17 8SN
Tel: 01298 871323

The Anglers Rest can be found tucked in a quiet corner, just off the main A6, in Millers Dale. The hostelry is over 250 years old and it retains a friendly traditional feel making it popular with locals and visitors to the area. This part of Derbyshire is popular with walkers, and they are made especially welcome, complete with muddy boots and dog, in the Hikers Bar! Open at every session the bar keeps four real ales on tap and the sensibly priced food is delicious.

Miller's Dale

On the pretty, sloping village green in Wormhill there is an ornate memorial to James Brindley, erected in 1895. This memorial is the centrepiece for the village's well-dressings at the end of August every year. The parish church of St Margaret was largely rebuilt in 1864, though it retains its medieval tower. **Wormhill Hall**, built by the Bagshawe family in 1697, is a late 17th century stone mansion (privately owned) which can be seen on the approach to the village from the Wye valley.

eight and a half miles. It is unsuitable for cycling and wheelchairs at its western half, with rocky diversions around tunnels. Level access is available from Miller's Dale Station, for half a mile west or 2 miles east.

WORMHILL
4 miles E of Buxton off the A6

The pretty hamlet of Wormhill was recorded in the *Domesday Book* and was a much more important settlement in the past. In Norman times it was one of the administrative centres of the Royal Forest of the Peak.

TUNSTEAD
3 miles E of Buxton off the A6

High in the hills above the valley of the River Wye, Tunstead is a small hamlet with a very famous son in James Brindley, born here in 1716. Known as the father of the canal system, Brindley never learned to read or write but became a millwright in 1742. His skills in engineering brought him before the Duke of Bridgewater, who commissioned Brindley to build the Bridgewater Canal to carry coal between Manchester and Worsley. Brindley went on to construct many more canals throughout Britain.

KING STERNDALE
2 miles SE of Buxton off the A6

King Sterndale is a charming limestone hamlet high above Ashwood Dale. The cosy parish church was built in 1847 in Gothic style, to a design by Bonomi. Inside the church there is a memorial to Miss Ellen Hawkins of the neighbouring village of Cowdale, founder of the church. Other memorials include those to the Pickford family, as the one commemorating William Pickford, a judge who later became Lord Sterndale, Master of the Rolls.

SOUTH OF BAKEWELL

SHELDON
5 miles W of Bakewell off the A6

Situated 1,000 feet up on the limestone plateau, black marble was also mined here, as it was at nearby Ashford in the Water, but Sheldon was not as successful as its neighbour as there was not enough water for the process. However, **Magpie Mine**, to the south of the village, produced lead for over 300 years. This important site of industrial archaeology has been preserved, from the Cornish-style chimney stack, engine house and dynamite cabin right down to the more recent corrugated-iron-roofed buildings. Now owned by the Peak District Mines Historical Society, guided parties are taken round to see the techniques used by the miners.

The village itself is chiefly a single row of mainly 18th century cottages lining the main street. The **Church of St Michael and All Angels**, with some notable features, is well worth a visit. Prehistoric monuments litter the limestone plateau above the village and, from Sheldon, numerous footpaths lead into the surrounding countryside to Monyash, Flagg and Monsal Dale.

FLAGG
5 miles W of Bakewell off the A515

The characteristic ridges and furrows of the medieval open fields, enclosed by stone walls in the 17th and 18th centuries, have been preserved in the farmland around Flagg. During the period of enclosure, hundreds of miles of stone walls were built, dividing the land into geometric patterns. Most of this can still be seen today, all over the Peak District, and is one of the particular features of the area. The Elizabethan manor house, **Flagg Hall**, is visible from the main road, and is well worth seeing, although it is not open to the public.

CHELMORTON
7 miles W of Bakewell off the A5270

The second highest village in the county, the remains of the narrow strips of land that were allotted to each cottage in medieval times can still be seen. Outside these strips lay the common land and then the parish boundary. Beyond the boundary can be seen the regular fields that were laid out after the first enclosures of 1809. The layout of the village is unchanged probably since Saxon times. It is a single street, with farms at intervals along the street.

To the north of the village, some 1,440 feet up on **Chelmorton Low** there is a Bronze Age tumulus and also the source of an unusually named stream, Illy Willy Water. The oldest part of the village lies near the top of this hill following the course of the stream, and curiously, the village church and inn now seem to be at the end of a cul-de-sac.

MONYASH
5 miles W of Bakewell off the B5055

Monyash was recorded in the *Domesday Book* as Maneis, thought to derive from 'many ash trees'. It is a picturesque village clustered around the village green. Farming and tourism are its main industries now but it was an important lead-mining centre from mediaeval times to the end of the 19th century and had its own Barmote Court. Its market charter was granted in 1340 and the old market cross still stands on the village green. Due to its isolated position, Monyash had for many years to support itself and this led to a great many industries within the village. As far back as prehistoric times there was a flint-tool "factory" here and, as well as mining, candle-making and rope-making, mere-building was a village speciality.

Chelmorton

Today, Monyash, which is situated at the start of Lathkill Dale, is busy, during the season, with walkers keen to discover the

SHELDON HOUSE

Chapel Street, Monyash, Nr. Bakewell, Derbyshire DE45 1JJ
Tel: 01629 813267 e-mail: steveandlou.fanshawe@virgin.net
Fax: 01629 815768 website: www.sheldoncottages.co.uk

Sheldon House is a large and typical of this area, stone-built property on the fringe of this unspoilt village, adjoining open fields, and home to Stephen and Louise Fanshawe. Here the charming couple offer bed and breakfast accommodation with two guest rooms with en-suite shower rooms. Within the grounds are two converted self-catering holiday cottages, furnished to a high standard and very well equipped. Both sleep up to five people, in two bedrooms. Children and well-behaved pets welcome. Weekly rental with short breaks also available. Sheldon House is also the home of a large Hawthorn Tree, comparable to any of those noted by The Tree Register of the British Isles.

THE OLD SMITHY TEA ROOMS

Church Street, Monyash, Nr. Bakewell, Derbyshire DE45 1JH
Tel: 01629 814510
e-mail: ed@drsicolls.freeserve.co.uk

As it's name suggests, **The Old Smithy Tea Rooms** are housed within a former blacksmiths, in a building that is over 250 years old, in the pretty Derbyshire village of Monyash. Ed and Ruth Driscoll created the tea rooms just ten years ago, and although the place is small, it has a good reputation for serving excellent food. The specialities are the all-day breakfasts and the delicious home-made cakes. Ed plays in a folk band that practise here and often perform locally.

surrounding countryside. The valley of the River Lathkill, **Lathkill Dale** is a road-free beauty spot with ash and elm woods that was designated a National Nature Reserve in 1972. The **River Lathkill**, like others in the limestone area of the Peak District, disappears underground for parts of its course. In this case the river rises, in winter, from a large cave above Monyash, known as Lathkill Head Cave. In summer, the river emerges further downstream at Over Haddon.

POMEROY
7 miles W of Bakewell off the A515

Pomeroy is a charming village with some lovely buildings, some dating back to medieval times. Parts of the Duke of York Inn in Pomeroy date back to the early 1400s. The chestnut tree in the car park was planted in the 1900s by the then-Prince of Wales, later King Edward VIII, on an occasion when he was visiting the area with Sir Thomas Pomeroy.

EARL STERNDALE
5 miles S of Buxton off the A515

At the less well-known northern end of Dove Valley, Earl Sterndale is close to the limestone peaks of Hitter Hill and High Wheeldon. Over 1,100 feet above sea level, it is surrounded by lovely farmland. A number of the farmsteads are called 'granges', a relic of the Middle Ages when the granges were where monks of Basingwerk Abbey lived. The parish **Church of St Michael**, built in the early 19th century, was the only church in Derbyshire to suffer a direct hit from a Second World War bomb. It was refurbished and restored in 1952, though it retains a Saxon font.

The village inn, the Quiet Woman, has a sign showing a headless woman, with the words 'Soft words turneth away wrath'. It is supposedly of a previous landlord's nagging wife, known as chattering Charteris, whose husband cut off her head.

CROWDECOTE
6 miles SE of Buxton off the B5053

Crowdecote is situated in the deep limestone valley of the River Dove, just on the border with Staffordshire. The limestone reef knolls of the upper part of the valley can be clearly seen from vantage points near the village. Seen as hills, such as **Chrome Hill** and **Parkhouse Hill**, they are as close to peaks as they get in the Peak

Chrome Hill and Parkhouse Hill

District. These knolls are actually the remnants of coral reefs - hard to believe, but perhaps not so puzzling when one remembers that much of this landscape has been formed by the action of water. The stone bridge over the River Dove, built in 1709 to replace an earlier wooden one, was a crossing point for the old pack horse route. The nearby Packhorse Inn dating back to 1723 was used by traders when this was the main road to Leek and Buxton.

LONGNOR
6 miles S of Buxton off the B5053

Over the county line into Staffordshire yet in the heart of the Peak District, on a ridge between the River Manifold and the River Dove, Longnor, with its old gritstone houses stands between the browns of the Dark Peak country and the bright greens of the limestone White Peak landscape. It was once the meeting-point of several packhorse routes. Then an important market town and the centre of a prosperous farming community, its **Market Hall** was built in 1873 - outside the hall there is a posting of the market charges of the time. The town's prosperity declined with the onset of the agricultural depression, and there was an accompanying fall in the population. However, this decline has in recent years been reversed. Longnor is now a conservation area and has attracted a good many craftspeople. The Market Square is one of the oldest in England, dating back to medieval times.

Main showroom for the work of local craftspeople and artisans, **Longnor Craft Centre** occupies the beautifully restored Market Hall in the centre of Longnor village. The village also has some fascinating narrow flagged passages, which seem to go nowhere but suddenly emerge into the most beautiful scenery.

Though the late 18th century **Church of St Bartholomew** is rather plain, the early Norman font of an older church is still within. The churchyard has a most interesting gravestone. The epitaph tells the tale of the life of William Billinge, born in 1679, died in 1791 - which made him 112 years old at the time of his death! As a soldier Billinge served under Rooke at Gibraltar and Marlborough at Ramilles. After being sent home wounded he recovered to take part in defending the King in the rebellions of 1715 and 1745. The village is the location for the filming of the TV series 'Peak Practice' and fans of the series will easily spot Dr Tom's House, The Beeches Surgery, The Black Swan among other familiar sights around Longnor village.

THE CREWE AND HARPUR ARMS HOTEL

Longnor, Nr. Buxton, Derbyshire SK17 0NS
Tel: 01298 83205

Opposite the village square in Longnor stands **The Crewe and Harpur Arms Hotel**, an imposing brick built structure, run by Pam and Alan Naden since 1993. They have created a comfortable inn which is ideally situated as a holiday base with seven guest rooms, three nearby holiday cottages, and a caravan and camping site. The bar is open at every session and all day at weekends, serving a selection of drinks and superb food. The menu is wide ranging and sure to cater to all.

OVER HADDON
1½ miles SW of Bakewell off the B5055

A former lead mining village Over Haddon is a picturesque village at the top of the steep side of the Lathkill valley. A typical rural settlement of the limestone plateau, it was at the centre of a gold rush in the 1850s when iron pyrites ("fools' gold") was found. The village is now visited by walkers as it lies on the **Lathkill Dale Trail** which follows the River Lathkill up the valley to beyond Monyash. Along the riverbank can be found many remains, some more hidden than others, of the area's lead-mining industry. There is an old engine house at **Mandale Mine** that was built in 1847 and further upstream from the mine are the stone pillars of an aqueduct, built in 1840, which carried water down to the engine house. Downstream from the village is the first National Nature Reserve established in the Peak District in 1972. Set mainly in an ash and elm wood, the reserve is home to many varieties of shrubs.

THE LATHKIL HOTEL

Over Haddon, Nr. Bakewell, Derbyshire DE45 1JE
Tel/Fax: 01629 812501
e-mail: info@lathkil.co.uk
website: www.lathkil.co.uk

Enjoying a peaceful location above Lathkil Dale, in the heart of the Peak District, is the charming **Lathkil Hotel**. Ideal for a special break, here you will find good old-fashioned hospitality, delicious food and a relaxing atmosphere. Situated in the village of Over Haddon, not far from Bakewell, the hotel enjoys spectacular views, surrounded by quiet valleys and rolling fields. For tourists there is plenty to see and do, with numerous pretty villages, historic houses and the spa towns of Ashbourne and Buxton to explore.

Home-cooked food is available at lunchtimes and in the evening in the light and airy dining room. In summer months lunch is in the form of a hot and cold buffet table, while packed lunches can also be provided on request. An extensive a la carte menu is served in the evenings complemented by an interesting wine list. The bar is open daily serving a choice of several real ales, including some local brews. The fine selection has been recognised by the Good Beer Guide, in which the Lathkil has featured for over 10 years. There are just four attractively furnished bedrooms, all doubles or twins, and complete with en-suite facilities. Little extras, such as the hot drinks tray, tv, clock/radio and personal bar, help make your stay even more comfortable.

BURTON MANOR FARM COTTAGES

Over Haddon, Bakewell, Derbyshire DE45 1JX
Tel: 01298 871429 or 01629 812236
Fax: 01298 871429
e-mail: cshirt@burtonmanor.freeserve.co.uk
website: www.burtonmanor.freeserve.co.uk

Burton Manor Farm Cottages can be found in the heart of the Peak District National Park, just a short drive from the pretty market town of Bakewell heading towards Over Haddon. This area is popular with visitors not only for the outstanding natural beauty of the surroundings and pretty villages but also for the nearby attractions of Chatsworth House and Haddon Hall.

Enjoying an elevated position, with superb views across the surrounding area, the cottages are located within a courtyard on a working dairy and beef farm. Owned and run by Ruth and Cecil Shirt, the couple are well known farmers in the area and have been renting out the holiday cottages for about four years. The six cottages have been converted from former farm buildings and provide modern, comfortable accommodation of an exceptionally high standard. The cottages are of a variety of sizes sleeping between two and eight people.

Ashford and Monsal Cottages are the two smallest and can sleep two adults in a twin or double room. Both are single level and are suitable for guests with limited mobility. One has a shower cubicle, the other a spacious bathroom, and both have a fully equipped kitchen. Brendan View is a first floor apartment and features exposed beams in the lounge/dining area. The main bedroom features a double bed, the second bedroom has twin beds, and there is a good sized bathroom with shower. Haddon Cottage again sleeps four with a double and a twin room, and is all on the ground floor. Lathkill Barn is at the gable end and features an impressive window extending the height of two floors. There is a double bedroom and a single room, and the bathroom has a bath and shower. Finally, Wragg Barn, has a spacious lounge, separate dining room and superb kitchen complete with dishwasher and freezer. Sleeping up to eight, there are two double bedrooms, one en-suite, and two twin rooms, and there is plenty of room for a large group. All cottages have access to a patio and/or garden area.

So that you can enjoy your holiday without worrying about life's little essentials, all the properties are provided with duvets, linen and towels and feature a cooker, fridge, microwave and colour TV with video. A cot is available on request and there is a central utility and games area with a washer/dryer, freezer and telephone. Gas fired central heating, electricity and power are all included in the price. Pets are welcome by arrangement and there is plenty of parking.

ROWSLEY
6 miles NW of Matlock off the A6

The older part of this small village, at the confluence of the Rivers Wye and Derwent, lies between the two rivers, while to the east is the 'railway village' around the former Midland railway station, now occupied by an engineering works. The two areas are quite distinct. The old part has gritstone cottages and farmhouses, while the newer part is clearly Victorian. The most impressive building in Rowsley is the Peacock Hotel. It was built in 1652 by John Stevenson, founder of the Lady Manners School in Bakewell, in 1636, and private secretary to Lady Manners, mother of the 8th Earl of Rutland. It is aptly named as above the entrance there is a magnificent ceramic peacock, made by Mintons of Stoke-on-Trent. It was at one time a dower house of Haddon Hall and the peacock is actually part of the family crest of the Manners family, whose descendents still live at nearby Haddon Hall.

On the banks of the River Wye lies **Caudwell's Mill**, a unique Grade II listed historic roller flour mill. A mill has stood on this site for at least 400 years; the present mill was built in 1874, powered by water from the River Wye, and was run as a family business for over a century up until 1978. Since then the Mill has undergone extensive restoration by a group of dedicated volunteers and, using machinery that was installed at the beginning of this century, the Mill is once again producing wholemeal flour. Other mill buildings on the site have been converted to house a variety of craft workshops, shops and a restaurant.

On Chatsworth Road near the terminus of the Peak Rail line, Peak Village is an extensive factory outlet shopping centre offering a range of ladies' and men's fashion, sports and outdoor wear, home furnishings, jewellery, toys and books, and eateries. Also on-site is the charming **Wind in the Willows** attraction, created by an award-winning team of craftsmen and designers to bring the adventures of Ratty, Mole, Badger and Mr Toad to life. Every scene from the classic English countryside tale is brought to life in an award winning indoor re-creation. After a short introductory film there is a walk along the River Bank, through the Wild Wood, into Badger's house, through all twelve chapters of the story. The setting is re-created from the original Shepard drawings and enhanced by lighting, sounds and smells.

BEELEY
6 miles N of Matlock off the B6012

This is another estate village to the great Chatsworth House which lies to the north. However, although much of the village was built for the 6th Duke of Devonshire by Paxton, there are some older buildings here including an early 17th century Hall (now a private farm) with stone mullioned and transomed windows, and Beeley Hill Top, a gabled 16th century house. The parish **Church of St Anne** is an inspirational sight, especially in the spring when the tree-lined churchyard is filled with daffodils. It has a Norman south door and a squat, square tower, but was over-zealously "restored" by the Victorians.

To the west of Beeley a small road climbs up onto Beeley Moor and here, along a concessionary path from Hell Bank, can be found **Hob Hurst's House**. Local folklore tells that this was the home of a goblin but it is only one of 30 or so Bronze Age barrows, which lie up here amongst the heather.

PLACES OF DERBYSHIRE

THE DEVONSHIRE ARMS

Beeley, Nr. Matlock, Derbyshire DE4 2NR
Tel/Fax: 01629 733259

Situated in the lovely conservation village of Beeley, this is one of the most picturesque and historic inns in Derbyshire. It sits almost at the gates of Chatsworth House and to this day forms part of the Duke's estate. **The Devonshire Arms** was built in 1747, of warm, mellow local stone, and by the late-18th century had become a prosperous coaching inn. The inside is as attractive as the outside with low, beamed ceilings and dark wood combining to create a welcoming atmosphere, and in the winter the crackle of log fires adds a warmth to this welcome. The inn has been managed by the Grosvenor family since 1962, and since 1988 has been under the guiding hand of John Grosvenor. The inn is renowned for its food and the superb menu ranges from simple sandwiches and salads to something just that little bit more special. Friday nights are a speciality fish night and booking for this, and at all times during the weekend, are essential. All the dishes are individually cooked from good, local produce wherever possible, and are reasonably priced. There's a comprehensive range of drinks available, including Bass and Marston's Pedigree, plus rotating ales as well as lager, stout and cider. There is a small but select wine list, which fully complements the dishes on the menu.

In July 1872 there was a tremendous flood in Beeley, and the nearby brook burst its banks and flooded the Devonshire Arms. The same thing happened in August 1997, and the height of the water is recorded on a beam in the bar.

THE DUKE WILLIAM

91 Church Street, Matlock, Derbyshire DE4 3BZ
Tel: 01629 582585

The Duke William can be found just over a mile from the centre of Matlock, heading towards Cromford, and is a fine old, stone building enjoying an elevated position. This is a friendly-run establishment with Peter and Louise Groves at the helm, ably assisted by mum and dad, Margaret and Alan. The pub is open at every session and all day Saturday and Sunday serving a wide range of real ales, including Mansfield Dark Cask and Mansfield Cask Bitter, Marstons Pedigree and Banks.

The food, mostly prepared by 'supercook' Margaret, is available each lunchtime and evening and is recommended far and wide. There is a regular printed menu of sandwiches, snacks and hearty meals supplemented by a specials board and children's menu, and everyone is sure to find something that appeals to their taste and appetite. The steaks are particularly fine and the Saturday night steak night is always popular, with all the beef sourced from a local butcher. On Saturdays you can enjoy some live music.

The cosy, traditional interior provides a separate non-smoking restaurant area, and there is also a hiker's bar where walkers with their muddy boots and well-behaved dogs are welcome. In warmer weather children can make use of the outdoor play area, and there is also plenty of parking. A separate function room is available for hire.

MATLOCK

Much of the southeastern Peakland area around Matlock lies outside the boundaries of the National Park, but the towns, villages and much of the surrounding countryside has plenty of the typical Peak District characteristics. Matlock and its various satellite settlements provide the focus and, after a period of decline, this essentially Victorian town is, once again, a busy and bustling place with plenty to offer the visitor as well as some fine views over the Lower Derwent Valley from its well planned vantage points.

Matlock lies right on the divide between the gritstone of the Dark Peak and the limestone of the White Peak. Though the hilltops are often windswept and bleak, the numerous dales, cut deep into the limestone, provide a lush and green haven for all manner of wild and plant life. Several of the rivers are famous for their trout, particularly the Lathkill, which was greatly favoured by the keen angler and writer Sir Izaak Walton.

Matlock is a bustling town nestling in the lower valley of the River Derwent, and is the administrative centre of Derbyshire as well as being a busy tourist centre bordering the Peak District National Park. There are actually eight Matlocks, which make up the town, along with several other hamlets. Most have simply been engulfed and have lost their identity as the town grew, but **Matlock Bath**, the site of the spa, still maintains some individuality.

Matlock itself is famed as, at one time, having the steepest-gradient (a 1-in-5½) tramway in the world; it was also the only tram system in the Peak District. Opened in 1893, the tramcars ran until 1927 and the Depot can still be seen at the top of Bank Street. The old Ticket Office and Waiting Room at Matlock station have been taken over by the Peak Rail Society and here can be found not only their shop, but also exhibitions explaining the history and aims of the society. The Peak Rail has its southernmost terminus just a few minutes walk from the mainline station.

Peak Rail is a rebuilt, refurbished and now preserved railway running between Matlock Riverside station (just a five-minute walk from the mainline station at Matlock) through the charming rural station of Darley Dale to the terminus Rowsley South. In future it is hoped that the line can be extended to Bakewell. Run entirely by volunteers, this lovely old steam train operates on different days throughout the year - please telephone for details. The full journey (one way) takes just 20 minutes, and passengers can alight to enjoy the picnic area at the entrance to Rowsley South Station, or the exhibition coach at Darley Dale platform (please ring for opening times) to learn about the

Matlock Park and Gardens

history of the re-opening of the line. The restaurant car offers Saturday evening meals, Sunday lunches and afternoon teas. Special events are held throughout the year, and engine-driving courses can be taken - the perfect gift for the steam enthusiast! As the countryside drifts by at a lovely pace, the journey in every way allows passengers to re-live the golden age of steam.

Inside Matlock's **Church of St Giles** can be seen the faded and preserved funeral garlands or "virgin crants" that were once common all over Derbyshire. Bell-shaped, decorated with rosettes and ribbons and usually containing a personal item, the garlands were made in memory of a deceased young girl of the parish. At her funeral the garland was carried by the dead girl's friends and, after the service, it would be suspended from the church rafters above the pew she had normally occupied.

View across Matlock

High up on the hill behind the town is the brooding ruin of **Riber Castle**. The castle was built between 1862 and 1868 and is often linked with the McCaig folly which overlooks Oban on the west coast of Scotland. The castle's creator, John Smedley, a local hosiery manufacturer who became interested in the hydropathic qualities of Matlock, drew up the designs for the building himself. Lavishly decorated inside, Smedley constructed his own gas-producing plant to provide lighting for the Castle and it even had its own well.

Following the death of first Smedley and then his wife, the castle was sold and for a number of years it was a boys' school. During the Second World War, the school having closed, the castle was used as a food store before it was left to become a ruined shell. Today the building and surrounding grounds are home to a

---

RIVERBANK GUEST HOUSE

Derwent Avenue, Matlock, Derbyshire DE4 3LX
Tel: 01629 582593 Fax: 01629 580885
e-mail: bookings@riverbankhouse.co.uk
website: www.riverbankhouse.co.uk

Riverbank is a family-owned period guest house enjoying a riverbank location within the conservation area of Matlock Bridge. Graham and Jennie Newberry have been here since 1999 and provide comfortable, relaxing bed and breakfast accommodation with six en-suite guest rooms. The unbeatable atmosphere results in a number of visitors returning time and time again and if it has a familiar feel to it, the house has been used as a filming location for the TV series Peak Practice.

sanctuary for rare breeds and endangered species; the **Wildlife Park** has been particular successful at breeding lynx, and boasts the world's largest collection of this magnificent animal.

To the west of Matlock, down a no-through road, can be found one of Derbyshire's few Grade I listed buildings, the secluded and well-hidden **Snitterton Hall**. Little is known of the history of this fine Elizabethan manor house, though it is believed to have been built by John Milward in 1631, around the same time that he purchased half the manor of Snitterton.

On the once busy old road between Matlock and Cromford, in an area once known as Starkholmes, The White Lion Inn was formerly called The Buddles Inn, after the habit of locals who would sit in the barn adjacent and "buddle" - the old word for washing lead.

NORTH OF MATLOCK

DARLEY DALE
2½ miles NW of Matlock off the A6

The charming name for this straggling village along the main road north from Matlock dates only from the 19th century, and was either devised by the commercially-minded railway company at work in the area or by the romantically-inclined vicar of the parish. Darley Dale makes up one of three stops on the Matlock-to-Rowsley South Peak Rail line.

One of the most unassuming heroines of this part of Derbyshire must be Lady Mary Louisa Whitworth. She was the second wife of Sir Joseph Whitworth, the famous Victorian engineer whose name is associated with the Great Exhibition of 1851 and who also invented the screw thread. Sir Joseph made a fortune manufacturing, amongst other items, machine tools, munitions and nuts and bolts. Following his death in 1887, Lady Mary undertook to bring sweeping changes to the lifestyle of the local poor and needy. She allowed the grounds of her home, Stancliffe Hall, to be used for school outings and events. In 1889, the Whitworth Cottage Hospital was opened under her auspices.

The **Whitworth Institute** was opened in 1890, bringing to the community a wide range of facilities including a swimming pool, an assembly hall, a natural history museum and a library. At a time when a woman was required to take a secondary role in society, Lady Mary was determined to credit her late husband with these changes, which so benefited Darley Dale. Lady Whitworth died in France in 1896, and is buried next to her husband at the parish Church of St Helen, in the hamlet of Churchtown. The churchyard is also home to the **Darley Yew**, one of the oldest living trees in Britain which has a girth of some 33 feet. The yew predates the Norman origins of the Church and may be older than the Saxon fragments found here earlier this century. St Helen's church dates from the 12th century and contains two fine examples of Burne-Jones stained glass windows.

Much of the stone used for building in the village came from nearby Stancliffe Quarry, which also supplied stone for the Thames Embankment and Hyde Park Corner in London and the Walker Art Gallery in Liverpool. To the north of the 15th century Darley Bridge, which carries the road to Winster over the River Derwent, are the remains of **Mill Close Mine**. This was the largest and most productive lead mine in Derbyshire until 1938, when flooding caused it to be abandoned.

Darley Dale has an extensive park which is very pretty in all seasons. Another of this small village's attractions is **Red House**

THE RED HOUSE COUNTRY HOTEL

Old Road, Darley Dale, Matlock, Derbyshire DE4 2ER
Tel: 01629 734854 Fax: 01629 734885
e-mail: enquiries@theredhousecountryhotel.co.uk
website: www.smoothhound.co.uk

One of the finest hotels in the whole Peak District is the **Red House Country Hotel** in Darley Dale, just to the north of Matlock. Under the ownership of David and Kate Gardiner it enjoys a reputation for elegant dining and superb accommodation, with a total of ten en-suite letting rooms. Patrick Stevenson has been the chef for over 20 years, and presents a tantalising menu of delicious dishes attracting diners from far and wide.

THE GROUSE INN

Dale Road North, Darley Dale, Matlock,
Derbyshire DE4 2FT
Tel: 01629 734357

Conveniently located on the A6 Matlock to Buxton road, in the village of Darley Dale, you will find **The Grouse Inn**. Recently under new management, the tradition of serving fine ales, all day in the summer months, is continued. There is also an excellent menu of dishes served each lunchtime and evening, with a roast lunch served at Sunday lunch (no food Sunday evening). Popular with the locals, there is plenty going on here, with a quiz each Wednesday and live entertainment once a month.

Stables, a working carriage museum featuring some fine examples of traditional horse-drawn vehicles and equipment. One of the finest collections in the country, it consists of nearly 40 carriages, including one of the very few surviving Hansom cabs, a stage coach, Royal Mail coach, Park Drag and many other private and commercial vehicles. Carriage rides are available, making regular trips through the countryside to places such as Chatsworth and Haddon Hall, and the carriages and horses can be hired for special occasions.

STANTON IN PEAK
5 miles NW of Matlock off the B5056

This is a typical Peak District village, with numerous alleyways and courtyards off its main street. A quick glance at the village cottages and the visitor will soon notice the initials WPT that appear above most of the doorways. The initials are those of William Paul Thornhill, the owner of Stanton Hall, which stands near the church and is still home to his descendents. There are some fine 17th and 18th century cottages, one of which has some of its windows still blocked since the window tax of 1697. The village pub, The Flying Childers, is named after one of the 4th Duke of Devonshire's most successful racehorses.

The gritstone landscape of **Stanton Moor**, which rises to some 1,096 feet and overlooks the village, is encircled by footpaths and is a popular walking area. There are also several interesting features on the moorland. The folly, **Earl Grey's Tower**, was built in 1832 to commemorate the reform of Parliament. There is also an ancient stone circle dating from the Bronze Age and with over 70 burial mounds. Known as the **Nine Ladies**, the stone circle has a solitary boulder nearby called the King's Stone. Legend has it that one Sunday nine women and a fiddler came up onto the moor to dance and, for their act of sacrilege, they were turned to stone.

The nearby **Rowtor Rocks** contain caves, which were carved out at some stage in the 17th century. Not only was the living space made from the rock but tables, chairs and alcoves were also made to create a cosy retreat for the local vicar, Rev Thomas Eyre. Prior to these home improvements, the caves were reputedly used by the Druids, who did not believe in such creature comforts.

ALPORT
5½ miles NW of Matlock off the B5056

This is an ancient village, much older than its delightful houses of the 17th to 19th centuries would at first suggest. Considered by many one of Derbyshire's prettiest villages, it stands at the confluence of the Bradford and Lathkill Rivers. The Lathkill cascades down through the village in a series of weirs to meet the Bradford coming down from Youlgreave. Named after the portway road which ran through the settlement, the Saxon inhabitants added the prefix "al", which itself means old.

The surrounding countryside, a lead-mining area, was owned by the Duke of Rutland and, by the end of the 18th century, the industry was running into problems. In order to prevent the mines filling up with water, the Duke had a 4½ mile sough (underground drainage canal) built to run the water off into the River Derwent. Begun in 1766, this project took 21 years to complete and, in an attempt to recover some of the construction costs, a levy was put on any more being taken from below a certain level.

Sometime after completion of the project, in 1881, the **River Bradford** disappeared underground for several years. As with other rivers in this limestone landscape, the river had channelled a route out underground, only this time the River Bradford was taking the route of the sough to the River Derwent. After sealing the chasm through which the river had joined up with Hillcar Sough, it was restored to the above-ground landscape.

Among Alport's many fine houses, **Monk's Hall** (private) is one of the best, dating from the late 16th or early 17th century and probably, at one time, was connected to a monastic grange. Another is **Harthill Hall Farm**, a gabled 17th century yeoman's farmhouse with stone mullioned and transomed windows.

YOULGREAVE
6½ miles NW of Matlock off the B5056

This straggling village, known locally as Pommey, lies in Bradford Dale. Once one of the centres of the Derbyshire lead-mining industry, fluorspar and calcite are still extracted from some of the old mines. The village **Church of All Saints**, one of the most beautiful churches in Derbyshire, contains some parts of the original Saxon building though its ancient font is, unfortunately, upturned and used as a sundial. Inside, the working font is Norman and still retains its stoop for holding the Holy Water. It is well worth taking the time to have a look at, as it is the only such font in England. The Church also contains a small tomb with an equally small alabaster effigy; dated 1488, it is a memorial to Thomas Cockayne, who was killed in a brawl when only in his teens. A fine alabaster panel in the north aisle, dated 1492, depicts the virgin with Robert Gylbert, his wife and seventeen children. There is a glorious Burne-Jones stained glass window, which was added in 1870, when Norman Shaw very sensitively restored the church.

Well Dressing, Youlgreave

Further up the village's main street is **Thimble Hall**, the smallest market hall in the Peak District and still used for selling goods today. Typical of the White Peak area of Derbyshire the Hall dates from 1656 and there are also some rather grand Georgian houses to be found in the village. Nearby the old shop built in 1887 for the local Co-operative Society is now a youth hostel. It featured in the film of DH Lawrence's 'the Virgin and the gypsy', much of which was filmed in the village. Standing opposite is the **Conduit Head**, a gritstone water tank that has the unofficial name of The Fountain. Built by the village's own water company in 1826, it supplied fresh soft water to all those who paid an annual fee of sixpence. In celebration of their new, clean water supply, the villagers held their first well-dressing in 1829. Today, Youlgreave dresses its wells for the Saturday nearest to St John the Baptist's Day (24th June). Such is the standard of the work that the villagers, all amateurs, are in great demand for advice and help.

The origin of the local name for Youlgreave is not known, but some say that it got this unusual name after a pig

The George Hotel

Church Street, Youlgreave, Nr. Bakewell, Derbyshire DE45 1VW
Tel: 01629 636292

The George Hotel is an attractive 17th-century coaching inn which is ideal for a quiet drink or bar lunch. The place has earned an enviable reputation for good service, a friendly welcome and value for money. You can enjoy tasty home cooked food every lunchtime and evening (all day April to September) from a wide-ranging menu of dishes, freshly prepared on the premises. The well-stocked bar offers up to three real ales with two guest beers. Three en-suite letting rooms available for bed and breakfast.

The Farmyard Inn

Main Street, Youlgreave, Derbyshire DE45 1UW
Tel: 01629 636221

The Farmyard Inn in Youlgrave dates back in parts to the 17th century and its unique name is a reminder of its days as a working farm. This traditional country inn serves a choice of real ales and an ever-changing menu available in either the bar or the non smoking restaurant, both of which have good disabled access. The large beer garden is just the place to relax in fine weather. No food Sunday night or Mondays. There is accommodation available in three comfortable chalets, all with en-suite facilities.

BAKEWELL, MATLOCK AND THE WHITE PEAK   67

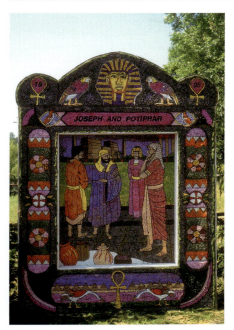

Well Dressing, Youlgreave

can really only be experienced by walking along the path by the banks of the quiet river, is noted for its solitude and, consequently, there is an abundance of wildlife in and around the riverbank meadows. The upper valley is a National Nature Reserve; those who are lucky enough many even spot a kingfisher or two. One of the country's purest rivers, the Lathkill is famed for the range of aquatic life that it supports as well as being a popular trout river. Renowned for many centuries, it was Izaak Walton who said of the Lathkill, back in 1676, "the purest and most transparent stream that I ever yet saw, either at home or abroad; and breeds, 'tis said, the reddest and best Trouts in England."

Two or three miles to the west of the village is **Arbor Low**, sometimes been referred to as the 'Stonehenge of the Peak District'. About 250 feet in diameter, the central plateau is encircled by a ditch, which lies within a high circular bank. On the plateau is a stone circle of limestone blocks, with a group of four stones in the centre cove. There are a total of 40 stones each weighing no less than 8 tonnes. Probably used as an observatory and also a festival site. It is not known whether the

joined the village band and was heard playing "Pom pom pom" down the village street. However colourful this derivation, the name more likely stems from the time of the Napoleonic Wars when French prisoners were brought to the area to work.

The Rivers Lathkill and Bradford are almost unique in Britain in that they both flow entirely through limestone country and their water quality, whilst being able to support crayfish, is also responsible for the formation of the unusual mineral tufa. **Lathkill Dale**, which

Arbor Low

stones, which have been placed in pairs, ever stood upright, although there is no archeological evidence to suggest that they did. Gaps in the outer bank, to the northwest and southeast could have been entrances and exits for religious ceremonies. Arbor Low dates to the Neolithic or Early Bronze Age period, and there is much evidence in the dales along the River Lathkill that they were inhabited in the Bronze Age. Nearby there is a large barrow known as Gib Hill, which stands at around 16 feet. When it was excavated a stone cist was discovered, containing a clay urn and burned human bones. This circular mound to the south of the stone circle, offers some protection against the weather and it is from this that Arbor Low got its name - "sheltered heap".

The Danes also occupied land here and their legacy is the name Lathkill, a Norse word meaning "narrow valley with a barn". For several centuries the valley was alive with the lead-mining industry that was a mainstay of the economy of much of northern Derbyshire, and any walk along the riverbanks will reveal remains from those workings as well as from limestone quarries.

MIDDLETON BY YOULGREAVE
7 miles NW of Matlock off the A5012

Just outside this leafy village is **Lomberdale Hall**, once the home of Thomas Bateman, the 19th century archeologist who was responsible for the excavation of some 500 barrows in the Peak District over a 20 year period - it is said that he managed to reveal four in one single day! Many of the artefacts he unearthed can be seen in Sheffield Museum. The village lies in the valley of the River Bradford, at the point where it becomes Middleton Dale, and is unusual among villages in this area of the Peak District in that it has a large number of trees.

WENSLEY
2½ miles W of Matlock off the B5057

There has not been a sudden leap into North Yorkshire - Derbyshire too has a Wensley and a Wensleydale, though the Derbyshire dale does not produce cheese. Lying just within the boundaries of the National Park, this quiet village does not feature on many tourist-favoured routes through the area, and as a result provides a peaceful and pleasant alternative to many other villages.

Wensley Dale can be easily accessed from the village and offers the opportunity for a charming walk. On the very edge of a limestone plateau, the valley is dry and its gently sloping grassed banks make a change from the dramatic limestone gorges nearby. Just down the Dale from Wensley is **Oker Hill**, the summit of which

EASTAS GATE
18 Main Street, Middleton, Matlock, Derbyshire DE4 4LQ
Tel: 01629 822790/ 822707
e-mail: eastasgate@hotmail.com

Eastas Gate overlooks open countryside and is set in a beautiful mature garden with ample off road parking. Kate Millwards family has lived in the house for nearly half a century with Kate providing quality bed and breakfast over the last nine years with an English Tourist Council four diamond rating. There are two comfortable en-suite letting rooms and a spacious guest lounge. There is no smoking in the house and pets are made welcome. Quality breakfasts are served and vegetarians catered for.

provides magnificent views over both Wensley and Darley Dale. Local legend has it that two brothers climbed the hill and each planted a tree before they separated to make their ways in the world. Only one of the two trees flourished, though it has been bent by the winds over the years. Wordsworth was so inspired by this evocative story that he wrote a poem about it.

BIRCHOVER
4 miles W of Matlock off the B5056

Birchover's main street meanders gently up from the unusual outcrops of **Rowtor Rocks** at the foot of the village, heading up towards neighbouring Stanton Moor. The name of this hillside village, which means "birch-covered steep slope", describes it perfectly.

Birchover was once home to father-and-son amateur antiquarians J C and J P Heathcote, who systematically investigated the barrows and monuments on Stanton Moor and kept a detailed and fascinating private museum in the old village post office in the main street. The Heathcote collection is now in Sheffield's Weston Park Museum.

The strange Rocks of Rowtor, behind The Druid Inn, are said to have been used for Druidical rites. The Reverend Thomas Eyre, who died in 1717, was fascinated by these rocks and built the strange collection of steps, rooms and seats which have been carved out of the gritstone rocks on the summit of the outcrop. It is said that the Reverend would take his friends there to admire the view across the valley below - a view, which nowadays is obscured by trees. Prehistoric cup-and-ring marks have been discovered on the rocks and several rocking stones can be moved by the application of a shoulder. One of these, weighing about 50 tons, could once be rocked easily by hand, but in 1799 fourteen young men decided to remove it for a bit of a lark. However when they put it back, they couldn't get the balance right.

Thomas Eyre lived at the Old Vicarage in the village below Rowtor Rocks, and also built the lovely little church known as the Jesus Chapel or **Rowtor Chapel**. The chapel had been demoted to the village cheese shop before Eyre's restoration, and it now features, among fragments of Norman work, unusual carvings and some wonderful decorative features, including modern stained glass by the artist Brian Clarke, who lived at the vicarage for a time during the 1970s.

The equally strange outcrops of **Robin Hood's Stride** and Cratcliff Tor can be found nearby. A medieval hermit's cave, complete with crucifix, can be seen at the foot of Cratcliff Tor hidden behind an ancient yew tree.

THE RED LION INN
Main Street, Birchover, Matlock,
Derbyshire DE4 2BN Tel/Fax: 01629 650363

If you are after a good old-fashioned country inn, then you need look no further than **The Red Lion**, situated in the picturesque village of Birchover. Dating back to the late 17th-century this is a traditional, stone-built inn, though it is perhaps hard to see now under its lavish covering of ivy! The cosy interior is friendly and welcoming, and here you can enjoy one of a range of five real ales together with selection of traditional pub fayre from a wide-ranging menu.

WINSTER
4 miles W of Matlock off the B5056

This attractive gritstone village was once a lead-mining centre and market town. Today, it is a pleasant place with antique shops in the high street and some fine late 18th century houses. Less splendid than the surrounding houses, but no less interesting, are the ginnels - little alleyways - which run off the main street. The most impressive building here, however, must be the **Market House**, owned by the National Trust and found at the top of the main street. The Trust's first purchase in Derbyshire, the rugged, two-storey Market House dates from the 17th and early 18th century and is an excellent reminder of Winster's past importance as a market town. Built from an attractive combination of brickwork and stone, the House is open to the public and acts as an information centre and shop for the Trust.

The **Ore House** at Winster is the best preserved ore house left in the Peak District. Up to 50 years ago miners used it to lodge lead ore in safety over night. It had a chute at the back for depositing the lead ore and a vaulted roof for security. The ore house has been preserved by the Peak Park Authority.

Winster Hall, built in 1628 by Francis Moore, has, like all good manor houses, its own ghost, which haunts the grounds. The ghost is said to be that of a daughter from the Hall, who fell in love with one of the coachmen. Her parents were horrified at her choice of husband and vowed to find a more suitable partner. However, before such a match could be made the girl and her lover climbed to the top of the Hall and jumped, together, to their deaths.

The annual Shrove Tuesday Pancake Race, from the Crown Inn to the Market House is a much-anticipated event that is taken seriously in the village. Small frying pans are issued to the men, women and children, it is an open event, and the pancakes are specially made with an emphasis on durability rather than taste.

Finally, although Morris dancing is traditionally associated with the Cotswold area, two of the best known and most often played tunes, The Winster Gallop and Blue-eyed Stranger, originate from the village. Collected many years ago by Cecil Sharpe, a legend in the world of Morris dancing, they were rediscovered in the 1960s. The Winster Morris men traditionally dance through the village at the beginning of Wakes Week, in June, finishing, as all good Morris dances do, at one of the local pubs.

ELTON
5 miles W of Matlock off the B5056

Situated at over 900 feet above sea level, the village lies on a ridge where limestone meets gritstone. The contrast of the vegetation, the lime-loving flowers and ash trees on one side with a scattering of oak trees on the other, is very marked. The two very different stones can also be seen in the buildings of the village, some of limestone, some of gritstone, though many are built using a combination of the two materials. To the north of the village, on Harthill Moor, is **Castle Ring**, an Iron Age hill fort behind Harthill Moor Farm. The landscape is dominated by Robin Hood's Stride, a natural gritstone crag, which was thought to have been used for ancient fertility rites. At twilight it looks like a large house, giving it its alternative name, 'Mock Beggars Hall'. It is popular with visitors and and rock climbers and is now covered with modern rock carvings and graffiti. Nearby to the north is the stone circle called **Nine Stone Close** or the Grey Ladies. It is the only circle in the Peak District that still has large standing stones although the stones are not on the same scale as those at Arbor Low. There were

BAKEWELL, MATLOCK AND THE WHITE PEAK 71

THE JUG AND GLASS

Lea, Matlock, Derbyshire DE4 5GJ
Tel/Fax: 01629 534232
e-mail: r.fretwell@btinternet.co.uk
website: www.thejugandglass.co.uk

The Jug and Glass public house in Lea, which dates back to 1782, was once used as a hospital for the employees of the Florence Nightingale's family who resided at nearby Lea Hurst. Roy and Gill have run the pub in recent years and the couple have created a friendly and welcoming establishment, where visitors can enjoy some fine ales and tasty food at every session. Bed and breakfast accommodation is available with two self-catering cottages for holiday rental.

originally nine stones, but only four now remain. A fifth stone is now a gatepost in the wall to the south of the circle.

SOUTH OF MATLOCK

LEA
4 miles SE of Matlock off the A615

The charming village is famous for its associations with Florence Nightingale, who spent many happy summers as a girl in nearby Holloway.

The building now home to **The Jug & Glass** (see panel above) in Lea was once a hospital for the employees of the Nightingale family, who resided at nearby Lea Hurst; it was perhaps here that Florence Nightingale discovered her vocation for tending the sick. The edifice dates back to 1782, though is older in some parts. **Lea Gardens** offer a rare collection of rhododendrons, azaleas, alpines and conifers in a superb woodland setting. This unique collection including kalmias and other plants of interest has been introduced from all over the world to this area in the heart of Derbyshire. The gardens provide a stunning visual display to enthral the whole family. Covering an area of some four acres, the site is set on the remains of a mediaeval millstone quarry and includes a lovely rock garden with dwarf conifers, alpines, heathers and spring bulbs. A mile of walks take visitors through a blaze of spring colour.

TANSLEY
1 mile SE of Matlock off the A615

This tiny and picturesque village has an eighteenth century mill, Tansleywood Mill and some good eighteenth century houses including Knoll House with an impressive carved doorway. It is well worth a visit by keen gardeners for its four garden centers and two horticultural nurseries.

THE GATE

Church Street, Tansley, Matlock, Derbyshire DE4 5FN
Tel: 01629 583838 Fax: 01629 57553

The Gate public house and restaurant is a large, impressive establishment, dating to the 17th century, which can be found in the centre of Tansley. Brian and Carole Rigby are your hosts and, together with their staff, have created a friendly atmosphere much enjoyed by locals and visitors. Open every day, at lunchtime and in the evening, there is a separate restaurant area serving an extensive menu of freshly prepared dishes. Children are welcome. Wide range of quality ales on offer. Quiz on Wednesdays.

SCOTLAND NURSERIES GARDEN CENTRE AND COFFEE SHOP

Stretton Road, Tansley, Matlock, Derbyshire DE4 5GF
Tel: Garden Centre 01629 583036
Fax: 01629 583013
e-mail: sales@scotlandnurserie.demon.co.uk
website: www.scotlandnurserie.demon.co.uk

On the B6104, one mile east of the junction with the A615 in Tansley, can be found **Scotland Nurseries Garden Centre**. Set within the beautiful Derbyshire countryside above the village, the garden centre is a well-established business specialising in hardy trees and shrubs, many of which are grown here at an altitude of nearly 1000 feet. The family-run business can boast that many of the Royal grounds and gardens are planted

with stock from this garden centre, and what better recommendation could you have! The garden centre stocks an excellent range of container-grown trees, shrubs, heathers, alpines, herbs and herbaceous plants together with water features, statues, stoneware, terracotta and glazed pots. The landscape supplies area, adjacent to the garden centre, has decking, paving slabs, fencing, turf, sheds and summerhouses. All in all, here you can find everything you could possibly need for creating or enhancing your garden. The garden centre shop, housed within a traditional Victorian barn, offers a superb selection of garden sundries, giftware and cards.

A visit to the centre would not be complete unless you sampled the culinary delights of **The Heathers Coffee Shop**, which serves morning coffee, full lunches and afternoon teas, with a full restaurant license. The specialities are the home-baked cakes, tea breads and mouthwatering puddings. The place can get quite busy and if you would like to take your lunch here on a Sunday then booking ahead is advisable. Overlooking the outdoor terraced area and surrounding garden centre, the Coffee Shop offers a relaxed and comfortable atmosphere. The Good Café Guide has classed The Heathers as Highly Recommended for quality and service.

Adjacent to the coffee shop there is the rather special chocolaterie, aptly named The Chocolate Tree. It stocks a range of hand made chocolates, many of which are from nearby Holdsworths of Bakewell. In addition there is a range of chocolate giftware products to buy, and you can also enjoy a range of select coffees and hot chocolate drinks, accompanied by chocolate torte, chocolate cake or ice cream on the premises.

Opened this summer, 'Lickpenny' is a 20-acre caravan park set within mature trees and rhododendrons within the nursery grounds. Each hard standing plot is individual, set within its own, beautifully planted boundary, with space for a car, caravan and awning, all with an electric hook-up point. There is an on-site modern, utility block with full washing and laundry facilities. The site boasts fantastic views towards neighbouring Riber Castle and woodland walks lead to the garden centre and coffee shop.

HOLLOWAY
4½ miles SE of Matlock off the A6

This tiny village has one famous daughter, Florence Nightingale, who lived here at **Lea Hurst**, a 17th century gabled farmhouse. Named after the Italian city where she was born in 1820, Florence was the second child of Edward William Shore, who later changed his name to Nightingale. Edward Nightingale began to alter and enlarge the house in 1825 and he also sold some land to Richard Arkwright so that he could build Willersley Castle, overlooking the River Derwent.

Florence's father left Lea Hurst to her in his will and, after her courageous work in the dreadful conditions of the Crimean War, she retired to the house and spent the next 50 years writing, specifically on the subject of hospital organisation. Florence died in London in 1910 and the house remained in the family until 1940. Still in private hands, as a home for the elderly, Lea Hurst is occasionally opened to the public.

MATLOCK BATH
1 mile S of Matlock off the A6

It is not known whether the Romans discovered the hot springs here, but by the late 17th century the waters were being used for medicinal purposes and the Old Bath Hotel was built. Like many other spa towns up and down the country, it was not until the Regency period that Matlock Bath reached its peak. As well as offering cures for many of the ills of the day, Matlock Bath and the surrounding area had much to offer the visitor and, by 1818, it was being described as a favourite summer resort. The spa town was compared to Switzerland by Byron and it has also been much admired by the Scottish philosopher, Dr Thomas Chalmers, and Ruskin, who stayed at the New Bath Hotel in 1829. Many famous people have visited the town, including the young Victoria before she succeeded to the throne.

The coming of the railways, in 1849, brought Matlock Bath within easy reach, at small cost, to many more people and it became a popular destination for day excursions. Rather than being a town for the gentility, it became a place for the genteel. Today, it is still essentially a holiday resort and manages to possesses an air of Victorian charm left over from the days when the puritanical Victorians descended on the town looking for a "cure".

One of the great attractions of the town is **The Aquarium**, which occupies what was once the old Matlock Bath Hydro that was established in 1833. The original splendour of the Bath Hydro can still be seen, in the fine stone staircase and also in the thermal large pool which now is without its roof (see panel on page 75).

Down by the riverbank and housed in the old Pavilion can be found the **Peak District Mining Museum and Temple Mine**, the only one of its kind in the world. Opened in 1978 and run by the Peak District Mines Historical Society, the Museum tells the story of lead mining in the surrounding area from as far back as Roman times to the 20th century. As well as the more usual displays of artefacts and implements used by the miners over the years, one of the Museum's most popular features are the climbing shafts and tunnels which allow the whole family to get a real feel for the life of a working lead miner. The Museum also houses a huge engine, dating from 1819, which was recovered from a mine near Winster. A unique survivor in Britain, the engine used water instead of steam to provide it with pressure. Adjacent to the Museum can be found the restored workings of Temple Mine.

For many, model railways are an interesting and absorbing hobby that friends and family find hard to understand, but **The Model Railway** on show in Temple Road is more a work of art than just another model railway. The brainchild of David White, this is a reconstruction of the Midland Railway Company's track through some of the most scenic areas of the Peak District. Combining magnificent dioramas with locomotives and carriages based on the designs of 1906, the trains, slowed down to a speed in scale with the models, travel the realistic route. This is a fascinating place for young and old, as well as a mecca for railway enthusiasts.

Being a relatively new town, Matlock Bath has no ancient place of worship, but the Church of the Holy Trinity is a fine early Victorian building which was added to in 1873 to accommodate the growing congregation. Of greater architectural merit is, however, the **Chapel of St John the Baptist**, found on the road between Matlock and Matlock Bath. Built in 1897, it was designed to be a chapel-of-ease for those finding it difficult to attend St Giles' in Matlock, but it also became a place of worship for those who preferred a High Church service.

Though on the edge of the splendid countryside of the Peak District National Park, Matlock Bath is surrounded by equally beautiful scenery. Found in the Victorian Railway Station buildings is the **Whistlestop Countryside Centre**, which aims to inform and educate the public on the wildlife of the county as well as manage wildlife conservation. Set up by the Derbyshire Wildlife Trust and run by volunteers, the Centre has an interesting and informative exhibition and a gift shop and the staff are qualified to lead a range of environmental activities.

For spectacular views of Matlock Bath,

HODGKINSON'S HOTEL AND RESTAURANT

150 South Parade, Matlock Bath, Derbyshire DE4 3NR
Tel: 01629 582170 Fax: 01629 584891
e-mail: enquiries@hodgkinsons-hotel.co.uk
website: www.hodgkinsons-hotel.co.uk

In the heart of the historic, picturesque town of Matlock Bath, you will find the equally historic **Hodgkinson's Hotel**. A Grade II Listed building it dates back to 1770, the height of the Georgian spa era, when it originally formed part of the much larger New Inn. It was later bought by local wine merchant John Hodgkinson. and it is his name that hangs above the door to this day. Much of the ground floor remains intact from that time and the rest has been carefully restored to its former Victorian splendour while at the same time satisfying the needs of the modern traveller.

The hotel offers seven en-suite guest rooms, each having been individually decorated in a period style. Some bedrooms are non-smoking and seasonal tariffs offer discounts for longer stays. The intimate candlelit restaurant is open Monday to Saturday evenings and as it is only small it is essential for non-residents to book ahead. Here you can enjoy some of the best local produce, imaginatively prepared by owner and head chef Antonio Carrieri. The superb menu changes regularly and attracts diners from across the area. Guests are invited to visit the hotel's caves which are former lead mines carved into the rock where wine and spirits were once stored.

Matlock Bath Aquarium

110 North Parade, Matlock Bath, Derbyshire DE4 3NS
Tel: 01629 583624 Fax: 01629 760793

All the attractions are set in a lovely Victorian building which was formerly the Matlock Bath Hydro, dating back to 1883. Reminders of its former splendour can be seen in the fine stone staircase, the drinking fountain and huge iron girders spanning the thermal pool.

The pool is fed by a spring from the hillside gushing 600,000 gallons a day, at a constant temperature of 20°C. This is where patients would immerse themselves in the pool or take the waters to relieve rheumatic ailments and improve digestive disorders.

Today, the health giving properties of the water are enjoyed by the famous collection of Large Mirror, Common and Koi Carp, weighing over 30 lbs. Visitors are welcome to feed the fish with food obtainable from the Aquarium.

The former Victorian consulting rooms are now home to the Aquarium containing a selection of British and Tropical freshwater species - Piranhas to Terrapins as well as many interesting fish from different regions of the world including the beautiful Malawi Cichlids.

Almost forgotten now, even in Matlock Bath where several Wells were once visited by thousands of Victorian trippers is the Petrifying Well. Here you can come and see the 'petrifying' process taking place in our working well as the famous Matlock Bath thermal water is sprayed onto objects gradually turning them to stone.

nothing beats a walk on **High Tor Grounds**. There are 60 acres of nature trails to wander around, while some 400 feet below, the River Derwent appears like a silver thread through the gorge. A popular viewing point for Victorian visitors to the town, today rock climbers practise their skills climbing the precipitous crags of the Tor. For the less energetic, the walk to the top is rewarded by the views and the chance of a cup of tea and a slice of home-made cake from the summit cafe.

On the opposite side of the valley are the beautiful wooded slopes of Masson Hill, the southern face of which has become known as the **Heights of Abraham** (see panel on page 76); this particular name was chosen after the inhabitants of Matlock had shown great enthusiasm for General Wolfe's victory in Quebec, this part of the Derwent valley being seen to resemble the gorge of the St Lawrence River and the original Heights of Abraham lying a mile north of Quebec. Today it is a well-known viewing point, reached on foot or, more easily, by cable car. The Heights of Abraham have a long history. For many years the slope was mined for lead but, in 1780, it was first

Ashdale Guest House

92 North Parade, Matlock Bath, Derbyshire DE4 3NS
Tel: 01629 57826
e-mail: ashdale@matlockbath.fsnet.co.uk
website: www.ashdaleguesthouse.co.uk

Ashdale Guest House can be found on the main North Parade in Matlock Bath and an ideal location for exploring Matlock and the surrounding area. Open all year round there are four comfortable en-suite guest bedrooms of which one, a family-sized room, is on the ground floor. Accommodation can be taken bed and breakfast, or on a room only basis.

Heights of Abraham

Matlock Bath, Derbyshire DE4 3PD
Tel 01629 582365 Fax 01629 580279
e-mail: office@hofa.co.uk
website: www.heightsofabraham.co.uk

Featuring steep rocky gorges, vast cavems, fast running rivers, wide panoramic views and a cable car, it is easy to understand why the Victorian's called Matlock Bath "Little Switzerland"; however, the **Heights of Abraham Country Park and Caverns** overlooks the famous spa town, and provides a unique aspect to a day out or holiday in the Derbyshire Dales and Peak District.

The journey to the summit of the country park is easily made by taking the cable car adjacent to Matlock Bath railway station and car park. The cable car ticket includes all the attractions in the grounds, as well as the two spectacular underground caverns. Tours throughout the day allow you to experience the exciting underground world within the hillside, with the "miner's tale' in the Great Rutland Cavern Nestus Mine, and the multivision presentation of the "story in the rock" at the Masson Cavern Pavilion.

The sixty acre country park also features woodland walks, the Owl Maze, the Explorers Challenge, play and picnic areas, Victoria Prospect Tower, plus the High Falls Rocks & Fossils Shop featuring Ichthyosaur remains. When you have worked up an appetite, why not relax with a drink on the terrace and take in the views, or enjoy a snack in the Coffee Shop or a meal in the Woodlanders Restaurant. So next time you are planning a trip to the mountains, remember The Heights of Abraham at Matlock Bath "Little Switzerland" is nearer than you think.

developed as a Pleasure Garden and since then trees and shrubs have been planted to make it a pleasing attraction for those visiting the town to take the waters. In 1812, the **Great Rutland Show Cavern**, on the slope, was opened to the public, a new experience for tourists of the time, and it was visited by many including the Grand Duke Michael of Russia and Princess Victoria. Following this success, in 1844, the **Great Masson Cavern** was opened and construction of the Victoria Prospect Tower was begun. Built by redundant lead miners, the Tower became a new landmark for the area and today still provides a bird's eye view over Derbyshire. The Heights of Abraham are today as popular as ever and provide all the amenities of a good country park.

To the south of the town centre is a model village with a difference; **Gulliver's Kingdom** theme park makes a great day out for all the family. Set on the side of a wooded hill, each terrace is individually themed with styles including Fantasy Land, the Old Wild West and the Royal Mine ride. There are plenty of fun rides, a monorail, water slides and other diversions, as well as a cafe and restaurant.

Life in a Lens is a museum of popular photography set in a beautiful renovated Victorian house. Displays include cameras of all ages, toy and novelty cameras, carte-de visite, postcards and much more.

Matlock Bath's Illumination and Venetian Nights are held annually from the end of August to the end of October.

CROMFORD
2 miles S of Matlock off the A5012

Cromford is a model village known the world over, which was developed by Richard Arkwright into one of the first industrial towns. In addition to housing, he also provided his workers with a market place and a village Lock-Up. Born in Lancashire in 1732, Arkwright was the inventor of the waterframe, a machine for spinning cotton that was powered by water. He built his first mill at Cromford in 1771, the project taking a further 20 years to complete. It was the world's first successful water-powered cotton spinning mill. The area he had chosen proved to be perfect: the River Derwent, described by Daniel Defoe as "a fury of a river", provided an ample power supply; there was an unorganised but very willing workforce, as the lead-mining industry was experiencing a decline, and probably most importantly, Cromford was away from the prying eyes of Arkwright's competitors. In 1792, Arkwright commissioned the building of the village church, where he now lies. The Mill proved to be a great success and became the model for others both in Britain and abroad, earning Arkwright the accolade "Father of the Factory System". His pioneering work and contributions to the great Industrial Age resulted in a knighthood in 1786, and one year later he became High Sheriff of Derbyshire. **Cromford Mill** and the associated buildings are now an International World Heritage site. Tours of the mill and Cromford village are available throughout the year. Continuing refurbishment and conservation by The Arkwright Society, who bought the site in 1979, ensures that future visitors will be able to follow the fascinating history behind this pioneering establishment. It is sponsored by Derbyshire County Council and the Derbyshire Dales District Council. Within the complex of the mill site there are a range of craft workshops and also the Mill Restaurant with its excellent home-cooked refreshment including a wide selection of wholefood dishes.

Cromford Canal

Cromford has a rather odd 15th century bridge, which has rounded arches on one side and pointed arches on the other. It was from this bridge, in 1697, so local folklore has it, that a horse and rider took a flying leap from the parapet, plunged into the river 20 feet below and lived to tell the tale. The **Cromford Venture Centre** is an ideal base for study visits, holidays, training and self-development courses. It offers self-catering accommodation for parties of up to 24 young people and four staff. It is run by the Arkwright Sociey in association with the Prince's Trust.

For lovers of waterways, there is an opportunity at **Cromford Canal** to potter along the five-mile stretch of towpath to Ambergate, or better still, to take a peaceful canal boat ride. The Cromford Canal Society, which organises the boat trips along the canal, also maintains the **Cromford Wharf Steam Museum**. Its exhibits include the 1902 Robey horizontal engine donated by Friden Brickworks from nearby Hartington. The Museum is open by arrangement for private steamings and working demonstrations. The old **Leawood Pumping Station**, which transferred water from the River Derwent to the Cromford Canal, has been fully restored. Inside the engine house is a preserved Cornish-type beam engine which is occasionally steamed up. Close by the Pump House is the **Wigwell Aqueduct**, which carries the Canal high over the River Derwent.

The High Peak Trail, which stretches some 17 miles up to Dowlow near Buxton, starts at Cromford and follows the trackbed of the Cromford and High Peak Railway. First opened in 1880, the railway was built to connect the Cromford Canal with the Peak Forest Canal and is somewhat reminiscent of a canal as it has long level sections interspersed with sharp inclines (instead of locks) and many of the stations are known as wharfs. After walking the trail it is not surprising to learn that its chief engineer was really a canal builder! The railway was finally closed in 1967; the old stations are now car parks and picnic areas; there is an information office in the former Hartington station signal box. Surfaced with clinker rather than limestone, the trail is suitable for walkers, cyclists and horses.

BONSALL
2 miles SW of Matlock off the A5012

In a steep-sided dale beneath Masson Hill, Bonsall was once a famous lead-mining centre and many of the fields and meadows around are still littered with the remains of the miners' work. This typical Peak District village has some fine 17th century limestone cottages clustered around its ball-topped 17th century cross. This is encircled by 13 gritstone steps in the steeply sloping market square. It is also one of the Derbyshire villages which continues the tradition of well-dressing, usually on the last Saturday in July.

Beside the market square cross stands The King's Head inn, dating from the late 17th century and said to be haunted. The other pubs in the village reflect the traditional occupations of its residents, as they are called the Pig of Lead and the Barley Mow. Above the village centre stands the battlemented parish church of **St James**, with its distinguished pinnacled tower and spire. Built mostly in the 1200s, it has a wonderful clerestory lighting the nave. The Baptist Chapel dates from 1824. From the Pig of Lead Inn, at one end of the main street, the road climbs up some 400 feet to the Upper Town which lies just below the rim of the limestone plateau. In order to cope with the steep hill, the village church is split-level.

Bonsall Brook, the power source for many of the textile mills in the village, also supplied power to the original Viyella mill, built in the 1790s by Philip Gell of Hopton Hall. Soon after building the mill, Gell constructed a road from his lead mines in Grangemill to the smelting house at Cromford. Called **Via Gellia** (and in the 19th century known locally as Via Jelly) it was the name of this road, which ran close to the mill, that was adapted to "Viyella" by the owners of the former Hollin Mill when they invented a new brand of hosiery.

MIDDLETON BY WIRKSWORTH
4 miles SW of Matlock off the A5012

Just to the north of the village, which is also known as Middleton, lies the **Good Luck Mine**, which is now a lead-mining museum. Usually open the first Sunday in the month, this old mine, found in the Via Gellia Valley, is typically narrow and, in places, the roof is low. Not a place for the claustrophobic, it does, however, give an excellent impression of a lead mine. The village also has another mine, where a particularly rare form of limestone is quarried. Hopton Wood Marble from here has been used in Westminster Abbey, York Minster and the Houses of Parliament.

Lying close to the Cromford and High Peak Railway, there was a particularly steep incline near the village, so steep in fact, that, as in other places, a steam engine was required to haul the wagon and carriages up the slope. **Middleton Top Winding Engine**, to the west of the village, can be easily picked out as the engine house has a distinctive tall chimney.

WIRKSWORTH
4 miles S of Matlock off the B5023

Nestling in the lush green foothills of the Peak District where north meets south, Wirksworth is home to a distinctive **Heritage Centre** (see panel below), housed in a former silk mill, which takes visitors through time from the Romans in Wirksworth to the present day. Quarrying, lead-mining and local customs such as clypping the church (a ceremony in which the parish church is encircled by the congregation holding hands around it) and well-dressing are explored with interactive and fascinating exhibits. One of the town's most interesting sights is the jumble of cottages linked by a maze of tiny lanes on the hillside between The Dale and Greenhill, in particular the area known locally as "The Puzzle Gardens". Babington House dates back to Jacobean Wirksworth. Another former lead-merchant's house, **Hopkinsons House**, was restored in 1980 as part of a number of restoration schemes initiated by the Civic Trust's "Wirksworth Project". The ancient **Parish Church of St Mary's** is a fine building standing in a tranquil close and bounded by Elizabethan "Gell Almshouses" and the former (Georgian) grammar school. The church holds one of

WIRKSWORTH HERITAGE CENTRE

Crown Yard, Wirksworth, Derbyshire DE4 4ET
Tel: 01629 825225

A visit to the **Wirksworth Heritage Centre** takes you from the Romans in Wirksworth to the present day. Housed in a former silk mill, the mysteries of the town's ancient lead

mining industry are, unveiled. Pit your wits against the computer and Rescue the Injured Lead Miner! Enter the Dream Cave and imagine how it felt to discover the remains of the prehistoric Woolly Rhino! Discover the local customs of Clypping the Church and Well Dressing. Learn about the regeneration of this historic market town and its George Eliot connections. Enjoy some of the best views of Wirksworth in town !

Carsington Cottages

Swiers Farm, Carsington, Derbyshire DE4 4DE
Tel/Fax: 01629 540513
e-mail riachclan@btinternet.com

Carsington Cottages are located in the heart of the beautiful Peak District close to the well-known Carsington Water, and are owned and run by Val and Doug Riach. There are two picturesque cottages, available all year round, and each sleeping up to four adults and two children. The buildings are nearly 300 years old and were former milking parlours which have been sensitively converted into cosy holiday cottages, retaining many original features. Stays of any duration are available and breakfast can be provided on request. Children welcome. No pets and no smoking in the cottages. English Tourist Board three star grading.

---

the oldest stone carvings in the country: known as the Wirksworth Stone, it is a coffin lid dating from the 8th century.

Wirksworth's well-dressing takes place during the last few days of May/first week of June.

The **National Stone Centre** tells "the story of stone", with a wealth of exhibits, activities such as gem-panning and fossil-casting, and outdoor trails tailored to introduce topics such as the geology, ecology and history of the dramatic Peak District landscape. Nearby, the **Steeple Grange Light Railway Society** runs along a short line over the High Peak Trail between Steeplehouse Station and Dark Lane Quarry at weekends between May and September. The former quarry is now overgrown with shrubs, trees and a profusion of wildflowers and birds. Power is provided by a battery-electric locomotive; passengers are carried in a manrider salvaged from Bevercotes Colliery in Nottinghamshire. Visitors to **North End Mills** are able to witness hosiery being made as it has been for over half a century; a special viewing area offers an insight into some of the items on sale in the Factory Shop.

Carsington Water just outside Wirksworth is one of Britain's newest reservoirs. This 741 acre expanse of water is a beauty spot that has attracted over a million visitors a year since it was opened by Queen Elizabeth in 1992. It can be reached on foot from Wirksworth along a series of footpaths and aims to be disabled friendly with wheel chairs available and access to as many attractions as possible. Sailing, windsurfing, fishing and canoeing can be enjoyed here, as well as just quiet strolls or bike rides. The Visitor Centre on the west bank offers visitors the opportunity to learn about Severn Trent Water and all aspects of water supply. An impressive exhibit in the courtyard is the Kugel Stone, a massive ball of granite weighing over 1 tonne, which revolves on a thin film of water under pressure. It can be moved with a touch of the hand! Some half a million trees and shrubs have been planted and are managed to attract wildlife and to enhance the landscape. There are two bird hides and a wildlife centre to help visitors understand the variety of wildlife and observe the birdlife that visits the reservoir. The reservoir is stocked for fishing either from the bank or boats available for hire. There is a large adventure playground and numerous open spaces for families to relax.

3 Dovedale and the Staffordshire Moorlands

This area of Derbyshire, which includes a southern section of the Peak District, is probably best known for the beautiful Dovedale. The large car park near Thorpe which gives general access to the Dale is often crowded, but there is plenty of room for everyone and the wonderful valley, just a few hundred yards from the car park, is well worth experiencing. It is also the place to have a go at crossing a river on stepping stones, something that has delighted children for many, many years, though there is a bridge just downstream, which ensures that the crossing can be made with dry feet, particularly when the water level is high.

The River Dove is also a mecca for keen fishermen. A favourite spot for Izaak Walton, who wrote his famous book, *The Compleat Angler,* in the area that was first published in 1653, and his influence is impossible to escape. An old farmhouse, at the head of the Dale, was converted, many years ago, into the well-known and much-loved Izaak Walton Hotel.

Dovedale is not the only dale worth exploring. The River Manifold offers some equally wonderful scenery and, in particular, there is Ilam. A beautifully preserved estate village, with a well established youth hostel, this is also a popular starting point from which to explore the Manifold Valley.

Dovedale

The ancient custom of well-dressing is almost exclusively confined to the limestone areas of the county. The porous rock, through which rainfall seeped leaving the surface completely dry just a few hours after heavy rainfall, meant that, for the people of these close knit communities, the well or spring was of utmost importance. If this dried up, the lives of the whole community were at risk. There are plenty of theories as to why well dressing began or was revived at Tissington. One centres on the purity of the Tissington wells during the Black Death, which swept through the country in the mid-1300s. During this time some 77 of the 100 clergy in Derbyshire died and the surviving villagers simply returned to the pagan custom of well dressing. Another plausible theory dates back only as far as the great drought of 1615, when the Tissington wells kept flowing though water everywhere was in very short supply. Whichever theory is true, one thing is certain, that in the last 50 years or so many villages who had not dressed a well for centuries, if ever, are now joining in the colourful tradition.

On the southern edge of the Peak District, the Staffordshire Moorlands certainly rival their neighbour in terms of scenic attraction. The undulating pastures of the moorlands, along with the fresh air and ancient weather-worn crags, make this the ideal place to walk, cycle or trek. It is also an area full of character, with charming scattered villages, historic market towns and a wealth of history, and many of the farms and buildings date back hundreds of years. The Industrial Revolution also left its mark on the landscape, though the two great reservoirs of Rudyard and Tittesworth, built to provide a water supply to the growing industry and population of the Midlands, now offer peaceful havens for a wide variety of plants, animals and birds as well as recreational facilities such as fishing and boating.

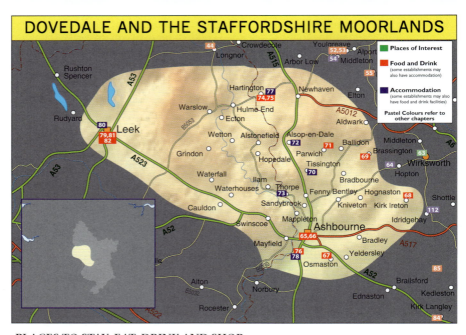

PLACES TO STAY, EAT, DRINK AND SHOP

65	The Horns Inn, Ashbourne	Pub with Food	Page 83
66	Earth Brand Café and Antiques, Ashbourne	Café and Antique Shop	Page 84
67	The Shoulder of Mutton, Osmaston	Pub, Food and Caravan Site	Page 86
68	The Barley Mow Inn, Kirk Ireton	Pub, Food and Accommodation	Page 87
69	The Miners Arms, Brassington	Pub with Food	Page 89
70	Bent Farm, Tissington, Nr Ashbourne	Bed & Breakfast	Page 91
71	The Sycamore Inn, Parwich, Nr Ashbourne	Pub with Food	Page 92
72	Church Farm Cottages, Alsop en le Dale	Self Catering	Page 93
73	Hillcrest House, Thorpe, Nr Dovedale	Guest House	Page 95
74	The Manifold Inn, Hulme End, Nr Hartington	Pub, Food and Accommodation	Page 99
75	Beresford Tearoom, Hartington, Nr Buxton	Tea Rooms and Gift Shop	Page 99
76	The Cock Inn, Clifton, Nr Ashbourne	Pub, Food and Accommodation	Page 100
77	Wolfscote Grange, Hartington, Nr Buxton	Self Catering and Bed & Breakfast	Page 101
78	Collycroft Farm, Clifton, Nr Ashbourne	Bed & Breakfast	Page 102
79	The Priory, Leek	Pub with Food	Page 104
80	The Green Man, Leek	Accommodation	Page 104
81	The Moss Rose Inn, Leek	Pub with Food	Page 104
82	Hare and Gate, Leek	Pub with Food	Page 104

Dovedale and the Staffordshire Moorlands 83

Ashbourne

ASHBOURNE

Ashbourne featured in the *Domesday Book* as "Essiburn", derived from the local stream with its many ash trees. It was originally a small settlement lying on the northern bank of Henmore Brook, which already had a church. It was a 13th century lord of the manor who laid out the new town to the east around its unusual shaped market place. Many of the town's traders, in order to continue to enjoy the benefits without paying the town's tolls, built themselves houses on the south side of the Brook. The area became known as Compton and it was slowly absorbed into the town. When writing *Adam Bede*, George Eliot based "Oakbourne" in "Stonyshire" on the town.

Often called The Gateway to the North, Ashbourne lies on the boundary of the old red sandstone of southern Derbyshire and the limestone which surrounds Dovedale and the White Peak. It is one of Derbyshire's finest old towns, with a wealth of wonderful Georgian architecture. It is a pleasure to visit, with plenty of shop-filled streets to potter up and down. The triangular cobbled **Market Square**, in the heart of Ashbourne, was part of the new development begun in the 13th century that shifted the town to the east, away from the Church. Weekly markets have been held in the square since 1296, and now take place every Saturday. It was from this market place, that used to be lined with ale houses, that Bonnie Prince Charlie proclaimed his father to be King James III, at the height of the Jacobite Rebellion of 1745. Though the old bull

---

THE HORNS INN

12/15 Victoria Square, Ashbourne,
Derbyshire DE6 1GG
Tel: 01335 300737

The Horns is a pretty, town centre inn which can be found in a small cobbled area in the heart of Ashbourne, not far from the market. Thought to date back to the 17th century it has a cosy interior though in warmer weather it is very pleasant to sit outside and watch the world go by. Open all day you can enjoy a refreshing drink from the well stocked bar, or some tasty food from the wide-ranging menu. (No food Wednesday evenings in winter months).

Gingerbread Shop, Ashbourne

ring no longer exists, the town boasts many fine examples of 18th century architecture as well as some older buildings, notably the Gingerbread Shop which is timber framed and probably dates from the 15th century. Traditional Ashbourne gingerbread is said to be made from a recipe that was acquired from French prisoners of war who were kept in the town during the Napoleonic Wars.

Also worthy of a second glance is the **Green Man and Black's Head Royal Hotel**. The inn sign stretches over the St John's Street and was put up when the Blackamoor Inn joined with the Green Man in 1825. Though the Blackamoor is no more, the sign remains and it claims to be the longest hotel name in the country. Of Georgian origin, the amalgamated Hotel has played host to James Boswell, Dr Johnson and the young Princess Victoria. Ashbourne was, in fact, one of Dr Johnson's favourite places; he came to the town on several occasions between 1737 and 1784. He also visited the hotel so often that he had his own chair with his name on it! The chair can still be seen at the Green Man.

A stroll down Church Street, described by Pevsner as one of the finest streets in Derbyshire, takes the walker past many interesting Georgian houses - including the Grey House, which stands next to the Grammar School. Founded by Sir Thomas Cockayne on behalf of Elizabeth I in 1585, the school was visited on its 400th anniversary by the present Queen. Almost opposite the Grey House is **The Mansion**, the late 17th century home of the

EARTH BRAND CAFÉ AND ANTIQUES

14 Church Street, Ashbourne, Derbyshire DE6 1AE
Tel: 01335 342518
e-mail: arthurjake@yahoo.co.uk

In the heart of Ashbourne, housed within a three storey, 18th-century building, you will find Hotspur Nimrod Antiques, and within it the **Earth Brand Café**. Both enterprises are owned and run by Anne and Philip Jarrett and are open seven days a week. The café serves fresh, natural, delicious food of the highest quality, using mainly local suppliers. The menu offers sandwiches, snacks, salads and coffees with the specialities being the home-baked cakes and pies. Very popular.

Reverend Dr John Taylor, oldest friend of Dr Johnson. In 1764, a domed, octagonal drawing room was added to the house, and a new brick facade built facing the street. Next to The Mansion are two of the many almshouses established in Ashbourne during the 17th and 18th centuries. Ashbourne also retains many of its narrow alleyways and, in particular, there is Lovatt's Yard where the town lock-up can be seen.

In **St Oswald's Parish Church** Ashbourne has one of the most impressive and elegant churches in the country, described by George Eliot as "the finest mere parish church in England". James Boswell said that the church was "one of the largest and most luminous that I have seen in any town of the same size". St Oswald's stands on the site of a minster church mentioned in the *Domesday Book*, though most of what stands today dates from rebuilding work in the 13th century. There is a dedication brass in the south transept dated 1241. The south doorway, with its dog-toothed decoration and ribbed moulding, reflects the church's classic Early English style. St Oswald's has chapels to its transepts, adding to the spacious feeling that is more reminiscent of a small cathedral than a parish church.

The alabaster tombs and monuments to the Bradbourne and Cockane families in the north transept chapel are justly famous. Perhaps the best-known monument is that to Penelope Boothby, who died in 1791 at the tender age of five. Thomas Banks' white Carrara marble figure of the sleeping child is so life like that she still appears to be only sleeping. The moving epitaph reads: "She was in form and intellect most exquisite; The unfortunate parents ventured their all on this frail bark, and the wreck was total." It is said that Penelope's parents separated at the child's grave and never spoke to each other again. The tower and gracious 212 foot spire of the church were erected between 1330 and 1350, at the crossing of the nave and transepts.

Ashbourne is home, too, to the famous Shrovetide football game played on Shrove Tuesday and Ash Wednesday. The two teams, the "Up'ards" (those born north of the Henmore Brook) and the "Down'ards" (those born south of it) begin their match at 2 p.m. behind the Green Man Hotel. The game continues until well into the evening. The two goals are situated three miles apart, along the Brook, on the site of the old mills at Clifton and Sturston. It is rare for more than one goal to be scored in this slow-moving game.

SOUTH AND EAST OF ASHBOURNE

YELDERSLEY
3 miles SE of Ashbourne off the A52

Yeldersley has long been the home of gentlemen farmers and those who love the countryside. This picturesque village offers many scenic delights. **Yeldersley Hall** is a spacious country house, which was built in 1760.

OSMASTON
2½ miles SE of Ashbourne off the A52

Osmaston is a sleepy, beautiful village just five minutes drive from Ashbourne. Neither crowded nor bustling, it offers the visitor a real haven of tranquility. It is the archtypical English village, with thatched cottages, village green, village pond, pub and church! It was originally an estate village built in the 19th century to house the workers at the Butterly Iron Works.

THE SHOULDER OF MUTTON

Osmaston, Nr. Ashbourne,
Derbyshire DE6 1LW
Tel/Fax: 01335 342371

Osmaston is a sleepy estate village just five minutes drive from Ashbourne, surrounded by rural Derbyshire. Forming part of the Walker-Okeover estate, this is an archetypical English village with thatched cottages, village green, village pond and church, and being neither crowded nor bustling, it offers the visitor a real haven of tranquillity. One highlight of the locals' calendar is probably the Ashbourne Shire Horse show.

The Shoulder of Mutton is a charming pub which can be found in the centre of the village. It has been personally run by Paul and Tina since 1993 with the couple previously having gained experience running a pub in Bournemouth. In such a small place it is perhaps inevitable that the pub occupies a unique position in the affections of the locals, forming a hub to village life. Sadly the records of the pub's history were destroyed in a fire and although a prominent date stone records a date of 1805, it is believed to be much older that that.

This fine establishment comes well recommended with a reputation that extends far beyond the parish boundaries. The Shoulder of Mutton is open each lunchtime and evening and all day Thursday to Sunday in summer months. Food is served from midday until 2pm and from 7 to 9pm, seven days a week, with snacks and cream teas available at other times. Meals can be taken either in the comfortable lounge, the recently refurbished bar, or outside in the picturesque garden. Customers can choose from the varied menu or from an excellent range of daily specials which offer something to tempt every palate. The home-made dishes are very popular, with the specialities including minty lamb and home-made curry. The Sunday roasts are particularly popular and also offer excellent value for money. The bar stocks a good choice of real ales, with two or three usually available, plus keg beers, mild, lager and cider. Paul and Tina – along with Tina's sister Karen – also run nearby Gateway Caravan Park, which is open all year round and can accommodate up to 200 caravans or campers. Set in 13 acres of flat land with woodland, it offers hard and soft pitches, electric hook ups, shop, showers, toilets, bar, TV room, games room and a function room for up to 300 people. On Saturday nights during July and August there is live entertainment.

The manor house, Osmaston Manor which was built in 1849 for Francis Wright, the owner of the ironworks, was demolished in 1964. The estate at Osmaston today is the location for the annual Osmaston Horse Trials and the Ashbourne Shire Horse Show.

BRADLEY
3 miles E of Ashbourne off the A517

A regular visitor to the Georgian Bradley Hall (private) was Dr Johnson, who would visit the Meynell family here when he was staying in Ashbourne with his friend, Dr John Taylor. The Meynells had come to Bradley in 1655 and bought the hall from Sir Andrew Kniveton, who had been financially ruined by the Civil War.

Opposite the hall stands the **Church of All Saints**, which is interesting in having a bell turret but no tower on its 14th century nave and chancel. The original wooden bell tower was struck by lightning. There are several memorials to the Meynell family in the church. The base and part of the shaft of a Saxon cross stand in the churchyard. The archway crossing the formerly gated road between cottages at Moorend is known locally as "The Hole in the Wall". The village pub has the distinction, common in Derbyshire, of having two official names, The Jinglers and the Fox and Hounds. Nearby **Bradley Wood** was given to the people of Ashbourne in 1935 by Captain Fitzherbert Wright.

KIRK IRETON
6 miles NE of Asbourne off the A 517

Kirk Ireton is a picturesque village, much of it built from locally quarried gritstone. In the hills near Carsington Reservoir it sits at 700ft above sea level. Much of the village is 17th century and one of the oldest buildings is the Barley Mow Inn. When decimalization was introduced in 1971, the 87 year old landlady refused to accept the new money. The Barley Mow was one of the last places in the country to go decimal.

KNIVETON
3 miles NE of Ashbourne off the B5035

This tiny village of grey stone houses, surrounding the small church lies close to Carsington Reservoir, sheltered in a dip in the hills. Its little church of St Michael has a 13th century tower, a Norman doorway, a 13th century font, small lancet windows, battlements and a short spire. The medieval glass in the chancel depicts the arms of the family of Kniveton. Sir Andrew Kniveton became so impoverished through his loyalty to Charles the First that he had to sell most of the family estates. A huge sycamore tree and an ancient yew stand in the churchyard. The yew has grooves in its bark, said to have been made by archers sharpening their arrows.

Just north of the village is the Bronze Age burial mound at Wigber Low which

THE BARLEY MOW INN

Main Street, Kirk Ireton, Ashbourne, Derbyshire DE6 3JP
Tel: 01335 370306

In the picturesque village of Kirk Ireton, **The Barley Mow Inn** is a real find. It looks much like a private house, with an attractive garden to the front, and has been run by Mary Short for the past 26 years. Open each lunchtime and evening, the bar serves ales in the traditional way, direct from the keg, with a couple of local brews usually available. Filled rolls are available at lunchtime, together with tea and coffee. Five en-suite letting rooms available.

has revealed some important remains from the village's past.

HOGNASTON
4 miles NE of Ashbourne off the B5035

The picturesque village of Hognaston stands on a hillside overlooked by Hognaston Winn, which rises to 1,000feet. It has been in existence for at least 1000 years and there is evidence of medieval field structures, where long demolished houses once stood. It used to be a busy place in coaching days when the London to Manchester coaches passed through the village. St. Bartholomew's Church, dating back to the twelfth century, has some extraordinary Norman carvings over the doorway and an early Norman font. Two of the bells date back to the thirteenth century. The clock and three of the other bells were a gift from John Smith and Sons, the famous Derby clock-makers as a memorial to John Smith who lived in the village. The village lies close to **Carsington Water**, Britain's newest reservoir, owned by Severn Trent Water. Opened by the Queen in 1992, the reservoir has already blended well with the local countryside. Unlike many of the Peak District reservoirs, which draw their water from the acid moorland, Carsington is different and the lake and surrounding area is able to support a whole host of wildlife. One controversial resident is the American ruddy duck. Once unknown outside wildlife reserves, the duck escaped and, in little over 50 years, the breed has become widespread throughout Europe.

Set in 8 acres of picturesque grounds overlooking Carsington Water is the famous **Knockerdown Inn**. The property dates back to the 17th century, and opened as a beerhouse in 1838, when it was known officially as The Greyhound but was given the affectionate name "The Nock". The famous stagecoach "The Devonshire" used to call here en route from Wirksworth to Ashbourne.

HOPTON
8 miles NE of Ashbourne off the B5035

This village, now by-passed by the main road, is dominated by the Carsington Water Reservoir. The land rises to the north of Hopton and here can be found the **Hopton Incline**, once the steepest railway incline in the British Isles. Lying on the **High Peak Railway** line, carriages were hauled up using fixed engines on their journey from Cromford to Whaley Bridge. It is now part of the High Peak Trail.

Until 1989 **Hopton Hall** was the home of the Gell family and in particular, the home of Philip Gell the owner of the Viyella mill at Cromford. Though the actual date of the original building is unknown, the Gell family have been known to have lived in the area since 1208 and they have held the manor of Hopton since the 15th century. The Gell family made their fortune in the nearby limestone quarries and they also were responsible for the construction of the Via Gellia, a road, which runs along a valley to the west of Cromford.

BRADBOURNE
4 miles NE of Ashbourne off the A5056

This is an ancient village, standing high on a ridge between the valleys of Bradbourne Brook and Havenhill Dale. Even at the time of the recording of the *Domesday Book* its name, Bradeburne (meaning broad stream) was well established. For more than 300 years the monks at Dunstable Priory grazed their sheep on the land round Bradbourne, and also supplied vicars to the parish Church of All Saints. Essentially Norman, but with some fragments of Saxon work - especially on the north side of the nave where typical long-and-short work is visible - the church is surrounded by its hilltop churchyard which contains not only the remains of a Saxon cross, dated approx 800AD, and containing a scene of the crucifixion. Originally the shaft would have been topped with a cross. The cross would be set up to mark a place, where people gathered to worship. This one was found in use as a squeeze stile into a nearby field before being identified and placed in the churchyard. Also found in the churchyard is the grave of Nat Gould. Nat worked on his uncle's farm opposite the Church and by the time of his death in 1919 he had written 130 horse racing novels.

The church's large, unbuttressed west tower is Norman and has an elegantly decorated south door. Most of the rest of this appealing little church dates from the 14th century, but there are some fine modern furnishings which owe much to William Morris' Arts and Crafts movement. Some of the wall paintings date from the 17th and 18th centuries. Whilst in the village it is also worth taking a look at the fine grey stone Elizabethen manor house Bradbourne Hall (private), with its three gables and beautiful terraced gardens. The Old Parsonage, which has a rather peculiar appearance as it was built in three completely different styles and materials, is also worthy of note.

BRASSINGTON
7 miles NE of Ashbourne off the B5056

This grey stone village, 800 feet above sea level and known to the locals as 'Brass'n', has its past firmly entrenched in the lead-mining and quarrying traditions of this part of Derbyshire. The hollows and bumps in the green meadows tell of 200 years of underground industry in pursuit of lead, and now lead-tolerant flowers such as mountain pansy, sandwort and orchids flourish here.

Protected from the wind by the limestone plateau that soars some 1,000 feet above sea level, the village sits by strange shaped rocks, the result of weather erosion, with names like **Rainster Rocks** and Harborough Rocks. Stone Age man found snug dwellings amongst these formations and there is evidence that animals like the sabre-toothed tiger, brown bear, wolf and hyena also found comfort here in the caves. As late as the 18th century families were still living in the caves. Once standing on the main London to Manchester road, this was once a prosperous village and many of the 17th and 18th century cottages survive from those days. Today's post office used to be the tollhouse on the Loughborough to Brassington road, which became a turnpike in 1738; the Gate Inn stood next to the turnpike gate. Brassington's oldest "resident" is a relief carving depicting a

The Miners Arms

Miners Hill, Brassington, Derbyshire DE4 4HA
Tel: 01629 540222

In the heart of the former mining village of Brassington you will find the traditional 18th-century hostelry that is **The Miners Arms**. Recently under the new management of Sandie and Clint Purcocks, here you can enjoy a pint of real ale with a good selection available from the well stocked bar. Quality food is served each lunchtime and evening from a wide ranging menu of traditional, English dishes. and proves so popular that booking is essential on Sundays. Occasional entertainment, usually at the weekends, with karaoke and quizzes.

man with one hand over his heart, which can be seen inside the Norman tower of the parish church of **St James**. It may date back to Saxon times, but most of the rest of the church is Norman, heavily restored by the Victorians. Nearby is the Wesleyan Reform Chapel, one of the so-called "Smedley Chapels" built by local millowner, Mr Smedley, in 1852. Smedley was a keen Revivalist and his two other chapels in the village are now the village hall and a private house respectively.

BALLIDON
5 miles N of Ashbourne off the A515

Ballidon is an almost deserted village, which, some 800 years ago, was a thriving community. All that can be seen today are four rather grand 17th century farms and the Norman Chapel of All Saints (much restored) standing isolated in a field surrounded by old crofts and tofts.

Overshadowed by its gigantic limestone quarry, the legacy of this tiny hamlet's days as a robust medieval village remain in the numerous earthworks, lynchets and evidence of ridge-and-furrow cultivation in its fields.

ALDWARK
9 miles NE of Ashbourne off the B5035

Close to the High Peak Trail, just inside the Peak Park boundary, Aldwark is one of the most unspoilt villages in Derbyshire. A quiet and tranquil backwater the highest recorded population was 97 inhabitants in 1831, although there is evidence of earlier occupation. A chambered tomb was discovered at Green Low, just to the north of the village, which contained pottery, flints and animal bones dating from 2000 BC.

SANDYBROOK
1½ miles N of Ashbourne off the A515

Sandybrook is a peaceful community not far from Ashbourne yet retaining an unspoilt, tranquil atmosphere.

FENNY BENTLEY
2 miles N of Ashbourne off the A515

Fenny Bentley is the first village of the Peak for visitors coming from the South, with its steep hill up into the Peak District and the old railway bridge where the Tissington Trail passes through the village. The Tissington Trail is a thirteen mile trail for walkers or cyclists from the old Ashbourne Station to The High Peak Trail at Parsley Hay.

Inside St Edmund's Church can be found the tomb of Thomas Beresford, the local lord of the manor who fought, alongside eight of his 16 sons, at Agincourt. The effigies of Beresford and his wife are surrounded by those of their 21 children - each covered by a shroud as, by the time the tombs were built nobody could remember what they had looked like! During the Civil War, much of the Church, and its rectory, were destroyed. On returning to his parish after the restoration of Charles II in 1661, the rector resolved to rebuild the rectory, which was all but rubble, and restore the Church to its former glory. Both of these he managed. The 15th century square tower of the fortified manor house, now incorporated into Cherry Orchard Farm, which belonged to the Beresford family and was once the home of Charles Cotton, is a local landmark that can be seen from the main road.

TISSINGTON
4 miles N of Ashbourne off the A515

Sitting at the foothills of the Pennines, Tissington is, perhaps, most famous for its ancient festival of well-dressing, a ceremony which dates back to 1350, or earlier. Today this takes place on Ascension Day, normally in the middle of May and draws many crowds who come to see the spectacular folk art created by the local people. The significance of the event in

Bent Farm

Tissington, Ashbourne, Derbyshire DE6 1RD
Tel/Fax: 01335 390214 website: bentfarm.co.uk

Bent Farm is a working dairy farm lying in a quiet and peaceful location within the picturesque village of Tissington and is home to Hilary and Michael Herridge. Here, within their pretty 17th-century farmhouse they offer comfortable bed and breakfast accommodation between Easter and October. There are just two en-suite guest rooms, both enjoying superb views across the surrounding countryside. A traditional, hearty farmhouse breakfast is included with vegetarian diets catered for on request. Guests can also make use of the comfortable lounge and delightful gardens. Stays of two or more nights are welcomed.

Tissington may have been to commemorate those who survived the ravages of the Black Death when it raged throughout the villages of Derbyshire. This was attributed to the purity and plentitude of the local spring waters, and the villagers were extremely lucky to have no fewer than five wells to choose from. A total of six wells are dressed at Tissington, the Hall, the Town, the Yew Tree, the Hands, the Coffin and the Children's Wells; each depicts a separate scene, usually one from the Bible. Visitors should follow the signs in the village or ask at the Old Coach House.

Very much on the tourist route, particularly in the early summer, Tissington has plenty of tea rooms and ice cream shops to satisfy the hot and thirsty visitor. The village, though often overlooked in favour of the colourful well-dressings, has some interesting buildings. The **Church of St Mary**, situated on a rise overlooking Tissington, has an unusual tub-shaped font, which dates back to the time of the original Norman Church. The pulpit too is unusual; converted from a double-decker type, it once had a set of steps leading out from the priest's stall below.

Home of the FitzHerbert family for 500 years, **Tissington Hall** is a distinguished and impressive stately home which was built by Francis FitzHerbert in 1609. The estate consists of 2,400 acres comprising 13 farms, 40 cottages and assorted lettings. The Hall boasts a wealth of original pieces, artwork, furnishings and architectural features tracing the times and tastes of the FitzHerbert family (now headed by Sir Richard FitzHerbert) over the centuries. The oak-panelled Main Hall has the original stone-flagged floor and is dominated by a stunning Gothic fireplace installed in 1757. Here visitors will also find a pair of late 18th century Chippendale bookcases, a rosewood piano and other fine pieces. The Dining Room, originally the old kitchen, is also panelled in oak and has an original Waring & Gillow table with a matching set of 13 chairs. The frieze work was added in the early 1900s. Paintings of country scenes and family portraits adorn the walls. The Library is a stunning repository of over 3,000 books, and is adorned with a superb frieze depicting a woodland scene. Other fine pieces include the bracket clock made by Jasper Taylor of Holborn in about 1907. Among the other wonderful rooms to explore are the East and West Drawing Rooms. Tissington Hall and Gardens are open to the public on 28 afternoons throughout the summer. Please call the Estate Office for details. In addition, the gardens are open on several days for charity including the National Gardens Scheme. Private groups and societies are welcome by written appointment throughout the year. The refurbished Old Coach House on the estate now houses comfortable and attractive tea rooms, opened in September 1997, it overlooks the handsome village church.

Following the old Ashbourne to Parsley Hay railway line, the **Tissington Trail** is a popular walk which can be combined with other old railway trails in the area or country lanes to make an enjoyable circular country walk. The Tissington Trail passes through some lovely countryside and, with a reasonable surface, it is also popular with cyclists. Along the route can also be found many of the old railway line buildings and junction boxes and, in particular, the old Hartington station, which is now a picnic site with an information centre in the old signal box.

PARWICH
5 miles N of Ashbourne off the A515

This typical Peak District village is delightful, with stone houses and an 1870s church around the village green. Conspicuous amongst the stonebuilt houses is **Parwich Hall**, constructed of brick and finished in 1747. The wonderful gardens at the Hall were created at the turn of the 20th century and it remains today a family home though, over the years, it has changed hands on several occasions.

Parwich Moor, above the village, is home to many mysterious Bronze Age circles, which vary in size. Though their function is unknown, it is unlikely that they were used as burial chambers. Close to Parwich is Roystone Grange, an important archaeological site where, to the north of the farmhouse, the remains of a Roman farmhouse have been excavated and, to the south, are an old engine house and the remains of the old medieval monastic grange. Both Roystone Grange and Parwich lie on the interesting and informative **Roystone Grange Archaeological Trail**, which starts at Minniglow car park. Some 11 miles long, the circular trail follows, in part, the old railway line that was built to connect the Cromford and the Peak Forest Canals in the 1820s before taking in some of the Tissington Trail.

ALSOP-EN-LE-DALE
5 miles N of Ashbourne off the A515

The old station on the Ashbourne-Buxton line, which once served this tiny hamlet is today a car park on the Tissington Trail. The tranquil hamlet itself is on a narrow lane east of the main road towards Parwich, just a mile from Dovedale. Alsop-en-le-Dale's parish church of St Michael is Norman, though it was rebuilt substantially during Victorian times. The nave retains Norman features, with

THE SYCAMORE INN
Parwich, Ashbourne, Derbyshire DE6 1QL
Tel: 01335 390212

The Sycamore Inn, dating back to the early 19th century, is a pretty stone-built country inn enjoying a picture postcard setting in the shadow of the church and overlooking the green in the village of Parwich. The present tenant, Janet Gosling, was born and brought up in the village. The well stocked bar offers a choice of real ales and Janet's home cooked meals are available each lunch time and evening. There is a quiz fortnightly on Thursday during the winter months and occasional musical entertainment throughout the year.

CHURCH FARM COTTAGES

Alsop-en-le-Dale, Ashbourne, Derbyshire DE6 1QP
Tel/Fax: 01335 390216
e-mail: churchfarmcottages.alsop@virgin.net
website: www.cressbrook.co.uk/ashborn/churchfarm

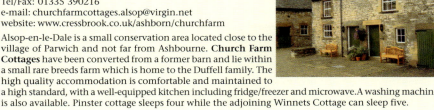

Alsop-en-le-Dale is a small conservation area located close to the village of Parwich and not far from Ashbourne. **Church Farm Cottages** have been converted from a former barn and lie within a small rare breeds farm which is home to the Duffell family. The high quality accommodation is comfortable and maintained to a high standard, with a well-equipped kitchen including fridge/freezer and microwave. A washing machine is also available. Pinster cottage sleeps four while the adjoining Winnets Cottage can sleep five.

impressive double zigzag mouldings in the arches, but the west tower is only imitation Norman, and dates from 1883. One unusual feature, which dominates this small church is its extraordinary 19th century, square mock-Gothic pulpit.

Opposite the church is the graceful and slender building known as **Alsop Hall**, constructed in the early 1600s. Though privately owned, it is worth seeing even for its exterior, as it is built in a handsome pre-classical style with stone-mullioned windows.

Alsop makes a good base for exploring the White Peak. It is also convenient for Dovedale. The renowned **Viator's Bridge** at Milldale is only a mile away to the west, as immortalised in Izaak Walton's *The Compleat Angler* in a scene in which the character Viator complains to another about the size of the tiny, two-arched packhorse bridge, deeming it "not two fingers broad".

NEWHAVEN
11 miles N of Ashbourne off the A5012

The High Peak Trail crosses Newhaven to link up with the Tissington Trail. This charming village is also along the White Peak tourist route, though it retains a tranquil air.

ARBOR LOW
13 miles N of Ashbourne off the A515

This remote stone circle is often referred to as the "Stonehenge of the Peaks", and it is still an impressive sight. There are several stone circles in the Peak District but none offer the same atmosphere as Arbor Low, nor the same splendid views (see page 67).

MAPPLETON
2 miles NW of Ashbourne off the A515

Mappleton is a village that has existed in some form or other since before 1086, when it is recorded in the *Domesday Book*. It is a secluded and charming village of the Dove Valley, with attractive views and a wealth of exciting natural beauty. The 18th century village church of St Mary's, is unusual in that it has a dome rather then a tower or a steeple. There has been a church here since at least the reign of Edward I.

Mappleton's main claim to fame is its annual New Years Day charity bridge jump, when 10 teams of 3 people paddle down 1/2 a mile of the river Dove and then jump off a bridge. The Dove is not easily navigable, the bridge is 30 feet high and after the jump there is a 500 yard sprint to the pub. It is a grand spectator sport and hundreds of people come to watch.!

THORPE
3 miles NW of Ashbourne off the A515

Thorpe was mentioned in the *Domesday Book* and is one of the few villages in the Peak, whose name has Norse origins, for

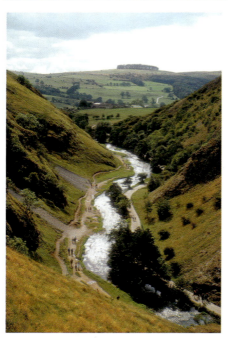

Dovedale

the Danish settlers did not generally penetrate far into this area. It lies at the confluence of the Rivers Manifold and Dove, and is dominated by the conical hill of **Thorpe Cloud**, which guards the entrance to **Dovedale**. Cloud is a corruption of the Old English word 'clud', meaning hill. The summit is a short but stiff climb from any direction, but whichever way you go the climb is rewarded by a panoramic view over Dovedale all the way to Alstonefield as well as Ilam and the lower Manifold valley. Although the Dale becomes over-crowded at times, there is always plenty of open space to explore on the hill as well as excellent walking. For much of its 45 mile course from Axe Edge to its confluence with the River Trent, the **River Dove** is a walker's river as it is mostly inaccessible by car. The steep sides to its valley, the fast-flowing water and the magnificent white rock formations all give Dovedale a special charm. Dovedale, however, is only a short section of the valley; above Viator Bridge it becomes Mill Dale and further upstream again are **Wolfscote Dale** and **Beresford Dale**. The temptation to provide every possible amenity for visitors, at the expense of the scenery, has been avoided and the village of Thorpe, clustered around the church, remains an unspoilt and unsophisticated limestone village. The beautiful little church with a Norman tower, was built about AD1100, with some Saxon work here and there. The nave was added in the 14th century, possibly replacing a Saxon construction, and a vestry in the 19th century. It has walls of limestone rubble which give the curious impression that the building is leaning outwards. If on horseback it is possible to read the curious sundial at the Church, but otherwise it is too high up! There is a fine tomb of the Millward family (1632) by the altar.

Close by the River Dove, not far from the village, is the 17th century farmhouse that has been sympathetically transformed into the Izaak Walton Hotel. The delights of trout fishing along this stretch of the river have been much written about, and most famously in *The Compleat Angler*, by Sir Izaak Walton. His fishing house, which he shared with his friend Charles Cotton, is preserved and can be seen in Beresford Dale. At this point along the river there is also a public car park, complete with other amenities useful to the walker and sightseer. A stroll up Dovedale from this point, as far as Milldale, will show the beauty of this stretch of valley to its fullest. The walking, along the river bank, is relatively easy (in many places wheelchairs will have no problem) but after a period of rain it can get quite muddy.

The Victorians delighted in visiting Dovedale, it was praised by such writers as Byron and Tennyson and soon became as popular as Switzerland. However, their enthusiasm for the Dale also had a down side and, as well as providing donkey rides up the Dale, in the late 19th century sycamore trees were planted along the sides of the Dale. Not native to this area, they overshadow the native ash and obscure many of the rock formations that make this such a special place. The National Trust are keeping the trees in check and encouraging the ash to grow. On higher, more windswept ground, the story would have been different as sycamore trees are ideal for providing a natural wind break.

The **Stepping Stones**, a delight for children, are the first point of interest, though for those who do not want to cross the river at this point there is a foot bridge closer to the carpark just below Thorpe Cloud. Further up the Dale is the limestone crag known as **Dovedale Castle** and, on the opposite bank, the higher hill known as Lover's Leap after a failed lover's suicide. Other interesting natural features with romantic names found along the way include the Twelve Apostles and the Tissington Spires.

Stepping Stones, Dovedale

ILAM
4 miles NW of Ashbourne off the A52

The village was inhabited in Saxon times and the church still displays some Saxon stonework as well as the tomb of the Saxon saint, Bertram, who lived as a hermit in this area. Now a model village of great charm, Ilam was originally an important settlement belonging to Burton Abbey. Following the Reformation in the 16th century, the estate was broken up and Ilam came into the hands of the Port family. In the early 19th century the family sold the property to Jesse Watts Russell, a weathly industrialist. He moved the village from its position near Ilam Hall and rebuilt it in its current location in 'Alpine style'. This explains both the unusual style of the buildings and the

HILLCREST HOUSE

Thorpe, Dovedale, Ashbourne, Derbyshire DE6 2AW
Tel: 01335 350436
e-mail hillcrest@freenet.co.uk
website www.ashbourne-town.com/accom/hilcrest

In the heart of Dovedale, in the historic village of Thorpe, is **Hillcrest House**. A former coaching inn, this has been home to Margaret and Dan Sutton for nearly four years and they have converted it into a high quality guest house. There are seven superb bedrooms, of varying sizes, most with en-suite facilities. Tasty farmhouse breakfasts are served each morning and packed lunches and evening meals can be provided. Spacious resident's lounge with bar available to all guests.

surprising distance between them and the village church. As well as building a fine mansion, **Ilam Hall**, for himself, Russell also spent a great deal of money refurbishing the village. Obviously devoted to his wife, he had the Hall rebuilt in a romantic Gothic style and, in the centre of the village, he had the Eleanor Cross erected in her memory. No longer a family home, Ilam Hall is now a Youth Hostel.

The ancient parish **Church of the Holy Cross**, with its saddleback tower, was largely rebuilt in 1855, and again the family are not forgotten as there is an enormous Watts Russell mausoleum dominating the north side. Opposite, on the south side, there is a little chapel which was rebuilt in 1618 and contains the shrine of a much-loved Staffordshire saint and local Saxon prince, Bertelin. The chapel became the object of many pilgrimages in medieval times. Another important Saxon item inside the church is the font in the nave whilst outside in the churchyard there are several Saxon cross shafts. As with many other churches in Derbyshire, it was the custom for garlands to be hung in the Church on the death of a young girl in the parish. The sad, faded "virgin crants", referred to by Shakespeare at the death of Ophelia, can still be seen.

Many places in the Peak District have provided the inspiration for writers over the years and Ilam is no exception. The peace and quiet found here helped William Congreve create his bawdy play *The Old Bachelor*, whilst Dr Johnson wrote *Rasselas* whilst staying at the Hall. In the valley of the River Manifold, and a much-used starting point for walks along this beautiful stretch of river, in summer the Manifold disappears underground north of the village to reappear below Ilam Hall. The village is also the place where the Rivers Manifold and Dove merge. Though Dovedale is, and probably deservedly so, the most scenic of the Peak District valleys,

the Manifold Valley is very similar and whilst being marginally less beautiful it is often much less crowded. The two rivers rise close together, on Axe Edge, and for much of their course follow a parallel path, so it is fitting that they should also come together.

WATERHOUSES
6½ miles NW of Ashbourne off the A523

Between here and Hulme End, the Leek and Manifold Valley Light Railway, a picturesque narrow-gauge line, used to follow the valleys of the Manifold and the Hamps, crisscrossing the latter on little bridges. Sadly trains no longer run but its track bed has been made into the **Hamps-Manifold Track**, a marvellous walk which is ideal for small children and people in wheelchairs, since its surface is level and tarred throughout its eight miles. The Track can be reached from car parks at Hulme End, Waterhouses, Weags Bridge near Grindon, and Wetton.

The **River Hamps** is similar to the River Manifold and, indeed, other rivers which pass over limestone plateaux, in that it too disappears underground for some of its course. In the case of the Hamps, it disappears at Waterhouses and reappears again near Ilam before it merges with the River Manifold.

WATERFALL
7 miles NW of Ashbourne off the A523

The tiny village of Waterfall is a small Staffordshire village, set on the moors, named after the way that the River Hemp, disappears underground through crevices in the ground. It was once the starting point of the Manifold Valley Light Railway, a narrow gauge railway from the main Leek-Ashbourne railway line, via Wetton to Hume End. The line has since been removed and now the track is the Manifold Trail, a well used tourist trail for walkers and cyclists.

The village church of **St James and St Bartholomew** is originally Norman but was largely rebuilt in the 19th century. However the Norman Chancel has been retained.

HOPEDALE
7 miles NW of Ashbourne off the A515

Hopedale is a charming hamlet just south of Alstonefield. It was the site of one of the first co-operative cheese producing factories in the country, with cheese being produced from 1874. They made a Derby cheese, but eventually greater demand and improved methods of distribution led to the closure of this small co-operative.

GRINDON
7½ miles NW of Ashbourne off the B5053

This unique moorland hill village stands over 1,000 feet above sea level and overlooks the beautiful Manifold Valley. Recorded in the *Domesday Book* as Grendon, meaning green hill, "an ancient manor in the 20th year of the reign of William the Conqueror", Grindon is reputed to have been visited by Bonnie Prince Charlie on his way to Derby. It was once a staging post on the packhorse route from Ecton Hill and the most productive copper mine in the country, where many of the local people would have worked.

The splendid isolation in which this village, like others nearby, stands is confirmed by a look around the churchyard. The names on the epitaphs and graves reflect the close knit nature of the communities. The Salt family, for instance, are to be seen everywhere, followed closely by the Stubbs, Cantrells, Hambletons and, to a lesser extent, the Mycocks. The church, with its soaring spire, dates only from the 19th century, but there has been a church here since at least the 11th century. Outside the church entrance there is a 'Rindle' stone. This records that: 'The Lord of the Manor of Grindon established his right to this rindle at Stafford Assizes on March 17th 1872'. A rindle is a brook which runs only in wet weather. In the church can also be found a memorial to six RAF men who were killed in 1947 when their Halifax aircraft crash landed during a blizzard on Grindon Moor when trying to parachute in food packages to the surrounding villages which had been totally cut off by the excessive snowfall.

WETTON
7½ miles NW of Ashbourne off the B5053

Wetton Mill has been sympathetically converted by the National Trust into a cafe, a very welcome sight for those walking the **Manifold Valley Trail**. There is also a car park here for the less energetic and a picnic area for those who would rather cater for themselves. Much of the hillside either side of the track also belongs to the National Trust and is a splendid place for walks.

Below the Mill can be found the ominous-sounding **Thor's Cave**, situated some 250 feet above the River Manifold. Though the Cave is not deep, the entrance is huge, some 60 feet, and the stiff climb up is well worth the effort for the spectacular views, all framed by the great natural stone arch. The acoustics too are interesting, and conversations can easily be carried out with people far below. In the village churchyard is the grave of Samuel Carrington, who, along with Thomas Bateman of Youlgreave, found evidence that Thor's Cave was occupied in Iron Age times. The openings at the bottom of the crag on which the Cave sits are known as **Radcliffe Stables** and are said to have been used by a Jacobite as a hiding place after Bonnie Prince Charlie had retreated from Derby.

Carrington also excavated the fields close to Wetton, where he was schoolmaster in the mid 1800s, and found an abandoned village, though neither he nor his friend Bateman could put an age to the settlement.

ALSTONEFIELD
7½ miles NW of Ashbourne off the A515

This ancient village, situated between the Manifold and the Dove valleys, lies at the crossroads of several old packhorse routes and even had its own market charter granted in 1308. The market ceased in 1500 but the annual cattle sales continued right up until the beginning of the 20th century.

Its geographical location has helped to maintain the charm of this unspoilt village. There has been no invasion by the canal or railway builders (it lies at 900 feet above sea level) and it is still two miles from the nearest classified road. One hundred and fifty years ago Alstonefield was at the centre of a huge parish which covered all the land between the two rivers. There has been a church here since, at least, AD 892 but the earliest known parts of the present Church are the Norman doorway and chancel arch of 1100. There is also plenty of 17th century woodwork and a double-decker pulpit dated 1637. Izaak Walton's friend, Charles Cotton, and his family lived at nearby Beresford Hall, now unfortunately no more, but their elaborate greenish pew is still in the church.

The village also retains its ancient **Tithe Barn**, found behind the late 16th century rectory. The internal exposed wattle and daub wall and the spiral stone staircase may, however, have been part of an earlier building.

ECTON
9½ miles NW of Ashbourne off the B5054

The tiny hamlet of Ecton, close to Hulme End, was once the site of great activity. The copper mines here were owned by the Duke of Devonshire and it is generally accepted that the profits from the ore extraction paid for his building of The Crescent at Buxton. One of the mines, Deep Ecton, to the north of **Ecton Hill**, was, at nearly 1,400 feet, one of the deepest in Europe. Work had ceased in the mines by 1900 but, so impervious was the surrounding limestone that the workings took several years to flood though now they are under water.

WARSLOW
9 miles NW of Ashbourne off the B5054

Situated opposite Wetton on the other side of the River Manifold, the village is one of the main access points to this dramatic section of the Manifold Valley. Lying below the gritstone moorlands this was an estate village for the eccentric Crewe family, who lived at Calke Abbey in south Derbyshire.

HULME END
9 miles NW of Ashbourne off the B5054

This is the ideal place from which to explore the **Manifold Valley**. From here to Ilam, the River Manifold runs southwards through a deep, twisting limestone cleft, between steep and wooded banks. For much of its dramatic course the Manifold disappears underground in dry weather, through swallow holes, which is typical of a river in a limestone area.

The village also lays at the terminus of the **Leek and Manifold Valley Light Railway**, which opened in 1904. Already aware of the tourism possibilities of the Peak District by the beginning of the 20th century, the other reason for constructing the railway was to transport coal and other raw materials to the surrounding settlements. A narrow-gauge railway, which left the standard gauge at Waterhouses, progressed through this seemingly inhospitable land of deep valleys by following the banks of the River Hamps - a tributary of the River Manifold.

THE MANIFOLD INN

Hulme End, Hartington, Nr. Buxton,
Derbyshire SK17 0EX
Tel: 01298 84537
website: www.themanifoldinn.co.uk

The Manifold Inn is a delightful 200-year old former coaching inn, which takes its name from the river on whose bank it sits. It makes an ideal base for exploring the area, and to take advantage of that there are five en-suite rooms available for bed and breakfast. This family-run hostelry offers a fine choice of ales together with a wide-ranging menu of meals and snacks. Food and drink are available each lunchtime and evening. A well-liked pub with many regular customers.

The line, however, was unable to pay its way, particularly after the creamery at Ecton, just a mile south of Hulme End, closed in 1933 and the following year the railway ceased operation. The tracks were taken up and, if it had not been turned into a semi-long distance footpath, the route of the railway might have been lost forever.

Considering that the buildings at Hulme End station were constructed using materials that were not designed to withstand the test of time, chiefly corrugated iron and wood, it is surprising to find that two of the three survive. Though the station, along with the railway closed in 1934, the sheds are still in use today.

HARTINGTON
10 miles NW of Ashbourne off the B5054

This charming limestone village was granted a market charter in 1203 and it is likely that its spacious market place was once the village green. Now a Youth Hostel

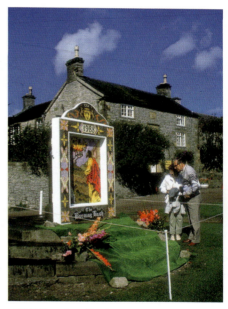

Well Dressing, Hartington

BERESFORD TEAROOM

Market Place, Hartington, Buxton, Derbyshire SK17 0AL
Tel: 01298 84418

In the village of Hartington, not far from Buxton and lying on the popular Tissington walking trail, you will find the **Beresford Tearoom**. Owned and run by Sue Wardle, with her business partner Bob, since 1987, the popular tearoom is open seven days a week through the summer from 10.30am until 5pm (open 10.30am-3.30pm most days in winter). She serves a delicious selection of home-made food with breakfasts, drinks, snacks, light meals and a range of delicious cakes. There is also a small gift shop selling local crafts.

The Cock Inn

Clifton, Nr. Ashbourne,
Derbyshire DE6 2GJ
Tel: 01335 342654

The Cock Inn at Clifton originally dates from the 17th century and is a hostelry that is full of history and character, housed within a solid, white-washed building of local stone, with good proportions and retaining many period features. It was originally a roadside coaching inn, which has inevitably been added to and altered over the years, but it still manages to retain the look and feel of those earlier times when a coach and horses would draw up at the entrance and life was lived at a less hectic pace.

Just as it was a staging point long ago, when coaches were the preferred mode of transport, today it continues to be an ideal stopping off point for a drink or a delicious meal. It can be conveniently found just off the A515 in the village of Clifton, just a mile south of Ashbourne, and there is ample car parking provided to the rear. The interior is well maintained, everything is spotlessly clean and the atmosphere is friendly and welcoming. There is plenty of room to find a cosy corner in which to enjoy a quiet drink, without feeling like you're party to your neighbours' conversation. The bar is well stocked and carries no less than three real ales with Bass and Pedigree being permanent features with a regularly rotated guest ale. You will also find draught bitter, mild, lager, stout and cider available, and being a roadside inn there is also a great range of cold and alcohol free drinks if you're behind the wheel.

The food is good, honest pub fayre with a selection of simple but beautifully cooked dishes which are all prepared on the premises using ingredients that are as fresh and full of flavour as possible. The portions are hearty and filling, and each dish on the menu is realistically priced to suit your pocket.

A recent addition to the facilities is the guest room upstairs, which is available for bed and breakfast as a double, twin or family room to suit your requirements. Like everything else at the Cock, it is neatly kept and comfortably furnished, and you can also enjoy an en-suite shower room. Children welcome.

The Cock Inn is owned and personally run by Delphe Gadsby and she works hard to provide a welcoming atmosphere that combines a sense of tradition and history with the modern concepts of efficiency and value for money. This hostelry is popular both with locals and visitors to the area.

DOVEDALE AND THE STAFFORDSHIRE MOORLANDS 101

WOLFSCOTE GRANGE
Hartington, Nr. Buxton, Derbyshire SK17 0AX
Tel/Fax: 01298 84342
e-mail: wolfscote@btinternet.com

Wolfscote Grange, home of Jane and Joe Gibbs, needs nothing more than its setting to help sell it as a perfect place to stay. The rural location is idyllic, surrounded by miles of rolling countryside and with picture postcard views in all directions. Here you will find high quality farmhouse bed and breakfast accommodation with three guest rooms. There are also four pretty self-catering holiday cottages, all in converted former farm buildings, fully equipped and comfortably furnished in a traditional style. Highly recommended.

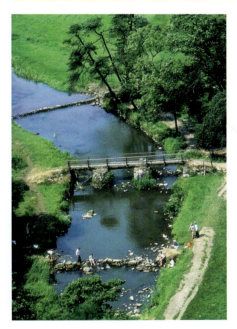

Beresford Dale

(the oldest in the Peak District, opening in 1934), **Hartington Hall**, built in the 17th century and enlarged in the 19th century, is typical of many Peak District manor houses and a fine example of a Derbyshire yeoman's house and farm. The village is also the home to the only cheese factory remaining in Derbyshire. From the dairy, not far from the village mere, Stilton, veined, plain or flavoured, is still made and can be bought at the dairy shop.

The village is very much on the tourist route and, though it is popular, Hartington has retained much of its village appeal. As well as the famous cheese shop, there are two old coaching inns left over from the days when this was an important market centre, which still serve refreshments to visitors. One of these goes by the rather unusual name of The Charles Cotton; named after the friend of Izaak Walton. Situated in the valley of the River Dove, Hartington is an excellent place from which to explore both the Dove and the Manifold valleys. To the south lies **Beresford Dale**, the upper valley of the River Dove and easily as pretty as its more famous neighbour Dovedale. It was immortalised by Izaak Walton and Charles Cotton when *The Compleat Angler* was published in 1653. Telling of their fishing experiences on this famous trout river, it is not surprising that the pair chose this Dale as their favourite site. Together they built a fishing temple on the banks of the River Dove in Beresford Dale bearing the inscription Piscatoribus Sacrum. The temple still stands on private land. Cotton was born and lived at Beresford Hall until financial difficulties forced him to sell it in 1681.

MAYFIELD
2½ miles SW of Ashbourne off the A523

Mayfield is a large village on the edge of

COLLYCROFT FARM

Clifton, Nr. Ashbourne, Derbyshire DE6 2GN
Tel: 01335 342187

A couple of miles south of Ashbourne, surrounded by picturesque countryside, you will find **Collycroft Farm**, a 250-acre working dairy farm. Here you can enjoy superb bed and breakfast accommodation within the charming 200-year old farmhouse, home of Mary and Ernest Hollingsworth. The three guest rooms are spacious and comfortably furnished in a traditional style, and all have panoramic views over the surrounding area. Hearty breakfasts are served in a pleasant breakfast room, with much of the produce sourced from Mary and Ernest's son's butchers shop.

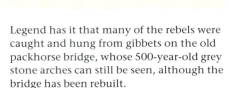

Ashbourne, divided into Upper Mayfield and Middle Mayfield. Mayfield is just "over the border" from Derbyshire and lies in Staffordshire.

Mayfield was originally a Saxon village, dating back over a thousand years and listed in the *Domesday Book* as Mavreveldt. The first Norman church was probably built about 1125 during the reign of Henry I, and the present parish church of **St John the Baptist**, illustrates the progressive styles of architecture since that date, with a 14th century chancel and a 16th century tower. In the churchyard there is an original Saxon cross. The ballad writer, Thomas Moore lived at Moore Cottage, formerly Stancliffe Farm. His young daughter, Olivia is buried in the local churchyard, her slate tombstone reading "Olivia Byron Moore, died March 18, 1815". Moore was friendly with Lord Byron, who visited him here.

On 7 December 1745 Bonnie Prince Charlie and his army passed through Mayfield on their retreat from Derby, terrorising the local populace. They shot the innkeeper at Hanging Bridge as well as a Mr Humphrey Brown, who refused to hand over his horse to them. Many of the terrified villagers locked themselves in the church. The soldiers fired shots through the door and the bullet holes can still be seen in the woodwork of the west door.

Legend has it that many of the rebels were caught and hung from gibbets on the old packhorse bridge, whose 500-year-old grey stone arches can still be seen, although the bridge has been rebuilt.

There is however a road out of the village, leading to the main Leek highway marked on the Ordnance Survey map as "Gallowstree Lane", suggesting that those to be hung went their way via the bridge and Gallowstree Lane to Gallowstree Hill.

Today it is a pleasant walk rewarded by a lovely view down the Dove Valley.

The Mayfield Mill site has the fairly rare distinction of a history of almost 200 years of textile production. The first mention of any sort of mill occurs in a property valuation of 1291: most of Mayfield then belonged to the Priory of Tutbury and it included a corn mill. By 1793 there had been various owners of the site which has developed to include two corn mills, two fulling mills and a leather mill. Textiles first appeared in 1795 when the cotton mill was completed. Unfortunately in 1806 the interior of the building, together with most of the machinery, was destroyed in a fire. When the mill was eventually rebuilt it was with a cast iron framework and brick vaulted ceilings, as can still be seen in the oldest of the buildings, to prevent a repetition of the fire.

The spinning of cotton continued in

Mayfield with various degrees of economic success until 1934 when it was sold to William Tatton and Company who used the mill to process silk. Since then it has seen changes of ownership and production but the mill remains.

SWINSCOE
4 miles W of Ashbourne off the A523

The peaceful hamlet of Swinscoe straddles the Derbyshire/Staffordshire border, not far from the River Manifold.

CAULDON
8 miles SE of Leek off the A52

This was the site of the quarry from which wagons travelled, down a railway track, to

Canal Boat, Cauldon

Froghall Wharf. In a former school building in the village can be found the **Staffordshire Peak Arts Centre**, which has a craft shop and a restaurant and holds regular exhibitions.

LEEK
15 miles NW of Ashbourne on the A523

Known as the 'Capital of the Moorlands', this is an attractive textile centre on the banks of the River Churnet. It was here that French Huguenots settled, after fleeing from religious oppression, and established the silk industry that thrived due to the abundance of soft water coming off the nearby moorland. Until the 19th century, this was a domestic industry with the workshops on the top storeys of the houses; many examples of these 'top shops' have survived to this day. Leek also became an important dyeing town, particularly after the death of Prince Albert, when 'Raven Black' was popularised by Queen Victoria, who remained in mourning for her beloved husband for many years.

William Morris, founder of the Arts and Crafts movement, lived and worked in Leek for many months between 1875 and 1878. Much of his time here was spent investigating new techniques of dyeing but he also revived the use of traditional dyes. His influence cannot only be seen in the art here but also in the architecture. **Leek Art Gallery** is also the place to go to find out more about the wonderful and intricate work of the famous Leek School of Embroidery that was founded by Lady Wardle in the 1870s. A replica of the Bayeux Tapestry, now on display in the Museum of Reading was first displayed here in 1886. She was Elizabeth Wardle along with thirty-five members of the Leek Embroidery Society and other embroiderers from the surrounding area completed the tapestry in just over a year. Each embroiderer stitched her name beneath her completed panel.

Leek is by no means a recent town that grew up in the shadow of the Industrial Revolution. An ancient borough, granted its charter in 1214, Leek was a thriving market centre rivalling Macclesfield and

The Priory

Abbots Road, Leek, Staffordshire ST13 6EZ
Tel: 01538 399988

The Priory is a superb, family-run hostelry, located just a short walk from the centre of Leek. The Victorian frontage is impressive, while inside you will find a spacious, open-plan style interior with plenty of tables and cosy seating. Open all day every day, the bar keeps three real ales on tap with plenty of other popular choices too. Quality food is available Saturday lunchtime only, with a menu of traditional English food. Live music or karaoke each Friday night and live entertainment each Saturday night.

The Green Man

38 Compton, Leek, Staffordshire ST13 5NH
Tel: 01538 388084
website: www.greenman-guesthouse.co.uk

Conveniently located in the centre of Leek, The Green Man is a former public house that now provides motel-style and guest house accommodation. There are two guest rooms within the main building, while a further four are in the adjoining annexe. The great attraction is that all guests in the annexe have their own doors and the freedom to come and go as they please. All rooms are en-suite. Accommodation is on a bed and breakfast, or dinner, bed and breakfast basis. Full restaurant licence.

The Moss Rose Inn

Buxton Road, Leek, Staffordshire ST13 7LN
Tel: 01538 398956

The Moss Rose Inn is a traditional country pub, enjoying a rural location just a short drive from the centre of Leek, and these attractive, whitewashed premises date back to the 18th century. The pub enjoys a super reputation for serving delicious food, and a wide ranging menu of home-made dishes is served each lunchtime and evening (no food Sunday and Monday evenings). The bar also stocks a good range with three real ales on tap. Popular pub quiz held each Sunday night.

Hare and Gate

Queens Drive, Leek, Staffordshire ST13 6QF
Tel: 01538 383507

Just a short drive from Leek town centre you will find the **Hare and Gate** public house. This relatively modern pub was built in 1963 and provides a spacious interior in which to enjoy a drink and a snack. Bass is permanently on tap and a selection of sandwiches and filled rolls are available at all times. Open at nearly every session (closed Thursday lunchtime) and all day Friday and Saturday. Live performers every Saturday night. Superb beer garden and large off-road car park.

Congleton. **The Butter Cross**, which now stands in the Market Place, was originally erected near the junction of Sheep Market and Stanley Street by the Joliffe family in 1671. Every road coming into the town seems to converge on the old cobbled Market Place and the road to the west leads down to the Parish Church. Dedicated to Edward the Confessor (the full name is St Edward's and All Saints' Church), the original Church was burnt down in 1297 and rebuilt some 20 years later though the building is now largely 17th century. The timber roof of the nave is well worth a second look and is the Church's pride and joy. It is boasted that each of the cross beams was hewn from a separate oak tree and, in the west part of the nave, an enormous 18th-century gallery rises up, tier on tier, giving the impression of a theatre's dress circle!

Although much has been altered inside the Church, most notably in 1865 when GE Street rebuilt the chancel, reredos, sanctuary, pulpit and stalls, there still remains a rather unusual wooden chair. Traditionally this is believed to have been a ducking stool for scolds, which was used in the nearby River Churnet. Outside, in the churchyard, can be found a rather curious inscription on a gravestone: "James Robinson interred February the 28th 1788 Aged 438"! To the north side of the Church is an area still known locally as 'Petty France', which holds the graves of many Napoleonic prisoners of war who lived nearby.

Another building worthy of a second glance is the imposing **Nicholson Institute**, with its copper dome. Completed in 1884 and funded by the local industrialist Joshua Nicholson, the Institute offered the people of Leek an opportunity to learn and also expand their cultural horizons. Many of the great Victorian literary giants, including George

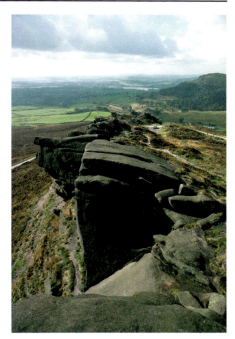

Ramshaw Rocks

Bernard Shaw and Mark Twain, came here to admire the building. The town's War Memorial, built in Portland stone and with a clock tower, has a dedication to the youngest Nicholson son, who was killed in the First World War. Leek was the home of James Brindley, the 18th-century engineer who built much of the early canal network. A water-powered corn mill built by him in 1752 in Mill Street has been restored and now houses the **Brindley Water Museum**, which is devoted to his life and work. Visitors can see corn being ground and see displays of millwrighting skills. Leek has a traditional outdoor market every Wednesday, a craft and antiques market on Saturday and an indoor 'butter market' on Wednesday, Friday and Saturday.

The **River Churnet**, though little known

outside Staffordshire, has a wealth of scenery and industrial archaeology. It is easily accessible to walkers and its valley deserves better recognition. The river rises to the west of Leek in rugged gritstone country, but for most of its length it flows through softer red sandstone countryside in a valley that was carved out during the Ice Age. Though there are few footpaths directly adjacent to the riverbank, most of the valley can be walked close to the river using a combination of canal towpaths and former railway tracks.

Four miles to the north of Leek on the A53 rise the dark, jagged gritstone outcrops of **The Roaches**, Ramshaw Rocks and Hen Cloud. Roaches is a corruption of the French word 'roches' or rocks and was reputedly given by Napoleonic prisoners: 'cloud' is a local word used for high hills. Just below The Roaches there is another delightful stretch of water, **Tittesworth Reservoir**, which is extremely popular with trout fishermen. It has some super trails, a visitor centre with an interactive exhibition, a restaurant and a gift shop.

RUDYARD
2 miles NW of Leek off the A523

In fond memory of the place where they first met in 1863, Mr and Mrs Kipling named their famous son, born in 1865, after this village. The nearby two mile long Rudyard Lake was built in 1831 by John Rennie to feed the Caldon Canal.

With steeply wooded banks the lake is now a leisure centre where there are facilities for picnicking, walking, fishing and sailing. The west shore of the Reservoir is also a section of the Staffordshire Way, the long distance footpath which runs from Mow Cop to **Kinver Edge**, near Stourbridge. This is a sandstone ridge covered in woodland and heath, and with several famous rock houses which were inhabited until the 1950s.

Back in Victorian days, Rudyard was a popular lakeside resort, which developed after the construction of the North Staffordshire Railway in 1845. The Rudyard Lake Steam Railway uses miniature narrow gauge steam trains to give a 3 mile return trip along the side of Rudyard Lake. Its popularity became so great that, on one particular day in 1877, over 20,000 people came here to see Captain Webb, the first man to swim the English Channel, swim in the Reservoir.

RUSHTON SPENCER
5 miles NW of Leek on the A523

This pleasant, moorland village nestles under the distinctive hill the Cloud and is the ideal starting point for a walk to the summit. It is also well known for its lonely church, the **'Chapel in the Wilderness'**, originally built of wood in the 14th century, which served both Rushton Spencer and neighbouring Rushton James. It has been almost rebuilt in stone.

4 The Trent Valley

In the valley of the River Trent, which runs through the southern part of the county, can be found many splendid stately homes, including Kedleston Hall and the eccentric Calke Abbey. The scenery affords ample opportunities to enjoy pleasant walks. This chapter also includes the western side of the region known as Erewash.

Derbyshire was at the forefront of modern thinking at the beginning of the Industrial Revolution. The chief inheritor of this legacy was Derby, and this city is still a busy industrial centre and home to the Industrial Museum. There are plenty of other places to visit in Derby, which is not, as is often supposed, the county town (that honour goes to Matlock).

Truly an area of hidden places, among the many explored in this chapter that are well worth a visit are the picturesque villages of Church Gresley and Castle Gresley, the welcoming centres of Melbourne and Hartshorne, quiet Repton on the River Trent and the "border" town of Swadlincote and the surrounding area.

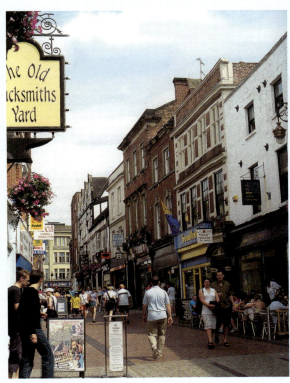

Derby Town Centre

108 THE HIDDEN PLACES OF DERBYSHIRE

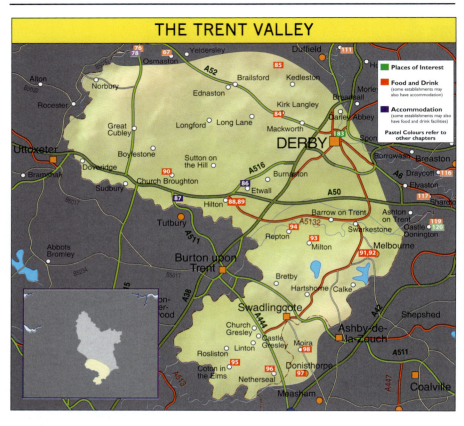

PLACES TO STAY, EAT, DRINK AND SHOP

83	Pickford's House, Derby	Museum	Page 110
84	The Bluebell Inn, Kirk Langley, Nr Ashbourne	Pub with Food	Page 113
85	The Cock Inn, Mugginton	Pub with Restaurant	Page 114
86	Blenheim House, Etwall	Guest House and Restaurant	Page 116
87	The Castle Hotel, Hatton	Hotel	Page 118
88	The White Swan, Hilton	Pub with Food	Page 119
89	The Old Talbot Inn, Hilton	Pub with Food	Page 119
90	Holly Bush Inn, Church Broughton	Pub with Food	Page 120
91	Bay Tree Restaurant, Melbourne	Restaurant	Page 122
92	Scarecrows, Melbourne	Restaurant	Page 124
93	The Swan Inn, Milton	Pub	Page 125
94	The Bulls Head, Repton	Pub with Restaurant	Page 126
95	The Queens Head, Coton-in-the-Elms	Pub, Food and Accommodation	Page 128
96	The Hollybush, Netherseal	Pub with Food	Page 128
97	The Turks Head, Donisthorpe	Pub	Page 129
98	Lakeside Lodge Tearoom, Moira	Tea Rooms	Page 130

DERBY

Essentially a commercial and industrial city, Derby's position, historically and geographically, has ensured that is has remained one of the most important and interesting cities in the area and, consequently, there is much for the visitor to see, whether from an architectural or historical point of view. There are, however, two things that most people, whether they have been to the city before or not, know of Derby: Rolls-Royce engines and Royal Crown Derby porcelain. When in 1906 Sir Henry Royce and the Hon C S Rolls joined forces and built the first Rolls-Royce (a Silver Ghost) at Derby, they built much more than just a motor car. Considered by many to be the best cars in the world, it is often said that the noisiest moving part in any Rolls-Royce is the dashboard clock!

The home of **Royal Crown Derby**, any visit to the city would not be complete without a trip to the factory and its museum and shop. The guided tours offer an intriguing insight into the high level of skill required to create the delicate flower petals, hand gild the plates and to hand paint the Derby Dwarves. The latest addition to the entrance to the factory is the illuminated ceramic window created by local artist Angela Verdon along with staff at Royal Crown Derby. Japanese influences were combined with the translucent quality of Royal crown Derby china to achieve this very innovative design, using simple images of the natural world . The museum houses the most comprehensive collection of Derby Porcelain to be seen anywhere in the world, including 18th century figurines, many interpretations of the Japanese designs for which the company is famous, the delicate "Eggshell China", by French Art Director, Desire Leroy and examples of the Crown Derby ware commissioned for the restaurants of the Titanic.

The city's **Cathedral of All Saints** possesses a fine 16th century tower, the second highest perpendicular tower in England and the oldest ring of ten bells in the world. The airy building was actually built in the 1720s by James Gibbs. Inside is a beautiful wrought-iron screen by Robert

Derby Cathedral

Bakewell and, among the splendid monuments, lies the tomb of Bess of Hardwick Hall. Originally Derby's Parish Church, it was given cathedral status in 1927. In the late 1960s the building was extended eastwards and the retrochoir, baldacchino and sacristy were added along with the screen. Only five minutes walk from the Cathedral, the beautifully restored medieval **St Mary's Chapel on the Bridge** is one of only six surviving bridge chapels still in use, and well worth a visit.

One of Derby's most interesting museums is **Pickford House**, situated on the city's finest Georgian street at number 41 (see panel on page 110).

Just a short walk from Pickford House is the **Industrial Museum**. What better place

PICKFORD'S HOUSE

41 Friargate, Derby DE1 1DA
Tel: 01332 255363

One of Derby's most interesting museums is **Pickford House**, situated on the city's finest Georgian street at number 41. It is a Grade I listed building, erected in 1770 by the architect Joseph Pickford as a combined family home and place of work. Pickford House differs from the majority of grand stately homes, in that unlike most, it does not have a wealth of priceless furniture and works or art. Instead, visitors are able to gain

an insight into everyday middle-class life during the 1830s. Pickford House is the epitome of a late Georgian professional man's residence. There is an exciting programme of temporary exhibitions as well as other displays, which deal with the history of the Friargate area and the importance of Joseph Pickford as a Midlands architect. The displays include a late 18th century dining room, breakfast rooms and an early 19th century kitchen and scullery. One special feature of Pickford House is the excellent collection of costumes, some dating back to the mid 1700s. A period 18th century garden is also laid out at the rear of the house.

to house a museum devoted to the preservation of Derby's industrial heritage than the beautiful old **Silk Mill**, a building, which stands on one of the most interesting sites in the country and which preceded Richard Arkwright's first cotton mill by over 50 years. The Silk Mill was badly damaged by fire in 1910 and had to be substantially rebuilt, however it still gives an impression of Lombe's original mill and tower. The whole of the ground floor galleries are devoted to the Rolls-Royce aero engine collection and illustrate the importance played by the aeronautical industry in the city's history.

Since 1915 Derby has been involved with the manufacture of engines, and this section of the Museum displays model aircraft and sectioned engines demonstrating how aircraft fly. A specially designed annexe houses a complete RB211 Turbo-fan engine. On the first floor of the building there is an introduction to other Derbyshire industries with displays of lead and coal mining, iron founding, limestone quarrying, ceramics and brick making. There is also a railway engineering gallery complete with a signal box and displays on the growth of the railway works in Derby since the 1840s. Since the coming of the railways in 1839, the railway industry has also played a large part in the life of the City. Along with Rolls Royce, British Rail Engineering Ltd (BREL) is one of the largest employers in Derby and its development is well documented within the Museum and allows visitors to broaden their knowledge.

The **City Museum and Art Gallery** is also well worth visiting. Opened in 1879, it

Derby Industrial Museum

City Museum and Art Gallery

is the oldest of Derby's museums and the displays include natural history, archaeology and social history exhibits. Derbyshire wildlife and geology feature in an exciting series of natural settings and hands-on exhibits. One section of the museum is devoted to a Military Gallery and relates to Derby's local historical regiments. The walk-in First World War trench scene attempts to capture the experience of a night at the front. The Bonnie Prince Charlie room commemorates Derby's role in the 1745 uprising.

A ground floor gallery houses the city's superb collection of fine porcelain, manufactured in Derby from the mid 18th century. The porcelain collection is displayed in a new, Lottery funded, gallery, complete with a colourful database of the collection. The museum is also home to a collection of portraits, landscapes, scientific and industrial scenes by the local painter Joseph Wright, ARA. On the second floor of the Museum are temporary exhibition galleries. These change every three or four weeks and cover not only the museum's own collection but also travelling exhibitions representing an exciting range of arts and crafts both modern and traditional in a variety of styles and techniques.

The **Derby Heritage Centre** has local history displays, tea room and souvenir shop housed in one of the city's oldest buildings. Opened in 1992 by local Historian, Richard Felix, visitors can book to go on various ghost walks around the city of Derby and now also Tutbury Castle. The city centre ghost walk takes in Derby city centre, including the site of Derby's first jail where witches, heretics and traitors were imprisoned, the scene of the brutal murder of a policeman and a subterranean trip into the barrel-vaulted tunnels beneath the Guild Hall.

Another of the city's treats, to which admission is free, is the **Derbyshire Constabulary Memorabilia Museum**, which has a display of police memorabilia dating from the mid 17th century to the present day. There is a fascinating collection of truncheons, handcuffs and police uniforms, as well as probably the largest collection of world-wide police badges in the country. It also includes records of the Force history, crime and punishment and much more.

Continuing with the theme of crime and punishment, **The Derby Gaol** is situated in the depths of the original dungeons of the Derbyshire County Gaol, dating back to 1756. The Derby Gaol offers a reminder of the city's grisly past. It includes the condemned cells and was the site of the last hanging, drawing and quartering in the country, after England's last revolution, the Pentrich Rebellion.

Pride Park Stadium, the home of Derby County Football Club, was officially opened in 1997, by Her Majesty the Queen. Visitors can take a 'behind the scenes' look at 'the Rams' new sporting arena. A guided tour includes visits to the director's box, corporate areas, crowd control centre and even the police cells. But the high point for any football fan has to be emerging from the players' tunnel on to the pitch.

The ancient custom of well-dressing, more commonly associated with the villages and towns of northern Derbyshire and the Peak District, has found expression here in Derby (in Chester Green, at Mansfield Street Chapel) since 1982, on the Saturday before the late Spring Bank Holiday (Whitsun).

AROUND DERBY

DARLEY ABBEY
2 miles N of Derby off the A6

Darley Abbey is a tranquil village of delightfully restored mill cottages, built in rows or around squares. The Augustinian **Abbey of St Mary** was founded by Robert Ferrers, second Earl of Derby, around 1140 and grew to become the most powerful abbey in Derbyshire and possibly in the whole of the Midlands. In 1538 the Abbey was surrendered as part of the Dissolution of the Monasteries. Sadly, few monasteries could have been so completely obliterated, so much so that what is now known as The Abbey public house is the only building remaining. The layout is of a simple medieval hall house and is thought to have been used as the Abbey's guest house for travellers and pilgrims during the 13th century. During renovation, 12th century pottery was unearthed.

Darley park, on the river Derwent, was landscaped by William Evans and has attractive flower beds, shrubberies and lawns. It once had a hall, built in 1727 but now demolished, that for 120 years was the home of the Evans family who built the cotton mill by the river in 1783.

The mill area is quite a large complex. The oldest parts, east mill, middle mill and west mill, are 5 storeyed and brick built. There is also a finishing house which has 3 storeys and sash windows, and an octagonal toll house in the mill yard. The Evans family built the red brick houses, still evident in the village, for the mill workers. They were typical paternalistic employers providing subsidised rents, coal, blankets in cold weather and even arranging burials and memorials for their workers.

BREADSALL
3 miles N of Derby off the A6

Breadsall began life as a small hamlet clustered around its Norman church. It is now known primarily as a residential suburb of Derby, with new estates that have sprung up around the original centre. The parish church of **All Saints** possesses one of the most elegant steeples in the country, dating from the early 1300s. The south doorway is Norman and the tower and chancel date back to the 1200s. The church was burnt down by suffragettes in 1914 and carefully restored over the next two years. Inside there is a touching pieta from the late 1300s. This beautiful alabaster depiction of the Virgin Mary with the crucified Christ lying across her knees was found under the floor of the church after another fire, and was restored to its present position by W D Caroe.

Opposite the west end of the church can be found **The Old Hall**, which has been part of village life for over 600 years. It was originally the manor house when the village was divided into the wards of Overhall and Netherhall. In later years it has been employed as a school, farmhouse, hunting box, public house, shop, joiner's shop and post office. It currently serves as a parish hall and is used by various village organisations.

As its name suggests, **Breadsall Priory** stands on the site of an Augustinian Priory which was founded in the 13th century. The only part of the original building extant is an arch in the basement. Most of what stands today dates back to the Jacobean period, with many early 19th century additions and embellishments. Breadsall Priory was home to Erasmus Darwin in his later years. A poet, physician

The Trent Valley 113

and philosopher, he is better known as grandfather of Charles Darwin. Born in 1731, he died in Breadsall in 1802, and there is a memorial to him in All Saints Church. The Priory is now a private hotel with golf course.

MACKWORTH
2 miles NW of Derby off the A52

Standing alone in a field near the village of Mackworth is a charming 14th century church. Although its position is unusual it is well worth taking a look inside to see the wealth of ancient and modern alabaster carving that it holds. This is not the only seemingly abandoned building in the village, as there is also a late 15th century gatehouse. This belonged to a castle built by the Mackworth family in 1495.

KIRK LANGLEY
4 miles north of Derby on the A52

Kirk Langley village has some fine 18th century stone houses, a mid 17th century gabled red brick rectory, an old village school and a church. The Church of **St Michael** is early 14th century, built on the site of an older Saxon church. There are monuments to the Meynell and Pole families, including a memorial to Hugo Frances Meynell, 'who was deprived of his life in a collision of carriages' in Clay Cross tunnel. The only pub is the Bluebell at Langley Common.

Kedleston Hall

KEDLESTON
4 miles NW of Derby off the A52

Kedleston Hall has been the family seat of the Curzon family since the 12th century and, until it was taken over by the National Trust, it had the longest continuous male line in Derbyshire and one of the longest in the country. Nothing remains of the original medieval structure and little is known about it other than details recorded in a survey of 1657 which state that one of the doorways was over 500 years old and that there was also a large hall and a buttery. The present

The Bluebell Inn
Adams Road, Kirk Langley, Ashbourne, Derbyshire DE6 4LW
Tel: 01332 824423

The Bluebell Inn, which can be found in the village of Kirk Langley, is a traditional, 18th-century former coaching inn. A later extension has ensured there is plenty of room inside in which to enjoy a refreshing drink and a tasty meal. There is a superb menu of food served each lunchtime and evening (no food Sunday night), complemented by a well-stocked bar. There is an attractive beer garden with children's play area, and a large car park. Popular quiz on Sunday evenings.

THE COCK INN

Mugginton, Weston Underwood,
Derbyshire DE6 4PJ
Tel: 01773 550293
e-mail info@thecockinn.fsnet.co.uk
website www.thecockinn.fsnet.co.uk

Enjoying scenic surroundings just outside the hamlet of Mugginton, between Derby and Ashbourne, you will find **The Cock Inn**. Dating back to the 17th century this is a former coaching inn and a place where teams of horses were stabled. It takes its name from the Cock Horse, which was the name given to the horse that led the team. Currently at the helm are Paul and Wendy who have been in residence for just a year and have firmly established the inn as a popular eating-place and watering hole. The reputation for quality food, ale and hospitality has spread far beyond the surrounding villages, with regular customers travelling from nearby towns to enjoy the fine food and friendly atmosphere.

The interior décor is traditional in its styling, complemented by fresh painted walls and a minimum of clutter. The welcome extended by all the local staff is friendly and warm and everyone is made to feel right at home. The bar is well-stocked with three real ales usually available. Marstons Pedigree is a regular feature with two ever-changing guest ales too. There is also a selection of draught lagers, cider and stout together with the usual spirits, soft drinks and some wines to choose from. Superb quality food is served daily at lunchtime and in the evening.

There is a superb, separate, non-smoking restaurant area, which can seat up to 60 diners, and bookings are recommended at weekends. There is an a la carte menu and a specials board, both offering an excellent choice of freshly prepared and home-cooked dishes. The steaks and fresh fish dishes are very popular, but other options may include Viennese Pork, Minty Lamb Steak, and for vegetarians a Caerphilly and Leek Tart or Stuffed Aubergines. Children are more than welcome and they also have a selection especially designed for smaller appetites. On Monday nights there is a

curry night, where the regular menu is supplemented by a delicious selection of curries of varying strengths, to suit all tastes. All major credit cards, except Diners Club, are accepted.

elegant mansion was built between 1759 and 1765 by Robert Adam and it remains one of the finest examples of his work. The façade represents an impressive Roman temple with six tall columns supporting a portico, and a double-armed stone stairway leading to the entrance. Inside, the elegant and extravagant Marble Hall is a massive open space, dominated by 20 pink alabaster Corinthian columns around a white marble inlaid floor with an intricate plasterwork ceiling above. As well as the design for the house and the 3-arched bridge across the lake, it is likely that Robert Adam had a hand in designing the park in the Serpentine Style. The three mile Long Walk was created in 1776. Edwin Lutyens designed the sunken rose garden.

Since taking over the property, the National Trust has embarked on a major restoration programme and many of the stately home's rooms have been beautifully furnished with contemporary pieces; modern photographs of the family can be seen mingled with priceless paintings and other treasures such as Blue John vases. Along with the house itself and the park with its lakes, there are the boat house and fishing pavilion to explore.

One member of the family, George Nathaniel Curzon, was the Viceroy of India from 1899 to 1905. When he returned to England he brought back numerous works of art, carvings and ivories that can be seen on display in the **Indian Museum**. Though he was out in India for some time, George would not have missed his family home, as Government House in Calcutta is a copy of Kedleston Hall. Once back in England, George did not have much time to enjoy his lands: he became a member of Lloyd George's inner War Cabinet, which met over 500 times during the First World War.

Nearby **All Saints Church**, the only part of the village that was allowed to remain when the rest was moved in 1765 to make way for the landscaped park around the Hall, dates from the 12th century. It is of an unusual design for Derbyshire in that it is cruciform in shape and the tower is placed in the centre. Inside are Curzon monuments dating from 1275 to the present day; the only brass in the church is to Richard Curzon, who died in 1496. The church has an unusual east facing sundial. Because of its orientation, the dial only catches the sun between the hours of 6 and 11am. The hour lines are parallel with each other, with half hour lines in between. The gnomon is in the form of a letter "T", the top bar of which casts a shadow across the dial. The inscription above the dial is "WEE SHALL", which cryptically links to sundial (soon die all) to make a sombre message. This is reinforced by the carvings on top of the dial, showing a skull between two hour glasses.

BRAILSFORD
8 miles NW of Derby off the A52

Brailsford is mentioned in the *Domesday Book* as having a priest and 'half a church'. The owner then was the Saxon Elfin, who appears to have managed to retain his lordship after the Conquest. The carved Saxon cross in the churchyard of **All Saints** parish church dates from Elfin's time. The church itself is an interesting building with much Norman work and an ashlar-faced diagonally buttressed tower. At nearby Mugginton can be found "Halter Devil Chapel", now part of a farm and built, so legend has it, by a reformed drinker who once tried to halter a cow in the mistaken belief that it was his horse. In his stupor the farmer, Francis Browen, thought he had haltered the Devil and is said to have built the chapel in 1723 in repentance.

BLENHEIM HOUSE

Main Street, Etwall,
Derbyshire DE65 6LP
Tel: 01283 732254
Fax: 01283 733860
e-mail: info@theblenheimhouse.com
website: www.theblenheimhouse.com

The village of Etwall is bypassed by the main A516, which runs between Derby and Uttoxeter, though it is well worth venturing into the village, if only to visit **Blenheim House**. This outstanding restaurant and guesthouse has been recently taken over by Peter and Carole Simpson and they have refurbished the whole place to the highest of standards. The main building dates back to the 18th century, when it was originally two houses, and these have since been knocked through to create a comfortable space in which to enjoy a drink and a superb meal.

Peter has many years experience in the catering trade, having worked in France for three years, and also at a top London restaurant. Blenheim House already enjoyed a fine reputation for serving excellent food, and Peter and Carole have built on this. Food is served each weekday lunchtime from 12 until 2.30pm with a delicious Sunday lunch served from 12 until 4pm. In the evening, snacks are served from 6pm with restaurant meals from 7pm. The menu is impressive, with plenty to inspire and tempt the palate. All the dishes are freshly prepared to order and use the best of locally available produce wherever possible. You may be lucky enough to find the duck and green peppercorn terrine served with fresh figs, among the starters, while the

chicken breast with asparagus and wild mushroom jus caught our eye among the choice of main dishes. A chop house menu includes some lighter meal options and sandwiches which are served with delicious homemade, chunky chips. The popular Sunday lunch can be selected from the fixed price menu, with a two- or three-course option, and in addition to a choice of roasts there is always a fish and vegetarian dish. To round off any meal to perfection there is a wickedly tempting range of desserts too. With the bar being open at each session, you can simply enjoy a refreshing drink, without eating, if you wish.

If you would like to stay over and make a night of it, in a separate building there are ten superb guest rooms available for bed and breakfast accommodation. There are single, double and twin rooms, and all have been individually decorated and furnished, making the most of the historic features of the building. All the rooms have en-suite facilities and some have four-poster beds. Children are welcome. There is a dinner inclusive rate and discounts for stays of more than four nights. Ring for full details.

EDNASTON
7 miles NW of Derby off the A52

This is an ancient manor which was recorded, in the Domesday Survey of 1086, as being in the ownership of Henry de Ferrers of Duffield Castle. The present manor house, **Ednaston Manor** on Brailsford Brook was built by Sir Edwin Lutyens at the turn of the 20th century. Unfortunately it is not open to the public.

LONG LANE
6 miles NW of Derby off the A52

Long Lane village is truly a hidden place, not found on most maps. It is south off the A52, and can be reached by heading for the village of Lees and then following the sign for Long Lane. It is set on the old Roman road bearing the same name and is not much more than a cluster of cottages, a school, a church and a pub. **The Three Horseshoes** in Long Lane dates back to 1750, when it was a grain store, where ale was brewed for the adjacent blacksmith's. Unusually, the property is owned by the village itself.

LONGFORD
8 miles W of Derby off the A515

Truly a hidden place, Longford lies very much off the beaten track, but it is well worth finding as the village has the distinction of being the home of the first cheese factory in England. Opened on the 4th May in 1870, its first manager bore the memorable name Cornelius Schermerhorn. Derbyshire, with its excellent rail and canal links, made the county an ideal centre for the mass production of cheeses for foreign markets.

Longford Hall is a late medieval house, renovated by Pickford in 1762 and restored after a bad fire in 1942. It was the family seat of the Coke family, after the Longfords. The Longfords settled here in the 12th century and the church, which is close to the hall, was built then. The church of **St Chads,** surrounded by magnificent lime trees, still retains many Norman parts, though the tower was added in the 15th century. There are some fine monuments to both the Cokes and their predecessors the Longfords in the church.

NORBURY
14 miles W of Derby off the B5033

Norbury lies on the river Dove and was recorded in the *Domesday Book* as Norberre or Nordberie, the 'norther' defence on the Dove. The mainly 14th and 15th century village church of St Mary and St Barlok is definitely worth a visit, as it houses the alabaster tombs of the 15th century FitzHerberts, one of the oldest families in Derbyshire. It is probable that the family contributed much towards the church building over the years. Those familiar with the works of George Eliot will feel much at home in this part of the county. The characters Adam and Seth from her famous novel *Adam Bede* were based on her father, Robert Evans, and his brother, and many of scenes from the book are set in this village. Members of Eliot's family are buried in the churchyard.

Norbury Manor and Hall, next to the church is a Grade I listed building. The original medieval Manor House is still attached to the later Hall. It was the seat of the Fitzherbert family from medieval times. Now owned by the National trust, it is open to the public by appointment only.

ETWALL
5 miles SW of Derby off the A516

This charming place has a fine range of Georgian buildings including some 17th century almshouses built by Sir John Port, the founder of nearby Repton College. The original site of **Etwall Hall**, where Sir John lived, is now the home of a large comprehensive school, which bears his name. For a village that derived its name

The Castle Hotel

Station Road, Hatton,
Derbyshire DE65 5DW
Tel: 01283 813396 Fax: 01283 520649

Just north of the historic village of Tutbury, noted for its castle and Norman church, you'll find the village of Hatton. On the southern edge, next to the bridge across the pretty River Dove, is a fine hostelry, **The Castle Hotel**. This substantial building constructed of old brick dates from around 1870 and offers a warm welcome to anyone who calls in for a quiet drink, a meal or a place to stay. It was built as a hotel and retains many of the original features though the whole place has been modernised to reflect today's demand for high standards of comfort and service.

This is a family-run establishment, with the owners Mike and Sue Freeman ably assisted by sister-in-law Trish and niece Joanne. They have been here for over twenty years, but only bought the property outright five and a half years ago, and have firmly established a fine reputation for The Castle in the surrounding area and attract a loyal following.

The whole of the interior has recently been refurbished to an exceptionally high standard and the main lounge is especially comfortable and welcoming. There is a well-stocked bar with usually three or four real ales on tap, together with a good selection of draught bitters, mild, stout, lager and cider.

Food is served in the bar at lunchtime and in the evenings with a menu of tasty bar meals and snacks on offer. There is also a superb, newly created, 75-seater, non-smoking restaurant, which is open from 12 midday until 9pm. Here they serve an a la carte menu, which ranges from tasty steaks to more unusual dishes, such as catfish. It is advisable to make reservations at the weekends to avoid disappointment. The Castle can boast eight, super en-suite letting rooms, which have also undergone some recent refurbishment. Decorated and furnished to a high standard they come fully equipped with a colour TV and tea and coffee making facilities. Two rooms also feature a swirl bath – make sure you ask at the time of booking. Children are welcome and all major credit cards are accepted.

In 1830, a hoard of 100,000 coins was discovered in the field between the fold and the River Dove. You won't find any ancient coins nowadays – what you'll find instead is a great inn that offers everyone a warm and friendly welcome.

from "Eata's Well", it seems strange that Etwall only took up the custom of well-dressing recently and by chance. To mark the centenary of the village primary school, the teachers dressed a token well while the Women's Institute, with the help of people from two villages within the Peak District, dressed the only true well in Etwall, Town Well. This was in 1970 and the event, in mid May, was so successful that it is now an annual occasion and a total of eight wells are decorated.

As there is no long-standing tradition of well-dressing in the village the themes for the dressings are not the more usual Biblical subjects but have covered a wide range of stories and ideas including racial unity and the life and times of Sir John Port. Etwall is also the most southerly village to take part in the custom of well-dressing and its position, well below the harsh uplands of Derbyshire's Peak District, has ensured that there is always a good supply of flowers even though the dressing takes place late in spring.

The Port Hospital Almshouses, fronted by wrought iron gates, made by Robert Bakewell of Derby, were rebuilt in 1681 and recently restored again. Until the 1960s, Almsmen and women wore special hats or bonnets and a dark blue cloak with a silver clasp.

HILTON
8 miles SW of Derby off the A5132

Wakelyn Old Hall is an unusual half-timbered house that can be found in this small village. Dating from the 16th century, when the Wakelyn family left in 1621, the building became The Bull's Head Inn. It was also, reputedly, one of the places that Mary, Queen of Scots stopped at on her way to Tutbury Castle. The Old Talbot Inn dates back to the 15th century. The old gravel works are now a bird sanctuary and a nature reserve.

THE WHITE SWAN
Eggington Road, Hilton, Derbyshire DE65 5FJ
Tel: 01283 732305

The White Swan enjoys a superb location in the village of Hilton, and lies set back from the main road with plenty of parking. Recently under new management, the pub is popular with locals and visitors to the area, who all come to enjoy the range of fine ales and tasty food, which is served all day until 9pm. The excellent menu and special board offer plenty of choice to suit all appetites. To the rear there is a huge beer garden and children's play area.

THE OLD TALBOT INN
1 Main Street, Hilton, Derbyshire DE65 5FF
Tel: 01283 733728

The Old Talbot Inn can be easily located directly on the main road, which runs through the village of Hilton. Dating back to the 15th century, a cosy, traditional feel has been retained throughout while also providing for the needs of today's customers. The well-stocked bar provides a selection of real ales and a superb menu of tasty, home-cooked food is served each lunch time and evening. Credit cards accepted. A pub quiz is held each Wednesday and there is occasional live music once a month.

HOLLY BUSH INN
Church Broughton, Derbyshire DE65 5AS
Tel: 01283 585345

The Holly Bush Inn is a substantial red brick building which enjoys a quiet setting in the picturesque village of Church Broughton. Husband and wife team Brian and Jean James have been tenants for the last 18 years and have made this one of the nicest places to enjoy a drink and bite to eat in the area. A full and varied menu is served at lunchtimes and in the evening each day, while the bar is kept well stocked with a fine selection of lager and beer.

SUTTON-ON-THE-HILL
8 miles W of Derby off the A516

Despite its name this is a sheltered spot, with the church standing above the village on the hill. The church of **St Michael** has a 14th century tower with a spire that was rebuilt in 1841. A few other parts are 14th century, but mostly, the church was rebuilt in 1863. It contains an unusual monument to Judith Sleigh, who died in 1634. It is a standing coffin carved in black stone with handles. Cricket fans will take special pleasure in visiting Sutton on the Hill, as it was the family home of G M and R H R Buckston, both of whom captained the Derbyshire cricket team.

CHURCH BROUGHTON
10 miles W of Derby off the A50

Church Broughton is a quiet village, which was, until the early part of the 20th century, part of the Duke of Devonshires Derbyshire estates. It is now mainly a commuter village for nearby towns. The parish church of **St Michael** dates back to the early 14th century. It has a large west tower with Victorian pinnacles and big gargoyles and is topped with a small spire. It also contains a long 14th century chancel.

SUDBURY
12 miles W of Derby off the A50

This is the estate village to **Sudbury Hall**, the late 17th century mansion and home of a branch of the Vernon family who lived at Haddon Hall. The house is intriguing, the garden restful. Gifted to the National Trust in 1967, the Hall is an unexpected mixture of architectural styles. A splendid example of a house of Charles II's time, inside Sudbury Hall contains elaborate plasterwork and murals throughout, wood carvings by Grinling Gibbons, and some fine examples of mythological paintings by Laguerre. The beautiful staircase of the Main Hall featured in the BBC's *Pride and Preudice*. Of particular interest is the **Museum of Childhood**, which is situated in the servants' wing and provides a fascinating insight into the lives of children down the ages. Fascinating displays range from a wealthy family's nursery and an Edwardian schoolroom to a "chimney climb" and coal tunnel for the adventurous. The formal gardens and meadows lead to the tree-fringed lake. Wildlife abounds, including kestrels, grey herons, grass snakes, dragonflies, newts, frogs, toads, little and tawny owls and woodpeckers. Special events are held throughout the year.

Next to the hall is the church of **All Saints**, which was recorded in Domesday but has been extensively restored in later years. The east window was donated by Queen Victoria and Prince Albert.

BOYLESTONE
8 miles S of Ashbourne off the A515

This isolated village amid gently rolling countryside south of Ashbourne is noted in history for an incident during the Civil War. Two hundred Royalist troops spent the night in the church of St John the Baptist on their way to Wingfield Manor. Rather foolishly they set no watch, and in the morning found themselves surrounded by Cromwell's men. The Royalists surrendered, were disarmed, and quietly filed out of the church.

The church tower is from the Victorian era and has an unusual pyramidal roof. Inside, the chancel is just as the Cavaliers would have seen it, as it dates back to the 1300s, as does a delicately moulded low recess in the chancel.

DOVERIDGE
15 miles W of Derby off the A50

As its name suggests, this village is situated on the banks of the River Dove and, although there is a fair amount of modern housing, Doveridge still retains a rural atmosphere. The village boasts a distinguished 13th century church and, in the churchyard, an old yew tree that is reputed to be one of the largest in Derbyshire.

SWADLINCOTE

Here at the extreme edge of Derbyshire, well south of the River Trent, Swadlincote shares many characteristics with Staffordshire. Among the town's thriving industries, based on the clay and coal on which it stands, are large potteries founded in 1795 as well as brickworks. Historically more a collection of villages though officially an urban district, it retains a rural feel that is charming and worth exploring.

NORTH OF SWADLINCOTE

HARTSHORNE
1 mile NE of Swadlincote off the A514

One of this lovely village's most renowned sons was George Stanhope, who grew up to be a famous preacher, a bold critic and a brave writer during the reign of Queen Anne.

Hartshorne's village church was rebuilt in 1835, though it retains its 15th century tower and 14th century font. A fine altar tomb shows the alabaster figures of Sir Humphry Dethick of 1599 and his wife. The Dethicks paid long and loyal service to the Royal family of their day - one of the Dethicks went to Cleves to find a fourth wife for Henry VIII, while his son Sir William is said to have laid a pall of rich velvet on the coffin of Mary, Queen of Scots.

CALKE
5 miles NE of Swadlincote off the B587

In 1985 the National Trust bought **Calke Abbey**, a large Baroque-style mansion built in 1701 on the site of an Augustinian priory founded in 1133. However, it was not until 1989 that the Trust were able to open the house to the public, for this was no ordinary house at all. Dubbed "the house that time forgot" since the death of the owner, Sir Vauncy Harpur-Crewe in 1924 nothing had been altered in the mansion! In fact, the seclusion of the house and also the rather bizarre lifestyle of its inhabitants had left many rooms and objects untouched for over 100 years. There was even a spectacular 18th century Chinese silk state bed that had never been unpacked.

Today, the Trust has repaired the house and returned all 13,000 items to their

BAY TREE RESTAURANT

4 Potter Street, Melbourne, Derbyshire DE73 1DW
Tel: 01332 863358 Fax: 01332 865545
website: www.baytreerestaurant.co.uk

Just eight miles south of Derby is the small Georgian market town of Melbourne. An attractive place to visit, there are a number of tourist attractions, pleasant places to walk within the town as well as in the surrounding countryside.

The parish church has been described as a miniature cathedral and the privately owned Melbourne Hall is open to the public through the month of August, and its gardens from April to September.

The Bay Tree Restaurant can be found in the heart of the town, close to the church and the main shops, and is generally considered to be the best restaurant in the area. It is housed within a building that is typical of the town. It dates back to 1790 and retains a wealth of original features, from the handsome Georgian exterior to the delightfully cosy and intimate interior.

The restaurant features in all the discerning food guides and bookings are required (especially for Sunday) months in advance. The secret of its success lies with the co-owners, chef Rex Howell and Vicki Talbott, who opened the place in 1988 and have built up a reputation for quality and service.

Winner of many well-deserved awards, the superb menu offers a wide range of dishes, described as the best of New World cuisine. The regular menu ranges from open bagels, baguettes and paninis to omelettes and egg dishes with light meal options and pasta dishes. All are exquisitely fresh and superbly presented. There is also an extensive a la carte and weekly updated table d'hote menu, all making the best use of seasonally available produce. You could enjoy some 'nibbles', such as nachos or garlic bread, lunchtime treats like fresh Scotch salmon and leeks with pasta or main courses such as fresh fish of

the day, crispy duckling with a plum sauce or mignons of prime beef with onion tart. To complement your meal there is also an outstanding wine list.

original positions so that the Abbey now looks just as it did when it was bought in 1981. The attention to detail has been so great that none of the rooms have been redecorated. Visitors can enjoy the silver display and trace the route of 18th century servants along the brewhouse tunnel to the house cellars. Calke Abbey stands in its own large park with gardens, a chapel and stables that are also open to the public. There are three walled gardens with their glasshouses, a restored orangery, vegetable garden, pheasant aviaries and the summer flower display within the unusual "auricular" theatre. Calke is home to lots of wildlife including fallow deer, weasels, stoats, barn, little and tawny owls, woodpeckers, common toads, butterflies and beetles.

Calke Abbey

Calke Abbey

Just over the Leicestershire border, the peaceful **Staunton Harold Church** is a few minutes from Calke Abbey. Built in an open act of defiance to Oliver Cromwell by Sir Robert Shirley, the church stands next to Harold Staunton Hall (private). Inside there are original 17th century cushions, painted ceilings and fine panelling.

MELBOURNE
6 miles NE of Swadlincote off the B587

This small town, which lent its name to the rather better-known city in Australia, is a successful market garden centre. A famous son of Melbourne, who started his working life in one of the market gardens, was Thomas Cook, who was born here in 1808. He went on to pioneer personally-conducted tours and gave his name to the famous worldwide travel company.

Full of Georgian charm, Melbourne has many fine buildings which include one of the finest Norman churches in the country, the church of **St Michael and St Mary**. This seems rather a grand church for this modest place and indeed, it is no ordinary parish church. In the 12th century, when the Bishopric of Carlisle was formed, there needed to be a place of safety for the clergy when Carlisle was being raided by the Scots. So this church was built at Melbourne and, while Carlisle was subjected to raids and violence, the Bishop retired to Melbourne and continued to carry out his duties. The church was built between 1133 and 1229

SCARECROWS
14 Derby Road, Melbourne, Derbyshire DE73 1FE
Tel/Fax: 01332 864536

Scarecrows restaurant stands on Derby Road in the heart of Melbourne and in a town well-known for its quality restaurants, this fine establishment stands out. Owner Laurence Duffy created this cosy and popular eating place, and since he opened in 1995 it has gone from strength to strength. The excellent menu boasts a range of tempting dishes with the fish being a speciality. Coffee and light meals are also served throughout the day. Bookings for weekend evenings are essential. Children welcome. Closed Sundays.

and, in 1299, the then Bishop built a palace on land that is now home to Melbourne Hall.

The birthplace of the 19th century statesman Lord Melbourne, and also the home of Lady Caroline Lamb, **Melbourne Hall** is another fine building in this area of Derbyshire. A modest building, the Hall is surrounded by beautiful gardens, the most notable feature of which is a beautiful wrought-iron birdcage pergola built in the early 1700s by Robert Bakewell, a local blacksmith from Derby. Bakewell lived in Melbourne for a time at the house of a widow named Fisher and her daughters. However when one daughter became pregnant, he moved hurriedly to Derby. Unfortunately the house is only open to the public in August, but the splendid and famous formal gardens are open throughout the summer season and are well worth a visit.

SWARKESTONE
9 miles NE of Swadlincote off the A5132

Excavations in the village of Swarkestone, at Lowes Farm, led to the discovery that the district was occupied in the Bronze Age and also in Saxon times. This small village has also been, quite literally, a turning point in history. The **Swarkestone Bridge**, with its seven arches and three-quarter-mile long causeway, crosses the River Trent. In 1745, during the second Jacobite Rebellion, the advance guard of Bonnie Prince Charlie reached the Bridge and, had they managed to cross the River at this point, they would have faced no other natural barriers on their 120-mile march to London. As it transpired, the army retreated and fled north, Bonnie Prince Charlie managed to escape and the Jacobite Rebellion was no more.

Legend has it that the original bridge at Swarkestone was built by two daughters of the Harpur family in the early 13th century. The girls were celebrating their joint betrothals when their fiancés were summoned to a barons' meeting across the river. While they were away torrential rain fell, flooding the river, and the two young men drowned as they attempted to ford the raging torrent on their return. The girls built the bridge as a memorial to their lovers. Both girls later died impoverished and unmarried.

BARROW-ON-TRENT
8 miles NE of Swadlincote off the A514

Barrow-on-Trent, as its name tells us, stands between the River Trent and the Trent and Mersey Canal in this rich agricultural part of south Derbyshire.

The row of parish cottages, built by parish levy in the 18th century, is an interesting feature of this attractive village. First rented for 30 shillings (£1.50) a year, the parish council still keeps them in a good state of repair.

The village **Church of St Wilfrid** is first mentioned in the *Domesday Book*, but the present building, which is approached down a pretty lane which also leads towards the river, dates mainly from the 13th century. The north arcade with its original columns is a notable feature. The plain glass windows lend the church a light and airy atmosphere. The base of the square tower and the north aisle date from the 1300s; there is also a Georgian east window.

The village chapel, unsurprisingly in Chapel Lane, was erected on arches so that it could reach the level of the road. This was not to everyone's liking: the marks of shots fired on the building can still be seen in the inscription stone set in the front of the building.

MILTON
5 miles N of Swadlincote off the A514

Milton is a small village, once owned by the Burdett family, who built the nearby church of St Saviour.

BRETBY
2 miles N of Swadlincote off the A50

Now a leafy rural backwater, Bretby was first mentioned in Domesday as an agricultural settlement around a green. There was once a castle in this quiet village until it was demolished and the stones used to build a mansion house. In the 18th century, that too was demolished and **Bretby Hall**, as seen today, was built in 1813 by Sir Jeffrey Wyatville, the designer of the 19th century extension at Chatsworth House.

REPTON
7 miles SW of Derby off the B5008

This village, by the tranquil waters of the River Trent, is steeped in history. The first mention of Repton came in the 7th century when it was established as the capital of the Saxon kingdom of Mercia. A monastery, housing both monks and nuns, was founded here sometime after 653 but the building was sacked by the Danes in AD874. A battleaxe, now on display in the school museum, was excavated a little distance from the church. It had apparently lain undisturbed for well over 1,000 years.

The parish **Church of St Wystan** is famous for its Anglo-Saxon chancel and crypt, but it also contains many of the major styles of medieval architecture. When the chancel and part of the nave were enlarged in 1854, the original Anglo-Saxon columns were moved to the 14th century porch. The crypt claims to be one of the oldest intact Anglo-Saxon buildings

THE SWAN INN

49 Main Street, Milton, Derbyshire DE65 6EF
Tel: 01283 703188
e-mail: stellasalt@aol.com

If you like the welcoming atmosphere of a popular, village hostelry, then **The Swan Inn** at Milton will be the place for you. The pub is under the management of Stella and Roger Salt, a local couple, who lived across the road for 30 years before deciding to take the place on themselves. Here you can enjoy some real ales and friendly hospitality, and children are made welcome with a play area in the garden. Occasional live entertainment and venue for some village events.

The Bulls Head

84 High Street, Repton, Derbyshire DE65 6GF
Tel: 01283 703297
Fax: 01283 704465
e-mail: rjcgold@aol.com

The outstanding **Bulls Head** inn dates back to the 18th century, and began life as a coaching inn with its own bakery. This characterful pub boasts wooden floors, exposed beams, and a wealth of bygone memorabilia, and retains a cosy, traditional feel. Your hosts are John and Anne Carter who have been here for two years and established a loyal following with regular customers from the local villages and surrounding area. The welcome is warm and friendly and all customers, whether old or new, are always made to feel right at home.

This is a spacious establishment with a large, open plan bar area, a blue pool table to help wile away a wet afternoon or evening, and you can be assured that the highest of standards are maintained

throughout. The pub is closed at Monday lunchtimes (except Bank Holidays) and opens every other lunchtime and evening, and all day Saturday and Sunday. The bar is stocked with some well-kept real ales with Marstons Pedigree, Bass, Adnams Broadside and the locally-brewed Bridge Bitter usually on offer. You will also find a range of popular beers and lager including Tetleys, Carlsberg, Stella and Murphys.

The upstairs restaurant is open each evening and Ricky, the chef, presents a superb menu of over 180 oriental dishes together with an a la carte selection of popular English dishes for those that prefer. The wide-ranging menu includes popular favourites, such as sweet and sour chicken, together with some more unusual selections, with a number of Thai dishes featuring. There is a well-priced set menu, and the whole lot is also available for take-away. The same menu is served in the bar in the evening, but all dishes are served plated. There is also a menu of bar snacks, with sandwiches, filled rolls and some hot meals, served Tuesday to Sunday lunchtimes and in the evening, in the bar. There is no food available on Mondays. Outside there is an attractive beer garden and meals can be taken outside, weather permitting. Children are welcome and they will enjoy the outdoor play area.

For a lively night out, why not visit on a Wednesday when there is a pub quiz held each week at 9pm. There is occasional live music, usually arranged once or twice a month, and held on a Friday or Saturday evening. There are also themed nights held once a month. Ring for full details.

in England. The burial place of the Kings of Mercia, including St Wystan in AD850, the crypt was rediscovered by chance in 1779 by a workman who was digging a hole for a grave in the chancel floor.

The ancient **Cross**, still at the central crossroads in the village, has been the focal point of life here for centuries and it has also stood at the heart of the Wednesday market. Right up until the late 19th century a Statutes Fair, for the hiring of farm labourers and domestics, was also held here at Michaelmas.

Parts of an Augustinian priory, founded in 1170, are incorporated in the buildings of **Repton College**, itself founded in 1557. Sir John Port had specifically intended the College to be a grammar school for the local poor children of Etwall, Repton and Burnaston. These intentions have somewhat deviated over the passing years and now Repton stands as one of the foremost public schools in the country. Interestingly, two of its headmasters, Dr Temple and Dr Fisher, went on to become Archbishops of Canterbury, while Dr Ramsey was a pupil at the school under Dr Fisher's guiding light. Film buffs will recognise the 14th century gatehouse and causeway, as they featured in both film versions of the popular story *Goodbye, Mr Chips*.

Just to the west of the village is **Foremark Hall**, built by Robert Adam in 1762 for the Burdett family. It is now a preparatory school for Repton College.

SOUTH OF SWADLINCOTE

CHURCH GRESLEY
2 miles SW of Swadlincote off the A444

This former mining village has a distinguished history dating back to the time of the Augustinian monks who settled here in the 12th century and founded a priory. The village's name, like that of nearby Castle Gresley, recalls the great Gresley family, said to have been the only Derbyshire family to have retained their lands from the time of the *Domesday Book* up until the 20th century.

The village church retains some links with the past. The priory and chancel buildings were pulled down during the Tudor age, and the church remained in a sad state of disrepair up until the early 19th century. A new chancel was built in 1872. Remains of the priory have been found, including fragments of painted glass, stone coffins and medieval tiles. What remains of the old church are the sturdy 15th century tower and two 14th century arches that lead to the church's north aisle.

An impressive alabaster monument depicts **Sir Thomas Gresley**, surrounded by arms showing the marriages of his ancestors dating back to the time of William the Conqueror. The church's treasure, though, are the 10 large and wonderfully carved stalls.

CASTLE GRESLEY
3 miles SW of Swadlincote off the A444

Unfortunately nothing is left of the castle built by the Gresley family which gives this attractive village its name - apart from the grassy mound on which it stood, still known as **Castle Knob**.

LINTON
2 miles SW of Swadlincote off the A444

Linton is a charming and restful village, within "The National Forest", which is mainly agricultural since the closure of the Coton Park colliery.

The Queens Head

Coalpit Lane, Coton-in-the-Elms,
Swadlincote, Derbyshire DE12 8EX
Tel: 01283 762573

The Queens Head is a traditional 16th-century inn retaining many of its original features, which add to the friendly and comfortable feel. Open every lunchtime and evening (closed Monday lunch), there is a tempting menu of meals and snacks served, and on fine days, food and drink can be enjoyed on the patio area. Bookings are advisable at weekends. Children are welcome and there are some non-smoking areas inside. The excellent ales include Bass and Marstons Pedigree. Also four lovely en-suite guest rooms available all year round.

ROSLISTON
5 miles SW of Swadlincote off the A444

Rosliston was recorded in the *Domesday Book* as Redlauseton, an Ango-Saxon name meaning farm of Hrolf. Rosliston is part of the National Forest and there are way-marked walks, a wildlife hide and childrens play equipment.

The church of St Mary the Virgin is mainly 19th century but the 14th century tower with its broach spire still remains.

COTON-IN-THE-ELMS
6 miles SW of Swadlincote off the A444

Mentioned in the *Domesday Book* as Cotune, it got its name from the elm trees which bordered every road into the village until they were obliterated by Dutch Elm disease. As befits a village with this much charm and character, Coton-in-the-Elms offers several quality eateries and inns.

NETHERSEAL
6 miles S of Swadlincote off the A444

Netherseal is a picturesque village on the banks of the river Mease, overlooking Leicestershire. Seal means forested and Netherseal was recorded in the *Domesday Book* as a wooded area on the edge of the Ashby Woulds. It was once a mining

The Hollybush

Main Street, Netherseal, South Derbyshire DE12 8DA
Tel: 01283 760390

In the heart of Netherseal, one of the prettiest villages in South Derbyshire, you will have no trouble spotting **The Hollybush**. Only very recently taken over by Nick and Barbara, the couple have quickly established a reputation for serving superb food, with French-born Nick bringing many years experience as a professional chef. The superb menu offers simple, superbly cooked dishes and bookings are essential at weekends. Well stocked bar with Marstons Pedigree on tap and a rotating guest ale. Closed Tuesdays.

community with a two-shaft colliery and several related industries. The mining industry has long gone and the centre of Netherseal village is now a conservation area with many listed buildings including the 17th century almshouses.

APPLEBY MAGNA
5 miles S of Swadlincote off the A453

The attractive village of Appleby has three pubs, a church, a handful of shops and a school, originally designed by Sir Christopher Wren. Originally agricultural, it has become a commuter village for the nearby towns. The centre of Appleby around the historic medieval Moat House is a Conservation Area,. The house, the moat and its fields on either side are scheduled as an Ancient Monument.

MEASHAM
3 miles S of Swadlincote off the A453

Just over the border into Leicestershire, Measham is well worth that short step over the county boundary. It is large enough to be lively yet retains the air of a lovely rural retreat. It also boasts some lovely 16th, 17th and 18th century buildings. The tiny Measham Museum opened in 1992. There is a collection of artifacts, pictures, letters and documents recording the history of the village through the eyes of two generations of local doctors covering nearly a century as well as items relating to the coal mining, terra-cotta and pottery industries. Mining was recorded in this area as early as the 13th century. There is also a display of Measham ware, traditionally associated with the canal people. All kinds of tea and table ware were made in the characteristic dark brown glaze covered in shiny sprigs of flowers and birds. Measham museum's earliest teapot is dated 1886 and the last known date of manufacture is 1914. They were sold by Mrs. Annie Bonas from her shop on the High Street.

DONISTHORPE
3 miles SE of Swadlincote off the A444

Donisthorpe is a famous old mining village right on the Derbyshire-Leicestershire border. Its inhabitants are justly proud of the village's industrial and historical heritage. The old colliery, the pit railway and the old British Rail line closed down by the 1960s. Left behind is a proud history and a tranquillity unknown in the days of the mines.

THE TURKS HEAD

Church Street, Donisthorpe, Derbyshire DE12 7PX
Tel: 01530 270220

The Turks Head is a popular public house that is renowned locally for its warm hospitality, the quality of its beer and the good entertainment. The historic premises date to the 18th century and retain many original features, while providing a cosy environment in which to enjoy a drink. A DJ appears each Friday night, there is a monthly quiz on Sundays and regular Ceilidh nights. Open Monday to Thursday evenings, Fridays from 3pm and normal opening hours Saturday and Sunday. No food.

Lakeside Lodge Tearoom

Shortheath Water, Moira, Swadlincote,
Derbyshire DE12 6BN
Tel: 01283 763777

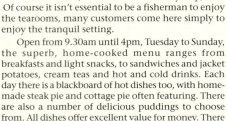

Close to the village of Moira, just a couple of miles south of Swadlincote, the **Lakeside Lodge Tearoom** is well worth seeking out. A cosy, traditional tea room, owned and personally run by Carol and Peter Mallen, together with daughter and son-in-law Joanne and Richard, it is the location that makes this stand out. Shortheath Water is a well-stocked coarse fishing lake where you can fish from dawn until dusk on a day or season ticket. There are twenty four pegs, some with disabled access, and the fish are mainly carp, with some roach, tench and bream for added interest. Of course it isn't essential to be a fisherman to enjoy the tearooms, many customers come here simply to enjoy the tranquil setting.

Open from 9.30am until 4pm, Tuesday to Sunday, the superb, home-cooked menu ranges from breakfasts and light snacks, to sandwiches and jacket potatoes, cream teas and hot and cold drinks. Each day there is a blackboard of hot dishes too, with home-made steak pie and cottage pie often featuring. There are also a number of delicious puddings to choose from. All dishes offer excellent value for money. There is seating for up to 36 people in the non-smoking dining area, with more room outside in fine weather.

MOIRA
6 miles SE of Swadlincote off the A444

Moira Furnace Museum is based in a 19th century iron blast furnace. There are interactive displays and information on how the furnace worked and its influence on the local economy and the lives of the workers.

5 The Amber Valley and Erewash

This chapter encompasses the regions of Derbyshire going by the picturesque names of the Amber Valley and the eastern part of the area known as Erewash. These two regions cover the eastern and southeastern parts of Derbyshire respectively. The Rivers Amber, Derwent and Trent run through this part of the county. Though the scenery is perhaps less dramatic than the popular Peak District, in which most of north Derbyshire lies, there are ample opportunities to enjoy pleasant walks in the extensive grounds of many of the estates.

Amber Valley

The southeast area of Derbyshire has been heavily influenced by the two towns of Derby and Nottingham. Originally small farming communities, many of the villages grew at the time of the Industrial Revolution and they can, in many cases, be characterised by rows of workers' cottages. However, notwithstanding this there are some interesting and unique buildings to be found in this corner of Derbyshire.

River Amber

Whilst a lot of the area did not escape from the growth of Derby and Nottingham, several villages remain, their centres almost intact, and, in particular there is Ockbrook, the site of a Moravian Settlement. Unlike the area to the west, there are no great stately mansions, except for one, Elvaston Castle, which, along with its extensive grounds, is an interesting and delightful place to explore. Dale Abbey is another of the region's attractions, a now ruined abbey founded here by Augustinian monks in the 13th century.

132 THE HIDDEN PLACES OF DERBYSHIRE

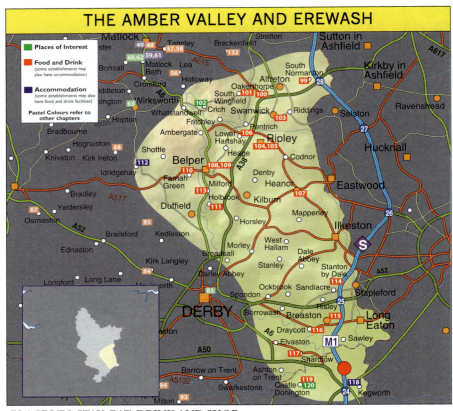

PLACES TO STAY, EAT, DRINK AND SHOP

99	The Clock Inn, South Normanton	Pub with Food	Page 133
100	The Peacock at Oakerthorpe, Oakerthorpe	Pub with Food	Page 134
101	The Blue Bell, South Wingfield	Pub with Food	Page 135
102	Crich Tramway Village, Crich, Nr Matlock	Historical Family Attraction	Page 136
103	The Steam Packet, Swanwick, Nr Alfreton	Pub with Food	Page 138
104	Butterley Park, Ripley	Pub with Food	Page 139
105	The Moss Cottage Carvery, Ripley	Pub with Food	Page 139
106	The Gate Inn, Lower Hartshay, Nr Ripley	Pub with Food	Page 140
107	Agatino's Restaurant, Heanor, Nr Derby	Restaurant	Page 142
108	Hill Top Inn, Belper	Pub with Food, Self Catering	Page 143
109	The Green Room Restaurant, Belper	Restaurant	Page 144
110	The Bluebell Inn and Restaurant, Belper	Pub with Restaurant	Page 145
111	The Wheel Inn, Holbrook, Nr Belper	Pub, Restaurant and Accommodation	Page 146
112	Garden Cottage, Idridgehay	Self Catering	Page 147
113	The Strutt Arms Hotel, Milford	Hotel	Page 147
114	Stanhope Arms, Stanton by Dale, Nr Ilkeston	Pub with Restaurant	Page 151
115	The Navigation, Breaston	Pub with Food	Page 153
116	Websters Restaurant and Take Away, Draycott	Restaurant and Take Away	Page 153
117	The Navigation Inn, Shardlow	Pub with Restaurant	Page 155
118	Kegworth House, Kegworth, Nr Derby	Bed & Breakfast	Page 156
119	The Nags Head Inn, Castle Donington	Pub with Food	Page 157
120	Grand Prix Collection, Castle Donington	Grand Prix Cars	Page 157

ALFRETON

This historic town dates back to Saxon times and, despite local legends to the contrary, Alfred the Great was not immortalised in the naming of the place. It would have belonged to a Saxon noble of the name of Alfred at some time and was named "Aelfredingtune", but there is nothing to suggest that King Alfred was based here. In the *Domesday Book* it is recorded as "Elstretune". This attractive former coal-mining town stands on a hill close to the Nottinghamshire border. The town benefited from the philanthropy of Robert Watchorn, a pit boy made good, who emigrated to America, became Commissioner of Immigration and made his fortune, much of which was used to rebuild the southern part of Alfreton. Along the charming High Street can be found the George Hotel, a fine Georgian building that looks down the length of the High Street. There are also a number of other 18th century stonebuilt houses. The parish church of St Martin is large and has an impressive fine western tower. The ground floor of the church dates back to the 1200s.

Among the many splendid old buildings in Alfreton, the most impressive is **Alfreton Hall** (private), the centrepiece of an attractive public park. In soft mellow stone, the Hall was built around 1730, with 19th century additions. Owned until fairly recently by the Palmer Morewood family, owners of the local coal mines, it is now used as an Arts and Adult Education Centre. The park is quite extensive, boasting its own cricket ground and a horse-riding track around its perimeters. In **King Street** there is a house of confinement, or lock-up, which was built to house lawbreakers and catered mainly for the local drunkards. The close confines of the prison with its two cells, minute windows and thick outer walls must have been a very effective deterrent.

The market at Alfreton was granted, in 1251, to Robert de Latham and Thomas de Chaworth, to be held on a Monday, together with a fair for three days at the festival of St. Margaret. There is still a bustling market and Afreton attracts visitors from quite a radius to its busy town centre.

AROUND ALFRETON

SOUTH NORMANTON
2 miles east of Alfreton the B6109

Normanton, meaning the farm of the north men or 'Northwegans' was a small holding belonging to William Peveril at the time of Domesday. Now a large, busy industrial village, it grew from a largely agricultural settlement with some tanning, framework knitting and small scale coal

The Clock Inn
Market Street, South Normanton, Derbyshire DE55 2AA
Tel: 01773 811396 Fax: 01773 784580
e-mail: thebar@theclockinn.co.uk
website: www.theclock.co.uk

They say you should never judge a book by its cover, and the same could well be applied to the family-run **Clock Inn**. The unpretentious exterior conceals a warm and friendly interior where regulars and new customers can enjoy a refreshing drink all day every day, with the bar offering three real ales, some unusual draught lagers and much more. The owner, Bob Skinner, is a superb chef and the varied menu of food is available at every session except Sunday evening.

THE PEACOCK AT OAKERTHORPE

Four Lane Ends, Oakerthorpe,
Derbyshire DE55 7LN
Tel: 01773 832088
Fax: 01773 521713
website: www.peacockoakerthorpe.co.uk

The Peacock is a historic and well-known public house situated within the village of Oakerthorpe on the B6013, close to the junction with the A615. This road was once the main coaching route between Sheffield and Derby and the hostelry was of great importance during this time. Teams of horses were changed here and the raised platform used by passengers can still be seen. Down in the cellars there is an ancient underground passage which links to Wingerfield Manor, used at one time as a prison for Mary Queen of Scots. There is also a crypt under

the stables which is linked to the main house by another underground passage. The interior of the inn also retains some interesting features, notably the ancient fittings of the post office, which can be seen in the bar parlour. At one time the hostelry was used as the post office for the district and letters for Alfreton would be addressed to 'Alfreton near the Peacock'.

Running the Peacock are Martin and Christine Gifford, who have been in the licensed trade for over 20 years, and arrived in Oakerthorpe just three years ago. They have successfully combined up-to-date modern facilities with a traditional style and there is a high standard of décor and furnishings throughout. Overall, there is seating for up to 150 customers, with two large non-smoking areas. Martin has brought his experience as a chef to the fore and created a superb menu of dishes, which is served between 12 noon and 8.30pm each day. All the dishes are home cooked and present a good choice catering to all tastes and appetites. If the regular menu is not enough to tempt your appetite, there is also a selection of classic favourites available each day, priced at just £2.95.

Never wanting a day to be overlooked, there is a special offer, meal deal or entertainment event every day of the week. For example on Monday there is a pub quiz, with beer at a pound a pint; Wednesday is curry night; Thursday there is a disco and on Saturday there is a live performer.

It is not surprising that The Peacock has become so popular with locals from the surrounding villages as well as visitors to the area. This place can be well recommended to customers of all ages, with friendly hospitality extended to all. There is also a function room – ideal for weddings, parties and christenings – with a full catering service available too. Plenty of off-road car parking.

mining. The village was transformed after the opening of 'A Winning' colliery in 1871 and 'B Winning' in 1875, by the Blackwell Colliery Company. By the 1881's 'A Winning' had the largest output of coal in Derbyshire and employed around 500 men. Terraced houses were built to accommodate the growing population, which doubled in the ten years from 1871 to 1881. Like many Victorian industrialists the Blackwell Colliery Company took a paternalistic attitude to its workforce, providing a reading room, library, tennis courts and playing fields as well as a cottage hospital. South Normanton Colliery closed in 1952, B Winning in 1964 and A Winning in 1969.

The present population is around 8000. Despite the unemployment caused by the closing of the coal mines, the community spirit, typical of mining villages continues. The village centre, around the old market place has moved to a new market area and housing covers the site of Jedediah Strutt's birthplace. New industries have taken over with the expansion of industrial estates around the village.

St Michaels Church dates from around the 13th century but most of the present building is 19th century. It contains a monument to a Robert Ravel who lived at the nearby Carnfield Hall, an early 17th century stone mansion built by the Revell family.

OAKERTHORPE
1 miles W of Alfreton off the B6013/A615/B5035

At Oakerthorpe Nature Reserve, subsidence from the Oakerthorpe coal mine has created a marshy area, which is now a nature reserve managed by Derbyshire Wildlife Trust.

SOUTH WINGFIELD
6 miles SE of Matlock off the A6

Above the village, on the rise of a hill, stand the graceful ruins of the 15th century **Wingfield Manor**. Built by Ralph Lord Cromwell, the manor house was used as Mary Queen of Scots' prison on two separate occasions in 1569 and 1584 when she was held under the care of the Earl of Shrewsbury. The local squire, Anthony Babington, attempted to rescue the Queen and lead her to safety but the plot failed and, instead, lead to them both being beheaded. One of the less well-known of Derbyshire's many manor houses and mansions, the history and architectural interest provided by the ruins make it one of the more fascinating homes in the area. A wander around the remains reveals the large banqueting hall with its unusual oriel window and a crypt which was probably used to store food and wine. Whatever its use, it is a particularly fine example and rivals a similar structure at Fountains

THE BLUE BELL
Church Lane, South Wingfield,
Derbyshire DE55 7NJ
Tel: 01773 520395

The Blue Bell in South Wingfield is a charming old pub that dates back in parts to the mid-18th century. Karen and Robert Menzies took over the running of the place in 2001 and have firmly re-established this as a popular eating and drinking place. Open each weekday evening and all day Saturday and Sunday for drinks, with good pub food served each evening and throughout the

weekend. Plenty of home-cooking with the meat and potato pie a popular choice. Live entertainment every other Saturday. Lovely beer garden.

Wingfield Manor

signposts, stone flags and gas lamps are all original and come from such diverse places as Liverpool, Oldham and Leeds. Today, in many towns and cities, trams are making a come back, but here the Museum gives visitors the opportunity to view the real thing. As well as those shuttling up and down the mile-long scenic route, there is an exhibition, which contains not only trams but much more besides, including some wonderfully colourful fairground organs. Throughout the year the museum holds many special events and, with their policy of no hidden extras, this is a great place to take all the family for a fun day out. The Museum stands on the site of a Abbey. High up in the tower can also be seen a single archer's slit, built the opposite way round so that only one archer was needed to defend the whole tower. The ruins have been used as a location for a number of film and TV productions, including *Peak Practice* and Zeffirelli's *Jane Eyre*.

CRICH

6 miles SE of Matlock off the A6

Probably best known as the village of Cardale in the TV series *Peak Practice*, this large village, with its hilltop church and market cross, is also the home of the **National Tramway Museum** (see panel). Referring to itself intriguingly as "the museum that's a mile long", it offers a wonderful opportunity to enjoy a tram ride along a Victorian Street scene. The

CRICH TRAMWAY VILLAGE

Crich, Matlock, Derbyshire DE45DP
Tel: 01773 853167 Fax: 01773 852326

Crich Tramway Village offers a family day out in the relaxing atmosphere of a bygone era. Explore the re-created period street with its genuine buildings and features, fascinating exhibitions and most importantly, its trams. Unlimited tram rides are free with your entry fee, giving you the opportunity to fully appreciate the Village and surrounding countryside.

Journey on one of the many beautifully restored vintage trams, as they rumble through the cobbled street past a traditional police telephone known as the 'TARDIS', the Red Lion Pub & Restaurant, exhibition hall, workshops, children's play and picnic area, before passing beneath the magnificent Bowes Lyon Bridge. Next it's past the bandstand, through the woods, and then on to Glory Mine taking in spectacular views of the Derwent Valley.

quarry that was owned by the great engineer, George Stephenson, who also owned the railway that carried the stone down the steep incline to his lime kilns alongside the Cromford Canal.

Back in the centre of the village is the tower of **Crich Stand**, a local landmark that looks rather like a lighthouse. In fact this is the Regimental Memorial for the Sherwood Foresters erected in 1923. It stands almost 1,000 feet above sea level and from its viewing gallery, on a clear day, it is said that seven counties can be seen. A lantern is lit in the tower at night and the regiment still holds an annual pigrimage to the tower on the first Sunday of July. A climb to the top certainly offers some fantastic views. This large, straggling village, which retains its medieval market cross, was also a flourishing knitting centre at one time; the telltale 18th century cottages with their long upper windows can still be seen. The part-Norman parish Church of St Michael has a built-in stone lectern, which, though common in Derbyshire, is rare elsewhere in the country.

WHATSTANDWELL
4 miles SW of Alfreton off the A6

This tiny village, of which it has been said "the loveliness of the English countryside is always here," was once owned by the monks of Darley Abbey. It nestles in the valley of the River Derwent. The highest hill surrounding the village is crowned by a War Memorial tower with a beacon that shines over Nottinghamshire and Derbyshire. Up across the valley is **Shining Cliff**, and along the village's steep lanes lie greystone cottages and farmhouses, built from the stone of its own quarries and merging gently into the background of woods and cliff. Florence Nightingale knew and loved the village, and took a keen interest in the local community.

FRITCHLEY
3 miles SW of Alfreton off the A610

This quiet hamlet was, during the 19th and early 20th centuries, an important meeting place for Quakers. A flourishing community survives today. Here also can be seen the remains of a pre-Stephenson tramway that was built at the end of the 18th century to carry stone to the lime kilns at Bull Bridge.

AMBERGATE
6 miles SW of Alfreton off the A6

Where the River Amber joins the mighty Derwent, Ambergate is one of the main gateways to the Peak District for travellers going north on the A6. A marvellous bridge crosses the Derwent. The village itself is surrounded by deciduous woodland, including the fine **Shining Cliff Woods**, an important refuge for wildlife. The railway, road and canal here are all squeezed into the tight river valley, and the railway station, standing 100 feet above the road, was one of the few triangular stations in Britain. Built in the late 19th century, the church of St Anne was a gift to the village from the Johnson family of the Ambergate Wire Works, now known as the business concern Richard Johnson and Nephew. Inside the church there is a marble figure depicting an angel protecting a child from a serpent; this was the creation of a Belgian sculptor who sought refuge in Ambergate during the First World War.

SWANWICK
2 miles S of Alfreton off the A38

Swanwick is an old Derbyshire village, which grew into a thriving industrial centre over the 18th and 19th centuries. Coal mining and stocking manufacture had provided work for centuries, but it was the arrival of the Butterley Company, the largest coal, iron and engineering concern

THE STEAM PACKET

Derby Road, Swanwick, Alfreton,
Derbyshire DE55 1AB
Tel: 01773 602172

In the heart of Swanwick, next to the church, you will find the comfortable **Steam Packet Inn**, a friendly pub which is open nearly all day, every day (closed Wednesday until 3pm) serving a good range of liquid refreshment. The bar offers three real ales – Adnams and two rotating guest ales – and sandwiches and snacks are served each lunchtime. There is an active programme of entertainment with live performers most Saturday nights and quizzes held each Tuesday and Thursday. Plenty of off-road parking.

in the East Midlands, in the late 18th century that changed the face of Swanwick. Despite the fact that it has lost much of its original industries, Swanwick has doubled its size to around 5000 during the 20th century, no doubt due to its easy access to the motorway and the large towns and cities nearby.

RIDDINGS
2 miles S of Alfreton off the A38/A610

Riddings, was first recorded in the 12th century as Ryddynges, meaning a clearing in the grove. Now a tranquil village, Riddings has twice been the scene of important discovery. In the mid 1700s, 800 precious Roman coins were uncovered here. The second time was in the mid 1800s, when James Oakes, a colliery proprietor and ironmaster, discovered a mysterious liquid flowing on his property. He called in the assistance of his brother-in-law, Lyon Playfair, one of the most brilliant practical scientists of his day. Playfair found the liquid to be petroleum - then an unknown product commercially, although it had been known as naphtha, "salt of the earth", from Biblical times.

Playfair summoned the help of his friend James Young, who soon after he came to Riddings approached Playfair in dismay to show him that the oil was in a turbid condition. Playfair recognised at once the presence of paraffin, and instructed Young to extract enough paraffin to make two candles - the first paraffin-wax candles ever produced. With one candle in his left hand and the other in his right, Playfair illuminated a lecture he gave at the Royal Institution. From these small beginnings date the enormous petroleum industry and the rich trade in paraffin and its wide range of products. Young, known thereafter as Paraffin Young, earned himself a fortune, and when the knowledge of his work spread about a worldwide search for petroleum began. Thus were sown the seeds of the motor-car and the aeronautical industries, and all the activities depending on the internal combustion engine.

RIPLEY

Ripley is an old industrial Derbyshire town, mentioned in the *Domesday Book* as Ripelie. Once a typical small market town, Ripley expanded dramatically during the Industrial Revolution when great use was made of the iron, clay and coal deposits found nearby. The town's Butterley ironworks, founded in 1792 by a group of men, which included renowned engineer Benjamin Outram, created the roof for London's St Pancras station. Outram's even more famous son Sir James enjoyed an illustrious career that saw him claimed

THE AMBER VALLEY AND EREWASH **139**

Bayard of India, and earned him a resting place in Westminster Abbey.

The village church was erected in 1820 to stem the tide of rebellion and "irreligion" that swept the area in the hard years after the Battle of Waterloo, when the local weavers and stockingers rebelled against their harsh living conditions. The insurrection saw three rebels brought to the scaffold and drove some into exile, and became a "cause celebre" throughout the nation.

Near to the town is the Midland Railway Centre, which is a railway museum to delight railway buffs or families looking for a diverting day out. There are working steam trains running along a line from Butterley to Riddings, through a 35 acre country park, which provides the habitat for an abundance of wildlife from herons to foxes as well as picnic areas for visitors. There is a Victorian railwayman's church, the "Tin Tabernacle", rescued from the railway village of Westhouses, which will be developed into a Victorian Street Scene. There is a working signal box, a collection of locomotives and farm and industrial machinery. As well as a model railway there is the Butterley Park Miniature Railway, a 3.5" and 5" gauge line with a circuit of approximately one sixth of a mile. The line is fully signalled using miniature examples of traditional railway signals controlled from a miniature Midland Railway signal box. The museum is open every weekend throughout the year, and most school holidays.

AROUND RIPLEY

PENTRICH
1 mile N of Ripley off the A610/B6013

Mentioned in the *Domesday Book* as Pentric, this hilltop village with its

BUTTERLEY PARK
Nottingham Road, Ripley, Derbyshire DE5 3QH
Tel: 01773 512334 Fax: 01773 741783

Butterley Park is a large modern, family-friendly public house that forms part of the Brewsters chain. Open all day every day, the emphasis is clearly on the well-priced food with a wide-ranging menu offering plenty of choice to suit all, with two menus specifically aimed at children, all available all day long. The bar is equally well stocked, with a number of popular ales and lagers on offer. Most of the interior is non-smoking and there is even an indoor children's play area. Ample car-parking.

THE MOSS COTTAGE CARVERY
Nottingham Road, Ripley, Derbyshire DE5 3JT
Tel: 01773 742555 Fax: 01773 741063
e-mail: mosscottagecarve@btconnect.com

On the edge of Ripley town centre, on the A610 Nottingham road, you will find the **Moss Cottage Carvery**. An ideal stopping place for those travelling by car, there is a large car park to one side. A popular eating and drinking place, here you can enjoy some tasty, well-priced food and a fine selection of ales. Regular special meal deals, occasional live entertainment and a quiz each Wednesday. Open at every session and all day at weekends and bank holidays.

brownstone gabled houses is very charming. Its sturdy church is approached via a picturesque flight of 48 steps. The Normans built the lower part of the church tower, the top of the tower was constructed in the 15th century, as were the battlements and most of the windows. A striking stained-glass War Memorial window created in 1916 depicts the warrior saints of England and France and a figure of St Michael.

Pentrich is famous historically as the site of the last revolution of England, which took place here in 1817. A small band of half-starved weavers, labourers and stockingers met and made plans for a march on London. The rebels' attempted riot was soon quelled. The trial of nearly 50 of them lasted 10 days. They were accused of high treason. A few were pardoned, 11 sent to Australia for life, three to Australia for 14 years and three were hung, drawn and quartered at Derby Gaol. The poet Shelley witnessed the scene and described the despair of the relatives and the disturbance of the crowd as the men were beheaded. The executioners were masked and their names were kept secret. The block is still to be seen in Derby Prison. The 1821 Census recorded a decrease of a third in the population of the parish because the Duke of Devonshire's agents had destroyed many of the houses after the insurrection.

LOWER HARTSHAY
2 miles W of Ripley off the A610

Lower Hartshay was on Ryknield Street, an important Roman military and trade route from the Fosse Way in Gloucestershire to the north. The line of Ryknield Street through Ripley, Pentrich and Lower Hartshay can still be seen and makes a pleasant walk with splendid views. Lower Hartshay was still on a main route for traffic until the 1970s. Now by-passed by the major trunk roads, it is a pleasant and tranquil backwater.

HEAGE
4 miles SW of Alfreton off the B6013

Heage was on the ancient pack horse route from Derby to Chesterfield and the old turnpike road passed through here. The village has no obvious centre and is scattered along the roads and lanes with some small estates of modern housing. The main occupation for centuries would have been farming and coal mining. Morley Park has been worked for coal and ironstone since 1372. The remains of bell-pits were discovered during recent opencasting. On Morley Park are the remains of two cold blast coke iron furnaces built by Francis Hurt in 1780 and the Mold Brothers in 1818, the older furnace was probably the first of its kind in

The Gate Inn

Main Road, Lower Hartshay, Nr. Ripley, Derbyshire DE5 3RP
Tel: 01773 742934

The Gate Inn is tucked away in the tiny settlement of Lower Hartshay, which is on a no through road signposted just off the A610. Well worth seeking out, this cosy inn is privately owned by Bob and Susan Starman and open at every session for fine ales. The food served here is also superb, with breakfasts served from 10am, and an excellent home-cooked menu offering superb choice at other times. The daily specials board occasionally features unusual dishes such as crocodile and bison. Well worth visiting. Children welcome.

THE AMBER VALLEY AND EREWASH 141

Heage Windmill

Derbyshire. There was also some framework knitting and weaving.

The Parish Church of St Luke has a medieval East window, the only part of the original church to survive a ferocious storm in 1545, the chancel was built in 1645-1661 and the main part of the church in 1886.

The oldest domestic building in the village is Heage Hall Farm, once the home of a branch of the Pole family. Crowtrees Farm was built in 1450 with three good crook beams and was refurbished in 1712.

Heage Windmill is situated west of the village between the villages of Heage and Nether Heage. It is a Grade II listed tower mill and the only one in Derbyshire to retain its six sails and fan tail and machinery. Standing on the brow of a hill, overlooking the village of Nether Heage, it is built of local sandstone and is over two hundred years old. It has been restored to full working order and is open to the public at weekends and bank holidays.

DENBY
2 miles S of Ripley off the A38/B6179

Denby was mentioned in the *Domesday Book* as Denebi, which means village of the Danes. Ryknield Street runs through the village.

Denby Pottery, one of the biggest attractions in Derbyshire not far from junction 28 of the M1, off the A38 towards Derby on the B6179, has a fascinating history. Derbyshire has a long tradition of stoneware pottery, closely associated with the natural clay deposits of the county. From a number of small buildings on the site of the clay bed, Denby Pottery was established in 1809. By 1994, classic ranges such as Imperial Blue and Regency Green were proving to be best sellers, and the Pottery had earned a reputation for the quality and durability of its wares. The business took on a new lease of life as the Visitor Centre was added - it now welcomes nearly 300,000 visitors a year. The site offers a chance to see the latest in ceramic technology. At the Factory Shop, seconds and discounts start at 20 per cent off the RRP. The Cookery Emporium offers cookery demonstrations and has in stock over 3,000 kitchen gadgets, supplies and

Denby Pottery

equipment. There are tours on offer as well, including a full tour of the pottery or the Craftsmen's Workshop Tour. Refreshments are available at the comfortable restaurant on-site. A factory shop for Dartington Crystal can also be found at this superb attraction.

As well as pottery, coal and iron have made Denby its name, though it remains an unspoilt retreat. A mile from the Pottery Visitor Centre, in Denby's oldest part, is its little church, set amid a lovely churchyard filled with trees. The church's round arches and pillars date from the late 12th century, while the chancel with its sedilia, piscina and aumbry is from the 14th century. The altar table is 17th century, and from the 20th century come the church tower and the spire, the fine porch with its stone roof, and the eight-sided font.

One of Denby's most famous sons was John Flamsteed, born here in 1646. A poor boy, he went on to become the first Astronomer-Royal at the then-new Observatory at Greenwich. Benjamin Outram, the railway engineer was also born here.

CODNOR
2 miles SE of Ripley off the A610

Codnor's surrounding billowy fields and woods make it easy to forget the coal and iron which have made this part of Derbyshire famous. Once it was a great park of nearly 2,000 acres, and the ruins at the gateway to Codnor were once a mighty castle, feudal home of the influential Grey family. Richard Grey was one of Henry III's loyal barons. Edward II visited another Richard here after fighting the rebels at Burton-on-Trent. Another was sent by Henry V to bring Hotspur's son from Scotland, while Henry, the last of them, busied himself with alchemy, in a vain attempt to change base metals into gold.

It is thought that the Greys built their castle with two courts, four enormous round towers and a great gateway. By the time the Zouch family sold it in the mid 1600s it was already beginning to decay. All that survives today is a length of boundary wall of the upper court, parts of the dividing wall and of the defending towers, and the odd doorway, window and fireplace, still standing tall and overlooking the Erewash valley into Nottinghamshire.

HEANOR
5 miles E of Belper off the A608

The hub of this busy town centres on the market place, where the annual fair is held, as well as the twice weekly market, which takes place on Fridays and Saturdays. Away from the bustle of the market are the **Memorial Gardens**. This

AGATINO'S RESTAURANT
7 Ray Street, Heanor, Derby DE75 7GE
Tel: 01773 710529

In the centre of Heanor, **Agatino's Restaurant** is open Monday to Saturday 8am-4.30pm (closed at 2pm on Wednesday) serving a superb menu ranging from snacks to main meals, breakfasts to cakes, and sandwiches to pizzas. All dishes are freshly cooked to order and there is a children's menu for the little ones. Run by Rosemary and Agatino Leto, the restaurant has become well known in the area for the superb home cooking, friendly service and reasonable prices. Seating for up to 60 diners.

peaceful setting always promises a magnificent spread of floral arrangements, herbaceous borders and shrubberies. Coal mining was once the dominant industry, but since all the pits have closed the scarred landscape has been reclaimed and restored. To the south of Heanor is the **Shipley Country Park**, on the estate of the now demolished Shipley Hall. In addition to its magnificent lake, the Country Park boasts over 600 acres of beautiful countryside, which should keep even the most enthusiastic walker busy. Well known as both an educational and holiday centre, there are facilities for horse riding, cycling and fishing. This medieval estate was mentioned in the *Domesday Book* and, under the auspices of the Miller-Mundy family it became a centre for farming and coal-mining production during the 18th century. Restoration over the years has transformed former railways into wooded paths, reservoirs into peaceful lakes, and has re-established the once-flowering meadows and rolling hills, which had been destroyed by the colliery pits. Here also can be found the American Adventure, a busy theme park with over a hundred thrill rides, gun fights, special events and boat trips on the lake.

The River Erewash passes through the area at Langley Mill and visitors are able to enjoy the restored boats, which travel to and from the 200 year old canal basin.

The ancient Parish Church of St Lawrence dates back to the 12th century, though little of the old church remains after rebuilding in 1868. The 15th century tower is still intact.

BELPER

Belper is a small, attractive market town 8 miles north of Derby. In 1740, the population of Belper was around 500. It grew rapidly at the beginning of the 19th century due to the industrial development of cotton mills. However the origins of the town go back much further than the Industrial Revolution. It was mentioned in the *Domesday Book* as "Beau Repaire", the beautiful retreat, in 1964 the remains of a Roman kiln were found here and its football team is called 'the nailers', for the nail makers who worked here when the area was part of the Royal Forest.

Famous for its cotton mills, the town is situated alongside the **River Derwent** on the floor of the valley. In 1776, Jedediah Strutt, the wheelwright son of a South Normanton famer, set up one of the earliest water-powered cotton mills here to harness the natural powers of the river to run his mills. With the river providing the power and fuel coming from the nearby South Derbyshire coalfield, the valley has a good claim to be one of the cradles of the Industrial Revolution. Earlier, in 1771 Strutt had gone into profitable partnership

HILL TOP INN
Belper Lane, Belper, Derbyshire DE56 2UJ
Tel: 01773 822569

Living up to its name, the **Hill Top Inn** enjoys an elevated position and superb panoramic views over the town of Belper and beyond. The present tenants, Martin and June, are a local couple that have brought a new lease of life to the pub, creating a friendly welcoming atmosphere in which customers can enjoy a quiet drink or a tasty bite to eat. Food is served at most sessions from a menu of home-made, traditional dishes. Self-catering holiday cottage, in nearby Ambergate, available for holiday lets.

with Richard Arkwright, to establish the world's first water-powered cotton mill at Cromford. Strutt and his son, William, retained the North Mill at Belper in 1872 when the partnership with Arkwright was dissolved, having added another at Milford in 1780. Great benefactors to Belper for 150 years, the Strutt family provided housing, work, education and even food - from the model farms they established in the surrounding countryside. Many parts of the town still reflect their influence.

Three hundred years later the mills are still standing and, along with them, are some unique mill-workers' cottages. To discover more about the cotton industry, the influence of the Strutt family on the town and of Samuel Slater, Strutt's apprentice who emigrated to America in 1789, built a mill there and went on to become "the Father of American manufacturers", a visit to the **Derwent Valley Visitor Centre** is a must. The oldest mill still surviving is the two-storey **North Mill** at Bridgefoot, near the magnificent crescent-shaped weir in the Derwent and the town's main bridge. Built in 1876, the mill has cast-iron columns and beams, and hollow tile floors which provided a warm-air central heating system. It is now the visitor centre. The massive, neighbouring redbrick East Mill was constructed in 1912, but now is largely empty. A Jubilee Tower in terracotta was erected on the mill site in 1897 to mark Queen Victoria's 60th anniversary on the throne.

Train travellers through Belper are among those treated to a glimpse of George Stephenson's mile-long cutting, walled in gritstone throughout and spanned by no fewer than 10 bridges. When completed in 1840 it was considered an engineering wonder of its day. There are also some lovely waterside

THE GREEN ROOM RESTAURANT

61 King Street, Belper, Derbyshire DE56 1QA
Tel: 01773 828800 Fax: 01773 828184
e-mail: julian@the-green-room.fsnet.co.uk

The Green Room is an outstanding restaurant, which can be found in the heart of the town of Belper, and just two minutes off the main A6. The present owner is Julian Mountney who actually started working here as an assistant chef, progressed to head chef, and a year ago bought the place himself. The superb menu is best described as modern British cuisine, with everything freshly prepared and cooked to order. There is a wide-ranging a la carte menu, a fixed price table d'hote menu, and a lunch menu where every dish is available as either a small or full size portion.

The starters range from a platter of smoked venison to roast mushrooms on toast, while the main dishes include such delights as baked fillets of sole and roast guinea fowl. Everyone is sure to find something that sounds tempting but try and leave room for the superb dessert selection. Once a month there is a gourmet evening – ring for details. Open for lunch Tuesday to Saturday, evenings Wednesday to Saturday and for Sunday lunch. There is seating for up to thirty in the elegant dining room and further seating on the attractive terrace, weather permitting. Large car park opposite. Children welcome.

walks in this bustling little town. Among Belper's other interesting buildings are the **Christ Church**, a lofty, spacious house of worship built in 1849, the parish church of St Peter with its pinnacled west tower (1824) and Chapel of St John the Baptist in The Butts, dating from 1683. A monument to George Brettle can be seen in St Peter's Church - **George Brettle's Warehouse**, in Chapel Street, is a distinctive and elegant building created in 1834.

The River Gardens were established in 1905 and today they are a pleasant place for a stroll among the beautifully tended gardens. Rowing boats can be hired for a trip along the Derwent. The Gardens are a favourite with the film industry, having been used in Ken Russell's *Women in Love*, as well as television's *Sounding Brass* and *In the Shadow of the Noose*. The riverside walk through the meadows is particularly rich in bird life.

AROUND BELPER

FARNAH GREEN
1 mile W of Belper on the A517

Farnah Green is a charming hamlet on the outskirts of Belper. It has no shops but has a pleasant old country pub, which serves food.

SHOTTLE
2 miles W of Belper off the A517

Shottle is a picturesque hamlet of a few farms, houses, a church and a chapel, surrounded by little lanes and footpaths. Unlike most of the surrounding villages it appears little changed since the 19th century. Shottle was the birthplace of Samuel Slater, the apprentice to Jedediah Strutt, who left Belper for the USA and built the first water powered cotton mill there. He is credited as the father of the

THE BLUEBELL INN AND RESTAURANT

Farnah Green, Belper, Derbyshire DE56 2UP
Tel: 01773 826495 Fax: 01773 881073

The Bluebell Inn can be found in the small hamlet of Farnah Green, just off the A517 Ashbourne road, a mile from Belper. This is more like a restautant with a bar than an inn, as the reason that most customers visit is for the fine dining in the elegant restaurant. Owner David Sandford is a highly experienced chef, and together with his wife Jules has created a well-liked restaurant with a far-reaching reputation. The menus are superb, offering a good choice of freshly prepared, delicious dishes, served each lunch time and evening.

Locally sourced ingredients are used as far as possible and the menus reflect seasonally available produce. Among the house specialities are the steak dishes, with the beef coming from naturally reared Scottish cattle. The restaurant is spacious and can seat up to 70 diners, however it advisable to book ahead at all times to avoid disappointment. To accompany your meal there is a good wine list. Children are more than welcome and all major credit cards are accepted. If you simply want a drink the bar is stocked with the usual selection, and there is also a bar menu of lighter meals and snacks.

It is anticipated that accommodation will shortly be available – ring for full details.

The Wheel Inn

14 Chapel Street, Holbrook,
Nr. Belper, Derbyshire DE56 0TQ
Tel: 01332 880006

The Wheel Inn is a genuinely lovely pub and restaurant enjoying a delightful setting within the small village of Holbrook, just a mile or so south of Belper. The small, quaint inn retains many original features inside and out and throughout the summer is a colourful display of hanging baskets and packed flower beds. The entrance is striking with bright red painted railings, a lamp post and the 'wheel' from which it takes its name making this place stand out on the street. To the rear there is a most attractive covered, terraced patio area which is covered in vines in the style of a Continental taverna, and with a large, well-tended and decorative beer garden. The interior is also very appealing with lots of exposed wood and open stone-built fireplaces in the two bar areas. There is also a cosy snug and a light and airy conservatory area.

This friendly and welcoming pub had become neglected and run down, but in 1996 it was tastefully and sympathetically refurbished – a move which seems to have agreed with the pub's two resident ghosts. The present owners, Andrea and Dave, are local and have only recently taken over. The Wheel inn is open each lunch time and evening (closed Monday lunchtime except for Bank Holidays) and all day Saturday and Sunday. The bar is well stocked with a fine selection of real ales, between five and seven are usually available at any one time. Regular features are Directors, Pedigree, and the home-brewed Wheel Inn Bitter, complemented by a range of rotating guest ales. The inn prides itself on the quality of its beer, and also holds regular beer festivals – sometimes up to three a year – with around 30 different real ales available for sampling. Ring for details of the next event. A superb menu of food is served at each session (no food on Mondays) and meals can be taken in the non-smoking restaurant, bars, conservatory and garden – weather permitting. Bookings are advisable for the restaurant at weekends, especially for the delicious and well-priced Sunday lunch. The menu offers a good selection of tasty, home-made dishes featuring the best of seasonally available produce. In summer months there are regular barbeques. If you prefer to tax the little grey cells, rather than your waistline, then a pub quiz is held each Sunday from 9pm.

Bed and breakfast accommodation is available with a lovely double, en-suite guest room. Ring for full details of price and availability.

Industrial Revolution in the USA and his original Slater Mill at Pawtucket is now a museum.

IDRIDGEHAY
10 miles NW of Derby off the B5023

This pleasant village is called "Ithersee" by the locals and it lies in the valley of the River Ecclesbourne. Formerly a working rural village, it is now purely residential. Part of the village is a conservation area including the half-timbered building, **South Sitch**, dating from 1621. The apparent Elizabethan mansion, **Alton Manor**, was in fact built by Sir George Gilbert Scott in 1846, when he moved from Darley Dale because of the coming of the railway.

MILFORD
1 mile S of Belper off the A6

Milford was a quiet hamlet until the cotton mills came. The village's first cotton mill was built by Richard Arkwright and Jedediah Strutt using stone transported from nearby Hopping Hill. It was only a year later that their partnership dissolved and both industrialists went their separate ways to forge individual empires. Housing was built for the workforce some of which still remain. Although most of the mill buildings are now gone, those that remain are used by small businesses.

HOLBROOK
2 miles S of Belper off the A6

The Saxon name for Hobrook was Hale Broc meaning Badger Hill. The ancient Roman Portway runs through the village and one of the toll houses for the turnpike road still stands in the village. In the early 1960s two Roman kilns were discovered in the village. Holbrook was once a busy industrial village well known for framework knitters, who supplied stockings for royalty. It is now a pleasant

GARDEN COTTAGE
Church Farm, Idridgehay, Derbyshire DE56 2SJ
Tel: 01773 550194 Fax: 01773 550814
e-mail: kiwibrendabutler@yahoo.com

Garden Cottage nestles in the picturesque country village of Idridgehay in the southern corner of the Peak District. Formerly the working forge for the adjacent farmhouse, now home to owner Brenda Butler, the cottage has been sensitively converted into luxurious holiday accommodation for up to four people. There are two double bedrooms, a fully fitted kitchen and a spacious living area with French doors leading to a patio and private garden. Weekly lets with short breaks subject to availability. Non-smoking. No children or pets.

THE STRUTT ARMS HOTEL

Derby Road, Milford, Derbyshire DE56 0QW
Tel: 01332 840240 Fax: 01332 841758

The Strutt Arms Hotel is one of the best-known hotels in Derbyshire, and enjoys a fine location on the A6 in the village of Milford, close to the river. An elegant, yet cosy, style can be found throughout, from the public bars and restaurant, to the ten, mostly en-suite, guest rooms. The food is of a superb standard, all home-cooked, and available each lunchtime and evening, and all day Friday to Sunday. The bar is open all day serving real ales. Ideal touring base.

village, with some attractive old houses, serving mainly as a commuter area for the nearby towns of Belper and Derby.

St Michael's Church was built in 1761 as a private chapel to Holbrook Hall. It was rebuilt as the parish church in 1841, but still retains the elegant classical lines of its predecessor. Holbrook Hall was built in 1681 although it looks later. The hall is now a residential home for the elderly.

DUFFIELD
2 miles S of Belper off the A6

This ancient parish is a charming place, with Georgian houses and cottages lining the banks of the River Ecclesbourne. For such a cosy place, it seems odd that the parish church of **St Alkmunds** is situated in isolation down by the river. It has a 14th century east tower with a recessed spire. It was much restored in the 19th century. Inside the Church there is an impressive monument dating from 1600, dedicated to Anthony Bradshaw, his two wives and their twenty children. Bradshaw was a barrister and the deputy steward of Duffield Firth, a former hunting forest between Duffield and Wirksworth. His great-nephew went on to officiate over the court, which called for the execution of Charles I.

Also in the village is a large mound, all that remains of **Duffield Castle** which was ransacked and burnt to the ground in 1266. However, excavations show that it must have been a massive building, with a large keep whose walls were over 16 feet thick. Following the Battle of Hastings, in 1066, William the Conqueror awarded Henry de Ferrers, one of his chief supporters, by giving him great areas of land. Controlling his estates from Tutbury Castle in Staffordshire, Henry built a motte and bailey castle here in around 1080 and installed his son Engenulph. The de Ferrers estates passed peacefully from father to son for nearly 200 years until they were inherited by Robert de Ferrers in 1254. Only 15 years of age at that time, by the age of 27 he had managed to ruin the family name and lose the estate and titles. The two-acre site on which the Castle stood is owned by the National Trust; the interesting relics that were excavated here between 1886 and 1957 can be seen in Derby Museum.

Duffield Hall is situated at the southern edge of the village. It is an Elizabethan building, enlarged in 1870 and once used as a girls boarding school. It is now the Head Quarters for the Derbyshire Building Society.

ILKESTON

The third largest town in Derbyshire, Ilkeston received its royal charter for a market and fair in 1252. Both have continued to the present day. The history of the town, however, goes back to the days when it was an Anglo-Saxon hilltop settlement known as Tilchestune. Once a mining and lace-making centre, its history is told in the **Erewash Museum**, housed in a fine Georgian house with Victorian extensions on the High Street. It was a family home and then part of a school before becoming a Museum in the 1980s. Many original features survive including a restored Edwardian kitchen and wash-house. The garden has unrivalled views across the Erewash Valley. Other fine examples of elegant 18th century houses can be found in East Street whilst, in Wharncliffe Road, there are period houses with art nouveau features.

Ilkeston commands fine wide views from the hillside above the valley of the **Erewash**, which here bounds the county. The town's church-crowned hilltop is a landmark that can be seen from far afield. This textile-manufacturing town in a colliery district has a fine church, which has undergone many changes since it was first erected in the 1300s. It is particularly notable for its window tracery, especially in the six windows in the older part of the church. A former tower and elegant spire were destroyed by storm in 1714. The tower only was rebuilt, to be succeeded by another on the old foundations in 1855. This tower was then moved westwards in 1907, at which time the nave was doubled in length. One intriguing feature it has retained throughout all these changes is its 13th century archway. The organ is also distinguished, in that it was built from one, which came from a London church and is known to have been played by the great Mendelssohn himself.

AROUND ILKESTON

MAPPERLEY
2 miles NW of Ilkeston off the A609

This historic village was first granted a market charter in 1267 and, though its old church was demolished due to mining subsidence, the modern church has some interesting stained glass windows. In the heart of Derbyshire mining country, any stroll from the village centre will take the walker past industrial remains.

To the south of Mapperley is the former branch line of the Midland Railway which served Mapperley Colliery as well as the old raised track which is all that remains of an old tramway which ran from the Blue Fly Shaft of West Hallam Pit to the **Nutbrook Canal** further east. The Canal, which opened in 1796, carried coal from the pits at Shipley to the ironworks at Stanton and beyond. Only just over 4 miles long, the Canal had some 13 locks but it fell into disuse after the Second World War and much of it has now been filled in. The relatively new "Nutbrook Trail" for cyclists and walkers follows the old Stanton to Shipley mineral railway line more or less parallel to the canal, from Long Eaton to Heanor. It is part of the Sustrans network of cycle ways and is very popular with both recreational users and commuters. The railway trail and the canal towpath can create a circular walk between West Hallam and Stanton Bridge. The Nutbrook Trail received grant aid from East Midlands Arts for three sculptures, which drew their inspiration from the social and industrial heritage of the Erewash Valley. The three sculptures represent vegetation found along the trail- Birch, Campion and Vetch and the collection is entitled 'Wild Weeds'.

WEST HALLAM
2 miles W of Ilkeston off the A609

West Hallam stands on a hilltop. Its church, set between the great expanse of **West Hallam Hall** and the rectory, is approached via a lovely avenue of limes. The rector's garden has a glorious lime tree, and looks out over the valley to a great windmill with its arms still working as they have done since Georgian times. St. Wilfred's Church is over 700 years old and has a very handsome tower, with a blue clock with gilt hands and figures.

The Powtrell family were historically important to the village of West Hallam. Their former home was offered as a hiding-place for fugitive priests during the 16th century. One priest taken at the house was condemned to death, but after long imprisonment his sentence was commuted to banishment. Another priest, sentenced for celebrating mass at West Hallam Hall, was sent to prison and later died there. On a stone on the chancel floor of the village church is an engraved portrait of Thomas Powtrell in armour of the 15th cenutry. A magnificent canopied tomb depicts Walter Powtrell, who died in 1598, and his wife

Cassandra. He wears richly decorated armour, she a gown of many folds. Around them are depicted their seven children.

One of the premier attractions in the area, **The Bottle Kiln** is a handsome and impressive brick built former working pottery, now home to contemporary art and craft. Visitors can take a leisurely look at exhibitions (changing throughout the year) of both British studio ceramics and contemporary painting in the European tradition. From figurative and descriptive to abstract, many styles and media are displayed here. In addition there is a selection of imaginative contemporary British jewellery and craftware on display in and around the old kiln. Two shops filled with jewellery, cards, gifts, objets-d'art, soft furnishings and housewares with an accent on style, design and originality can also be found at this superb site. At the Egon Ronay-recommended Buttery Cafe, visitors can enjoy a wide choice of freshly prepared and hearty food, along with a tasty selection of teas, coffees and cakes. Visitors can also take their meals in the tranquil Japanese tea garden on fine days.

West Hallam has a well dressing ceremony each year, normally held during the second week of July.

HORSLEY
6 miles west of Ilkeston on the A609

Horsley is a charming little village with a population of around 500. It has a main street lined with mature trees and a village green. The church of **St Clement and St James** is a real gem dating back to the 13th century. It has a broach spire and mid 15th century battlements and a pretty porch with a medieval crucifix. The interior is much restored but there are some scraps of ancient glass in one window.

MORLEY
4 miles SW of Ilkeston off the A608

Morley is essentially a rural village with working farms around it. There are four parts to the village, Brackley Gate and the Croft, the Smithy and Brick Kiln Lane, Almshouse Lane and Church Lane.

Brackley Gates has some disused quarries and marvellous views to the north. It is now a wildlife reserve, managed by the Derbyshire Wildlife Trust. The Croft has a cluster of 17th and 18th century cottages. The 17th century almshouses in Almshouse Lane were originally provided by Jacinth Sitwell, then Lord of the Manor of Morley for '6 poor, lame or impotent men'.

The **Church of St Matthew** has a Norman nave, with the tower, chancel and north chapel being late 14th, early 15th century. It is perhaps best known for its magnificent stained glass windows. Originally in the Abbey Refectory at Dale, the windows were acquired by Sir Henry Sacheverell in 1539. There are monuments and brasses to important local families like the Sacheverell's and the Sitwell's, including one to John Sacheverell, who died at Bosworth Field in 1485 and the beautifully carved tomb chest of Henry Sacheverell, who died in 1558 and his beautiful wife Katherine Babington, who died in 1553 with its recumbent effigy and kneeling figures.

DALE ABBEY
3 miles SW of Ilkeston off the A6096

The village takes its name from the now ruined abbey that was founded here by Augustinian monks in the 13th century. Beginning life in a very humble manner, local legend has it that a Derbyshire baker came to the area in 1130, carved himself a niche in the sandstone and devoted himself to the way of the hermit. The owner of the land, Ralph FitzGeremunde, discovered the baker and was so impressed by the man's devotion that he bestowed on him the land and tithe rights to his mill in Borrowash. The sandstone cave and the romantic ruined 40 foot high window archway (all that now remains of the original abbey) are popular attractions locally and a walk around the village is both an interesting and pleasurable experience. Nearby **Hermit's Wood** is an ancient area of woodland with beech, ash, oak and lime trees. It is wonderful at any time of year, but particularly in the spring when the woodland floor is covered with a carpet of bluebells.

The village **Church of All Saints**, which dates back to the mid 12th century, must be the only church in England, which shares its roof with a farm. The church has a pulpit that dates from 1634 and the whole interior appears rather crammed with its box pews and open benches. The farmhouse was once possibly used as an infirmary for the Abbey and then as an inn. The adjoining door was blocked up in the 1820s to prevent swift transition from salvation to damnation. To the north of the village is the **Cat and Fiddle Windmill**, built in the 18th century and a fine example of the oldest type of mill. The stone roundhouse is capped with a box-like wooden structure which houses the machinery and which is fitted onto an upright post around which it can rotate to catch the wind.

STANLEY
3 miles SW of Ilkeston off the A609

Stanley is a pleasant little rural village, whose main industry was coal mining until the closure of Stanley colliery in 1959.

All that is left of **Stanley's chapel** that was here over 800 years ago is a Norman priests' doorway, now in the wall. Some of the buttresses and a small lancet date from the 1200s. The font dates back to the 1300s, and the pulpit from the 17th century. A brass tablet on the floor by the pulpit is dedicated to Sir John Bentley of Breadsall, who was buried here 20 years before the Civil War.

STANTON BY DALE
2 miles S of Ilkeston off the B6002

Stanton-by-Dale is mentioned in the *Domesday Book* and derives its name from the nearby stone quarries. The houses in the village are mainly 18th and 19th century brick or stone cottages built to house the workers of the Stanton Ironworks, which still continues to provide employment as Stanton PLC. The village pump, erected in 1897 to commemorate Queen Victoria's jubilee, had fallen into a sad state of dilapidation. It is now repaired, completely renovated and returned to its original green and gold. The village church of **St Michael and All Angels**, is 13th century in origin but there is a fine modern stained glass window depicting Stanton Works.

SANDIACRE
4 miles S of Ilkeston off the B6002

Sandiacre is situated on the border with Nottinghamshire. Although it has been all but incorporated into the ever-expanding

STANHOPE ARMS

15/17 Stanhope Street, Stanton by Dale, Ilkeston, Derbyshire DE7 4QA
Tel/Fax: 0115 932 2603

The Stanhope Arms is a cosy village inn run by a charming couple. Alan and Christine have only been here a year, yet this place has quickly proved to be a hit with locals and visitors to the area. There is a well-stocked bar, but it is the quality and range of food that impresses everyone. The well priced menu is extensive, catering to all tastes and appetites, and is available each lunchtime and evening, (except Sunday evenings). Bookings advisable for the restaurant at weekends.

Nottingham conurbation, it maintains many village features including a picturesque 14th century church up a narrow lane at the top of a hill. In the churchyard four stones remain of the remarkable Charlton family. One was an MP as far back as 1318. Sir Richard was slain on Bosworth field. Sir Thomas was Speaker in 1453. Edward was a commissioner in the Civil War.

RISLEY
4 miles S of Ilkeston off the B5010

This small village has once again become a quiet backwater now that the main Derby to Nottingham road bypasses it to the south. Apart from ribbon building along the former main road, Risley consists of no more that a small group of old buildings, but they are unique and well worth a visit. In 1593, Michael Willoughby started to rebuild the village church. Although small, even by the standards of the day, it is charming and essentially Gothic in style. In the same year his wife founded a school and, although none of the original school houses exist, those seen today date from the early 18th century and were constructed by a trust founded by the family. The central school building is a perfect example of the Queen Anne style and acted as both the school and school house, with the boarders sleeping in the garrets. The trustees still maintain this wonderful building, along with the Latin School of 1724, the English School of 1753 and another School House built in 1771.

OCKBROOK
4 miles SW of Ilkeston off the A52

This quiet village close to, but hidden from, the busy main road between Derby and Nottingham, is quite a place and well worth a visit. The old part of Ockbrook was established by Occa an Anglo Saxon, around the 6th century but the village is unusual in that, in the mid 18th century, a Moravian Settlement was founded here when a congregation of the Moravian Church was formed. The Settlement has several fine buildings, including The Manse, built in 1822, and the Moravian Chapel. Within the Settlement there is also a girls boarding school. Historical research has discovered that Ockbrook may have been a Pagan religious site well before **All Saints' Church** was built. It became the parish church in the mid 1500s and its most interesting features include a Saxon font, the 12th century tower, some fine windows and the oak chancel screen dating from around 1520. This is farming country and many of the ancient hedgerows remain, sustaining all manner of wildlife that has disappeared from many other areas. Several old farm buildings also remain, including an impressive 17th century timber-framed building at Church Farm. Little but the ground floor, however remains of **Ockbrook Windmill**, one of only 10 windmill sites extant in Derbyshire.

BORROWASH
6 miles SW of Ilkeston off the A6005

Close to the River Derwent, this once quiet place, separated from its neighbour, Ockbrook, by the main Derby to Nottingham road, has developed into a commuter village. Pronounced "borrow-ash", the village has lost its railway station and canal, which was filled in during the early 1960s. P H Currey designed the small redbrick church of **St Stephen** in 1899. The interior features a low, 18th century ironwork chancel screen, believed to be the work of Robert Bakewell of Derby.

SPONDON
5 miles SW of Ilkeston off the A52

This village, with many Georgian brick houses, is now almost engulfed by Derby, but the older parts can still be picked out. The church, damaged by fire in 1340, was completely rebuilt and has also undergone restoration work in 1826 and again in the

1890s. Nearby is **Locko Park**, the privately-owned ancestral home of the Drury-Lowe family since 1747. The present Hall was built by Francis Smith in the mid 1700s, and since then it has been given an Italian appearance. Today, the Hall houses one of the largest private collections of Italian paintings in Britain. The chapel is earlier than the Hall, having been built in 1669. Way back in medieval times a leper hospital stood here.

BREASTON
5 miles S of Ilkeston off the A6005

On the southern borders of the county, close to Nottinghamshire and Leicestershire, Breaston occupies the flat countryside near the point where the River Derwent joins the River Trent before continuing on its long journey to the North Sea. The mainly 13th century church of **St Michael** boasts the "Boy of Breaston" - a small, chubby-faced child immortalised in the 13th century by the mason of the nave arches. He has smiled down on worshippers and visitors for the past seven centuries. The story has it that this boy would come in and watch the masons at work while the church was being built. The master mason decided to make the child part of the church, so that he could always have a good view of it!

Coffins had to be carried to neighbouring **Church Wilne** for burial up until the early 1800s, as there was no burial ground at Breaston until that time. For this reason the footpath over the fields of Wilne continues to be known by villagers as the 'Coffin Walk'. The now-drained Derby Canal passed through the village at one time. The basin where the narrowboats were turned can still be seen.

DRAYCOTT
7 miles S of Ilkeston off the A6005

Having strong connections with the Nottingham lace trade, Draycott's **Victoria Mill** was built in 1888 and was established

THE NAVIGATION
Risley Lane, Breaston, Derbyshire DE72 3BP
Tel: 01332 872880

In the centre of the village of Breaston, on the banks of a disused canal, stands **The Navigation**. Not far from Derby, a delightful country walk leads from behind the pub to the city. Your hosts Peter and Lisa have been here since May 2000 and they have refurbished much of the interior to create comfortable, relaxed surroundings in which to enjoy a refreshing drink and a tasty meal. The menu is varied and offers delicious, home-cooked dishes which use mainly local produce. No food Saturday or Sunday evenings.

WEBSTERS RESTAURANT AND TAKE AWAY
29 Victoria Road, Draycott, Derbyshire DE72 3PL
Tel: 01332 874253

Websters Restaurant and Take Away was created by Doreen and George Webster, together with assistance of the rest of their family, just eight years ago. This popular eating place serves good value, home-cooked food until 3pm each day (closed Mondays), together with an efficient take-away and home delivery service. The Sunday lunches are exceptional value at £5.95 and there are regular French, Greek and Italian themed nights for which bookings are essential. Well known locally and well worth a visit.

as one of the most important lace factories in the world. The four-storey building, with its green-capped ornamental clock tower, still dominates the Draycott skyline though it is now the home of an electrical component manufacturer. Draycott House, designed by Joseph Pickford, was built in 1781. It remains a private residence.

ELVASTON
8 miles SW of Ilkeston off the B5010

Elvaston is gathered around the edge of the **Elvaston Castle** estate, home of the Earls of Harrington. The magnificent Gothic castle seen today replaced a 17th century brick and gabled manor house; part of the original structure can be seen on the end of the south front. Designed by James Wyatt, the castle was finished in the early 19th century but, unfortunately, the 3rd Earl died in 1829 and had little time to enjoy his new home.

It is, perhaps, the grounds, which make Elvaston Castle famous today. They were originally laid out and designed for the 4th Earl by William Barron. Barron, who was born in Berwickshire in 1805, started work in 1830 on what, at first, appeared to be an impossible task. The 4th Earl wanted a garden 'second to none', but the land available, which had never been landscaped, was flat, water-logged and uninspiring with just two avenues of trees and a walled kitchen garden (but no greenhouses or hot houses). First draining the land, Barron then planted trees to offer shelter to more tender plants. From there the project grew. In order to stock the gardens, Barron began a programme of propagation of rarer tree species and, along with the tree-planting methods he developed specially to deal with Elvaston's problems, his fame spread. The gardens became a showcase of rare and interesting trees, many to be found nowhere else in Britain. Barron continued to work for the 5th Earl, but resigned in 1865 to live in nearby Borrowash and set up his own nursery. Now owned by Derby County Council, the gardens, after years of neglect, have been completely restored and the delights of the formal gardens, with their fine topiary, the avenues and the kitchen garden can be enjoyed by all visitors to the grounds, which are now a Country Park.

As well as fine formal gardens and the walled kitchen garden, there are gentle woodland walks and, of course, the man-made lake. However, no visit to Elvaston would be complete without a walk down to the **Golden Gates**. Erected in 1819 at the southern end of the formal gardens, the gates were brought from the Palace of Versailles by the 3rd Earl of Harrington. Little is known of the Gates' history, but they remain a fine monument and are the symbol of Elvaston. Around the courtyard of the castle can be found a restaurant as well as an information centre and well-stocked gift shop. All manner of activities take place from the castle, which can provide details.

SHARDLOW
9 miles SW of Ilkeston off the A6

There was a settlement at Shardlow at the time of the *Domesday Book*, when the area belonged to the Abbey of Chester and the village was known as Serdelov. Shardlow was once an important port on the river Trent and a horse drawn ferry was used to cross the river. This was replaced in 1760 by a toll bridge and the stone giving the toll charges can still be seen on the roadside approaching the modern Cavendish Bridge. This replaced the old bridge, which collapsed in 1947. After 1777, when the **Trent and Mersey Canal** was opened, Shardlow became a canal port, one of only a few in the country. With Liverpool, Hull and Bristol now linked by water, the warehouses here were

The Navigation Inn

143 London Road, Shardlow, Derbyshire DE72 2HJ
Tel: 01332 792918

The Navigation Inn in Shardlow is a 300-year old, former coaching inn which is thought to be the oldest in the area. Recently taken over by Ian Pascoe, the traditional interior has been updated to provide comfortable surroundings which are much enjoyed by all customers. The bar offers three real ales and there is an excellent bar menu served each lunchtime and evening, with the 60-seater restaurant serving an a la carte menu in the evenings too. Accommodation will shortly be available – ring for details.

quickly filled with heavy goods of all descriptions that could be carried at half the cost of road transport and with greater safety. Many of the homes of the canal carriers and their warehouses survive to this day and the port is now a modern marina, linked to the River Trent, and filled with all manner of pleasure barges. Many of the old cottages in Shardlow were swept away by 1960s development but some were saved when much of the canal side was designated a conservation area in 1978. There are still some fine houses remaining that were built by the wealthy canal merchants. Broughton House, built in the early part of the 19th century is an example.

The outstanding **Shardlow Marina** covers 46 acres, of which the Marina itself covers 12 acres, set in beautiful rolling countryside. The marina has moorings for up to 365 boats, with berths available for up to 70-foot narrow and wide-beam boats.

ASTON-ON-TRENT
9 miles S of Ilkeston off the A6

Aston stands on the River Trent, marking the border between Derbyshire and Leicestershire. Aston's **All Saints Church** is mainly Norman, though also boasts parts of a Saxon cross with beautifully interlaced carving. The cross is built into the outer wall of the south aisle. There is an octagonal font dating from the 1200s inside the church, and a moving, early 15th century alabaster tomb chest of a husband and wife holding hands, she with a small dog at her feet.

Aston Hall dates from 1753; much enlarged over the centuries, it was originally a fine Georgian mansion with no fewer than five bays and central Venetian windows.

CASTLE DONINGTON
10 miles S of Ilkeston off the A6

Castle Donington (pronounced Dunington) is just over the Leicestershire border on a hill above the Trent River. The castle from which Castle Donington takes its name is now merely a mound on the northern edge of the village. It was built in the eleventh or twelfth century, demolished in 1216, rebuilt later that century and was finally demolished in 1595. The oldest part of the church of **St Edward, King and Martyr**, dates back to 1200 but it was probably built on the site of an older Saxon church. The spire, rising to a height of 160 feet, is a landmark for miles around.

A 17th century stone farmhouse in the centre of Castle Donington is now a museum tracing its fascinating history. **Donington Park** museum (see panel on page 157) on the edge of the racing circuit features more than 130 vehicles from motor racing history, most in working order.

KEGWORTH HOUSE

42 High Street, Kegworth,
Derby DE74 2DA
Tel: 01509 672575 Fax: 01509 670645
e-mail: tony@kegworthhouse.co.uk
website: www.kegworthhouse.co.uk

Tucked away in the interesting village of Kegworth, from which it takes its name, you will find the outstanding **Kegworth House**, home to Di and Tony Belcher. This charming, Georgian property was completely renovated and refurbished by the couple when they arrived nine years ago, and access through eleven-foot high gates mean this is a real haven of tranquillity. Inside they have created eleven, individually styled, spacious guest rooms, each with en-suite bath or shower room, and provided with telephone, colour TV and courtesy hot drinks tray. The decoration and furnishings are of an unbeatably high standard throughout, much of it in the period style.

The pretty walled garden is a colourful display of mature shrubs and well-stocked flower beds and provides a peaceful spot in

which to relax when the weather is favourable. There is an elegant dining room where you can enjoy breakfast and evening meals are also available.

A bar and comfortable guests' lounge, where you can relax with the newspapers or enjoy a drink in the evenings, will shortly be opened. Di and Tony offer their guests the ultimate in service and facilities, while maintaining a personal touch, and you can be assured of being well looked after in this lovely old house.

THE AMBER VALLEY AND EREWASH **157**

THE NAGS HEAD INN

Hill Top, Castle Donington, Derby DE74 2PR
Tel: 01332 850652   Fax: 01332 850435
e-mail idavisonc@aol.com

The Nags Head Inn can be found just a little way from the centre of Castle Donington, heading towards the East Midlands Airport. Business partners Ian and Jennie have been here for over eleven years and have created a far-reaching reputation for serving superb food which uses only the freshest ingredients, with every dish freshly prepared to order. Bookings essential (no food on Sundays). To enjoy on its own, or with your meal, the bar offers a choice of real ales.

THE DONINGTON GRAND PRIX COLLECTION

Donington Park Castle, Donington, Derby DE74 2RP
Tel: 01332 811027   Fax: 01332 357188
e-mail: alison@imageereative.co.uk   website: www.doningtoncollection.com

More Grand Prix cars, under one roof, than anywhere else in the world. Driven by more famous names than you could possibly imagine! It's all at the Donington Grand Prix Collection, located at Donington Park, the World famous Grand Prix circuit, in Leicestershire, containing over 130 exhibits within five halls, depicting motor sport history from the turn of the 1900s to the present day.

The Collection now features the World's largest collection of McLaren Formula One cars on public display. An incredible array of cars are on display including Vanwalls, BRMs, Ferrari, Jordan, Williams and also those driven by Tazio Nuvolari, Sir Henry Segrave, Stirling Moss, Damon Hill, Nigel Mansell and many more! Just arrived is also the Lancia D50 Ferrari! Plus there's the World's biggest collection of helmets including those worn by Mansell, Senna, Coulthard, Nuvolari and Ascari.

The Collection is the work of Tom Wheatcroft, who for over 40 years has collected the cars which reflect his love of the sport which started when, as a young boy, he himself witnessed the amazing spectacle of the awesome Mercedes Benz and Auto Unions, in the pre war Donington Grands Prix. During the War, the circuit was taken over by the War Office and became the biggest base in the country for military vehicles. After the War, the circuit became neglected, and it was Tom Wheatcroft, by this time a very successful builder, who bought the circuit in the early 1970s, and racing returned there in 1977.

2002 marks Tom's 80th birthday year and the 25th, Anniversary of the re opening of Donington Park circuit. A number of celebrations will be taking place and these will be revealed soon at www.doningtoncollection.com.

Vehicles on show include Ascari's Ferrari, Jim Clark's Lotus 23 and Nigel Mansell's Williams.

LONG EATON
7 miles SE of Ilkeston off the A52

Long Eaton, straddling the Derbyshire and Nottinghamshire border, has a history that goes back earlier than the 7th century. Lying close by the River Trent, the name came from the Anglo Saxon 'Aitone' meaning town by the water. Visited by the Romans and settled by the Danes, this medieval village remained undisturbed for centuries. A national census of 1801 recorded that only some 504 people lived here.

It was the machine age

that transformed Long Eaton from a small market town into a boom town by the mid 19th century. The arrival of the railway in 1847 triggered the expansion, and the hosiery and lace-making factories, escaping the restrictive practices in nearby Nottingham, brought employment for many and wealth for some. By the 1870s the population was recorded at over 3,000; it then doubled in the following 10 years. In 1915 construction began on the National Shell Filling Factory sited just over a mile away from Long Eaton's ancient market place. A staggering 19 million large shells were filled to aid the war effort, and it was not until there had been some 19 explosions at the plant, the worst with a death toll of 140, that the operation ceased. The lace industry, forever associated with this area, gave way to furniture, narrow fabrics and electrical wiring manufacture which reflected the interests and activities of a stream of entrepreneurs drawn to the town. The most famous of these men was Ernest Tehra Hooley - lace-maker, property dealer, builder, benefactor and company director. Hooley was responsible for the flotation of such well-known names as Dunlop, Raleigh, Humber and Bovril before he went bankrupt.

Although Long Eaton has no castles, cathedrals or impressive buildings, it does reflect perfectly the growth of industrial England. However, the Erewash Canal and, in particular, **Trent Lock**, the first lock on the Canal, are popular local attractions.

SAWLEY
8 miles SE of Ilkeston off the B6540

Situated close to the county border with both Nottinghamshire and Leicestershire, Sawley is an attractive village standing on the banks of the River Trent. Over 1,000 years ago a small collective of monks boated down the Trent from Repton to the green meadows of Sawley. Parts of the church they built remain in the edifice between the road and the river. Much of the church is 14th century, with 15th century tower and spire and much 15th century timbering. The chancel arch is Saxon. The interior boasts an impressive group of monuments, a 600 year old font, a 500 year old screen, a Jacobean pulpit and 17th century altar table.

In the late 1400s the Bothes (or Booths) settled at Sawley in a house of which some of the timbers remain in the cellars of **Bothe Hall**, near the church. Sawley's most noted son was John Clifford. Born here in 1836, he became one of the most powerful voices of Non-conformity, known as "the greatest Free Churchman of his day".

6 Derbyshire Coal Mines

This area of northeast Derbyshire and the District of Bolsover, with the Peak District to the west, South Yorkshire to the north and Nottinghamshire to the east, centres around Chesterfield. This was the heart of the county's coal-mining area, and many of the towns and villages reflect the prosperity the mines brought in Victorian times. Sadly, the vast majority of the collieries are now closed; there was for a while a period of decline, but visitors today will be surprised at the wealth of history and fine architecture to be seen throughout the region. Geologically this area makes up one of Derbyshire's four distinct regions, with sandy coal east of Derby and Chesterfield and a band of magnesium limestone around Bolsover and Whitwell.

Barrow Hill Roundhouse

Sometimes overlooked, this part of Derbyshire is well worth exploring, and there are many new and interesting sights and attractions to discover. The ancient custom of well-dressing is just as popular and well executed here as elsewhere in the county, plus there are curiosities such as a 'castle that isn't a castle despite its battlements, a church clock that has 63 minutes in an hour and an Italian-style garden in the grounds owned by a famous English family', according to the North East Derbyshire District Council. The area boasts two exceptional Norman churches, at Steetley (near Creswell) and Ault Hucknall.

Chesterfield Canal

Despite appearances that many of the places in and around Chesterfield only date from the Industrial Revolution, the area is rich in history. From medieval times this has been an area of trade and the weekly markets were an important part of the local economy. Though some have been lost over the years, these traditional centres and meeting-places remain.

160 THE HIDDEN PLACES OF DERBYSHIRE

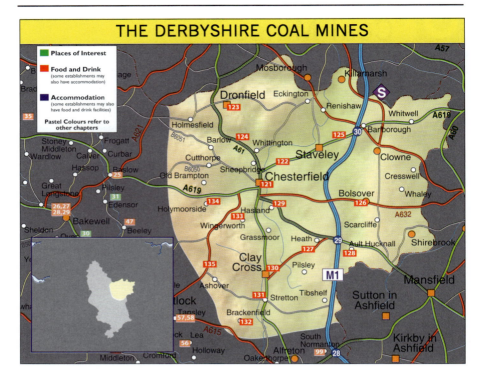

PLACES TO STAY, EAT, DRINK AND SHOP

121	Buddy's Diner, Chesterfield	American Style Diner	Page 162
122	The Red Lion, Brimington, Nr Chesterfield	Pub with Food	Page 164
123	Coach and Horses Inn, Dronfield	Pub with Food	Page 166
124	Fleur de Lys, Unstone	Pub, Restaurant and Accommodation	Page 166
125	The Gate Inn, Mastin Moor, Nr Chesterfield	Pub with Camping Site	Page 168
126	The Anchor Inn, Bolsover, Nr Chesterfield	Pub with Food	Page 170
127	The Alma Inn, North Wingfield	Pub	Page 171
128	Hardwick Inn, Nr, Nr Chesterfield	Pub with Restaurant	Page 172
129	Winsick Arms, Hasland, Nr Chesterfield	Pub with Food	Page 174
130	Aristocrats Café, Clay Cross	Café	Page 175
131	The White Bear, Stretton, Nr Alfreton	Pub with Food	Page 177
132	The Plough Inn, Brackenfield	Pub with Restaurant	Page 177
133	The Barley Mow Inn, Wingerworth	Pub with Food	Page 178
134	Chander Cottages, Chander Hill	Self Catering	Page 179
135	Kelstedge Inn, Kelstedge	Pub, Restaurant and Accommodation	Page 180

CHESTERFIELD

This friendly, bustling town on the edge of the **Peak District National Park** grew up around its open-air market, which was established over 800 years ago and claims to be England's largest. As the town lies at the crossroads of England, the hub of trade routes from all points of the compass, the town's claim seems easily justified. Life in Chesterfield has revolved around this market since the town's earliest days. It was earning Royal revenue in 1165, as the Sheriff of Derbyshire recorded in the Pipe Rolls and, in that year, the market earned the princely sum of £1 2s 7d for the Crown. The Pipe Roll of 1182 also mentions a fair in Chesterfield. Such fairs were large markets, usually lasting for several days and drawing traders and buyers from a much wider area. Chesterfield's formal charter, however, was not granted until 1204, but this charter made the town one of the first eight free boroughs in the country. Escaping the prospect of redevelopment in the 1970s, the markets are as popular as ever and are held every Monday, Friday and Saturday, with a flea market each Thursday.

The town centre has been conserved for future generations by a far-sighted council, and many buildings have been saved, including the Victorian **Market Hall** built in 1857. The traditional cobbled paving was restored in the Market Place, and New Square was given a complete facelift. There are several Tudor buildings in the heart of Chesterfield, most notably the former Peacock inn which is now home to the **Peacock Heritage Centre** and the tourist information office - built in 1500 for the wealthy Revell family, who later moved to Carnfield Hall near Alfreton. The black-and-white timbering in Knifesmithgate, however, was built only in the 1930s, to resemble the famous rows in Chester.

Visitors to the town are drawn to a peculiarly graceful spire reaching high into the skyline; twisting and leaning, it is totally confusing to the eye. Recognised as one of Chesterfield's landmarks, the **Crooked Spire** of St Mary & All Saints' Church has dominated the skyline for so long that local folk have ceased to notice its unusual shape. Superstition surrounds it, and sadly the real story to its unusual appearance has been lost over the years. The truth probably lies in the wake of the

Crooked Spire of St Mary & All Saints' Church

BUDDY'S DINER

21 Soresby Street, Chesterfield, Derbyshire S40 1JW
Tel: 01246 556969 Fax: 01246 554222

Buddy's Diner is one of the newest, and already one of the most popular, eating places in Chesterfield. It can be found on Soresby Street, next to the Town Hall car park where parking is free of charge after 5pm. Owned and personally run by Mike and June Hyman, the place opened in March 2001 and has proved to be a hit with the local clientele.

As its name suggests this is an American themed diner with the décor having a distinctive feel. Decorated in red, white and blue throughout, the dining area is divided up into numerous cosy booths, giving an intimate feel. Stars and Stripes, together with music, film and sports posters, adorn the ceiling and walls.

The menu is absolutely superb and it could easily take you half an hour to decide what to try, as it all sounds delicious. They have brought together a mixture of American and Mexican-style cuisine with a touch of English flair, which is sure to cater to all tastes and appetites. The starters include Thai glazed prawns, stuffed chilli peppers and the popular chilli nachos, enough to tempt any palate. But this really is only the beginning. The rest of the menu ranges from a selection of specials, fish, steaks and vegetarian dishes, with burgers, salads and sandwiches too. All the burgers are 100% pure beef and the specially imported baby rack ribs are the finest available. These can be enjoyed as a small, starter portion, or as a main course, and are cooked to perfection with the chef's own BBQ sauce. Other tempting choices are the swordfish with garlic and red onions; Tennessee Jack

Black Chicken, cooked with honey mustard and pecans; and the mushroom stroganoff-filled brioche. There is a good selection of steak dishes, and for the more hearty appetite the mega-specials menu includes a 30oz rump steak – not for the faint hearted! To round off your meal to perfection there is a delicious selection of wicked desserts, including pancakes, waffles and Key Lime Pie. Buddy's is fully licensed so you can enjoy a beer, or some wine, with your meal.

Open Monday to Saturday, from 10am until 11pm, last orders for food are taken at 10.30pm. On Tuesdays there is an all-you-can-eat buffet, Wednesday night is rib night and on Monday there is often live music. It is advisable to book for these nights and at weekends. Superb food, fabulous hospitality and lively surroundings – all in all, Buddy's Diner is hard to beat.

Black Death during the 14th century, when the people of Chesterfield were building their beautiful new church and awe-inspiring steeple. Many must have fallen to the plague and, among them, skilled craftsmen who knew how to season wood. The survivors built the spire out of green timber, which, over the years, has distorted under the heavy lead covering. However, some stories say it was the Devil, who, pausing for a rest during one of his flights, clung to the spire for a moment or two. Incense from the Church drifted upwards and the Devil sneezed, causing the spire to twist out of shape.

This magnificent spire rises to 228 feet and leans 9 feet 4 inches from its true centrepoint. It is eight-sided, but the herringbone pattern of the lead slates trick the eye into seeing 16 sides from the ground. The Crooked Spire is open most Bank Holidays and at advertised times; the church, the largest in Derbyshire, is open all year, Monday to Saturday 9 a.m. to 5 p.m. (9 a.m. to 3 p.m. January and February), and Sundays at service times only.

Opposite the Church is **Chesterfield Museum and Art Gallery**, home to exhibitions depicting the story of the town, from the arrival of the Romans to the first days of the market town, the industry of the 18th century and the coming of the "Father of the Railways", George Stephenson. The Art Gallery displays paintings by local artists such as Joseph Syddall (who lived at nearby Whittington).

In the heart of Chesterfield, **The Spread Eagle** stands opposite the new shopping mall in Beetwell Street. The premises date back some 400 years and once had stables to the rear - the archway where the carriages and carts used to pull in can still be seen. Once upon a time prisoners would be held in the cellars here when the police station cells were full. The old police

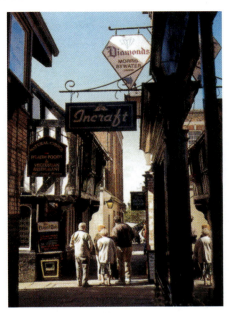

Chesterfield Shambles

station used to stand across the road, in what is now the library, and an underground tunnel linked the two buildings.

Chesterfield owes much of its prosperity during the industrial age to the great railway engineer George Stephenson. His home, Tapton House, lies just outside the town and it was to here that he retired and carried out his experiments in horticulture. Buried in Holy Trinity Church, where one of the windows was created in his memory, his death, in 1848, was announced by one local newspaper with the headline "Inventor of Straight Cucumber Dies".

Perhaps surprisingly, Chesterfield is home to one of the earliest canals in the country, the Chesterfield Canal. After seeing the success of the Bridgewater Canal in 1763, the businessmen of Chesterfield, which was at the start of its rapid expansion, looked to link the town with

THE RED LION

Church Street, Brimington, Chesterfield,
Derbyshire S43 1JE
Tel: 01246 273628

A popular local hostelry within the village of Brimington is the centrally located **Red Lion Inn**. Run by Margaret and Mike since June 2001, the 18th-century, former coaching inn has a cosy traditional feel inside and an attractive beer garden to the rear with children's play area. Adjoining the main bar is an area for younger customers, and there is a disco each night at weekends. Superb quality home cooked food is available using locally grown produce wherever possible.

the River Trent via Worksop and Retford in Nottinghamshire. Construction work began in 1771, just a year before its builder, James Brindley, died whilst surveying the Caldon Canal. The biggest engineering project along the length of the new canal was the Norwood Tunnel, which took four years to build. The Tunnel was officially opened on 9 May 1775. It was 2884 yards long, 9ft 3ins wide, and 12ft high. The entire canal was officially opened in 1777. The most famous item carried on the canal was stone to rebuild the Houses of Parliament in the 1840s. The stone was loaded into canal boats at Dog Kennels Bridge, carried to West Stockwith, and transferred to Trent sloops for the journey to Westminster, via the Humber, North Sea, and Thames. In October 1907 the roof of Norwood Tunnel collapsed, cutting the canal in two. Coal cargoes from Shireoaks colliery continued until the Second World War, but after that there was little boat traffic apart from brick cargoes from the kilns at Walkeringham. All the working boats on the Chesterfield Canal were horse-drawn until, by 1962, virtually all the boat traffic had gone. The whole length of the Canal is in the process of restoration and is open to walkers and, though some sections border onto busy roads, much of the waterway runs through quiet and secluded countryside. The Chesterfield Canal Trust runs boat trips on

the canal, and one of the boats has wheelchair access.

Finally, although the custom of tap-dressing took place in Chesterfield in the 19th century, it was not until 1991 that the tradition, this time of well-dressing, was revived. Initially with help from local experts from Holymoorside, the Chesterfield dressers are developing their own styles and customs and, while the well-dressing at the Peacock Centre takes its inspiration from buildings, their colleagues at St Mary and All Saints Church follow the theme of the stained glass windows within the church.

AROUND CHESTERFIELD

SHEEPBRIDGE
3 miles N of Chesterfield off the A61

Dunstan Hall, below Newbold Moor, was built in the 17th century and extended in the 18th century. In an excellent parkland setting, the Gothic-style park railings mirror the Gothic revival details that were added to the Hall in 1826.

WHITTINGTON
3 miles NE of Chesterfield off the B6052/A61

During the 17th century, **Revolution House** was part of an alehouse called the Cock and Pynot ("pynot" being the local

THE DERBYSHIRE COAL MINES

Revolution House

Despite the growth of Chesterfield, Whittington has managed, on the whole, to retain its village centre, though one of its best buildings (apart from Revolution House), Manor Farm, was demolished in the 1970s. However, the farm's barns still survive and can be found to the west of St Bartholomew's Church.

dialect word for magpie). It was here that three local noblemen - the Earl of Devonshire, the Earl of Danby and John D'Arcy - met to begin planning their part in the events which led to the overthrow of James II in favour of his daughter Mary and her husband, William of Orange. The Glorious Revolution took place later in the same year, November 1688, and it was in the year of its 250th anniversary that this modest house was turned into a museum. Both the 100th and the 200th anniversary of the Revolution were keenly celebrated at the Revolution House; the inhabitants of Whittington and Chesterfield being proud that they had provided the venue where the plot was hatched to overthrow the Catholic King James.

Revolution House, a tiny cottage with thatched roof, flower border and charming garden gate which belies its rather incendiary name, is now open to the public and features period furnishings and a changing programme of exhibitions on local themes. A video relates the story of the Revolution and the role, which the house played in those fraught and dangerous days.

DRONFIELD
5 miles N of Chesterfield off the A61

An important market town which has since developed industrially, there are some fine 17th and 18th century buildings in the town's conservation area. Centred around the Peel Monument, the church and the cruck barn, **The Hall** here is also worthy of a second glance as it has an attractive balustrade and a fine Queen Anne facade. In front of the early 18th century Manor House, now the home of the town library, is a highly elaborate Town Cross. Erected in 1848, it commemorates the repeal of the Corn Laws.

The prosperity of Dronfield in the early years of the Industrial Revolution was such that an unexpectedly large number of mansions were built in and around the town. Of those that remain today, **Chiverton House**, built in 1712, and Rose Hill, dating from 1719, are worthy of note.

To the east of the town can be seen a large group of 19th century coke ovens, once a common sight in this part of Derbyshire. The forty eight seen here, arranged in two groups, were part of the Summerley Colliery complex; the tall engine house also survives.

ECKINGTON
6 miles NE of Chesterfield off the A616

This large, sprawling village built of local Derbyshire stone, lies close to the Yorkshire county border. The name Eckington is of Saxon origin, meaning the township of Ecca. In medieval times it was a small but important settlement, whose main occupations were farming and then mining. Since the decline of coal mining in the late 20th century several light industries have become established and much farmland has been lost.

The parish church of **St Peter and St Paul** dates from the year 1100 and still retains the original Norman doorway. In a field at the back of the church, near the river stands the Priest's Well where the

COACH AND HORSES INN
Sheffield Road, Dronfield, Derbyshire S18 2GD
Tel: 01246 413269

As its name clearly suggests, the **Coach and Horses Inn** was once a busy 17th-century coaching inn. Found on the outskirts of Dronfield town centre it is believed that in his day Dick Turpin frequented the establishment. Your hosts are Neil and Victoria and they open the pub each lunchtime and evening serving a good selection of ales and some tasty home-cooked food with a traditional menu supplemented by a specials board (no food Sunday evening). Children welcome. Quiz on Sunday night.

FLEUR DE LYS
Main Road, Unstone, Derbyshire S18 4AB
Tel: 01246 412157

The **Fleur de Lys** public house stands on the A61 at Unstone, just north of the town of Chesterfield. Dating back to the 17th century, the premises were a well known coaching inn with stables, where teams of horses would have been changed, while travelling between Derby and Sheffield. The pub also proved to be popular with the labourers who worked on the construction of the Derby to Sheffield railway line.

Today, the pub continues to be as popular and as welcoming as it was in times past and it is owned and personally run by Pauline and Gordon Austin. Despite the minor setback of a fire in January 2001, the whole place has since been completely refurbished and there has also been the addition of a delightful conservatory dining area. Open at every session, the well stocked bar offers plenty of choice, complemented by an extensive menu of tasty meals and snacks. Food is available each lunchtime and evening except Sunday and Monday nights. There is an attractive beer garden, where drinks and meals can be enjoyed in fine weather, and ample off-road car parking.

If you would like to linger in the area a while, five en-suite letting rooms will shortly be available, one with full disabled access. Ring for full details.

THE DERBYSHIRE COAL MINES 167

Renishaw Hall

parish priest used to draw water as did the travelling people, who used the field as a camp until the 1930s.

The Sitwell family had their home close by. **Renishaw Hall**, situated midway between Eckington and neighbouring Renishaw, was built by George Sitwell in 1625 after he had re-established his fortune with the success of the Renishaw Iron works. The massive house was greatly transformed under the first baronet, Sir Sitwell Sitwell, and in the grounds can be found the world's most northerly vineyard. The Sitwell family and, in particular, Dame Edith, Sir Sacheverell and Sir Osbert, have, over the years, become famous for their literary leanings - perhaps there is something in the wine that promotes success in this field! The Hall is also said to be haunted by a number of ghosts, though few houses of any great age seem to escape the interest of some form of poltergeist. In particular there is the little boy in pink, known as the Kissing Ghost because it seems that this is just what he likes to do to any guests at the Hall. The grounds of the village Rectory, a handsome late Georgian building, are also worth a second glance. Though not laid out by the Reverend Christopher Alderson, he set about improving them in the late 18th century. A magazine of the time said that the Reverend "was so renowned as a garden improver that he was employed at Windsor as well".

RENISHAW
6 miles NE of Chesterfield off the A616

The village lies close to the Sitwell family home and was the home of the family iron works, which helped to re-establish their fortune.

STAVELEY
4 miles NE of Chesterfield off the A619

Staveley lies to the south of the great **Staveley Iron Works** and has its fair share of large 20th century housing estates. However, this is not altogether a modern village and has some fine earlier structures, including its 13th century church dedicated to St John the Baptist and **Staveley Hall**, built in 1604 and now the District Council Offices. The name of Frecheville is one that crops up from time to time in this part of Derbyshire, and the church has a selection of tombs and monuments to the family. As well as the tomb-chest of Peter Frecheville, dating from around 1480, there is also an early 16th century monument to Piers Frecheville. In the Frecheville Chapel is a memorial to Christina Frecheville, who died in childbirth in 1653.

BARLBOROUGH
7 miles NE of Chesterfield off the A619

Lying close to the county borders with both Nottinghamshire and Yorkshire, this village still retains its manor house. Lying just north of the village centre, **Barlborough Hall** (private) was built in 1584 by Lord Justice Francis Rodes to plans

THE GATE INN

28 Worksop Road, Mastin Moor, Chesterfield,
Derbyshire S43 3DN
Tel: 01246 472554

The Gate Inn is a well-stocked, popular watering hole situated between Chesterfield and the M1, on the A619. Open each evening and all day at the weekends, the bar offers Marston's Pedigree and a local ale together with usual lager, cider and other beers. The friendly owners have created a friendly, relaxed atmosphere where everyone is sure to feel right at home, but apparently there are some mischievous ghosts. Caravan and camping site can be found to the rear. Food will be introduced shortly.

drawn up by the designer of Hardwick Hall, Robert Smythson. Those who visit both houses will notice the strong resemblance. As well as building houses, Rodes was also one of the judges at the trial of Mary, Queen of Scots. The Hall is supposed to be haunted by a grey lady, said to be the ghost of a bride who received the news of her groom's death as she was on her way to the 12th century village church. Barlborough Hall should not be confused with Barlborough Old Hall: this is an easy mistake to make as Barlborough Old Hall is actually the younger of the two! Built in 1618, as the date stone over the front door states, the Old Hall is of a large H-plan design and has mullioned windows.

Although there is a lot of new development, particularly around Barlborough Links, the village also boasts some fine old stone houses with pantile roofs. The village **Church of St James** dates from the beginning of the 13th century, though it was heavily restored in 1899. Among the medieval work extant is the four-bay north arcade. The church contains the effigy of a grieving woman. This is said to be Lady Furnival, who died in 1395. The monument was probably brought here from Worksop, where she is buried.

The custom of well-dressing was started anew in 1975 when the Young Wives' Group produced a modest picture to dress the village well for St James' Day (25 July). From such humble beginnings, well-dressing in Barlborough is now an annual event that coincides with the church flower festival.

CLOWNE
7½ miles NE of Chesterfield off the A616

This small town has grown up around the county's coal-mining industry though, away from the centre, the part-Norman Church of St John the Baptist can be seen. It is now mainly residential, but retains its own identity and sense of community. It is well known locally for its dazzling Christmas Lights display.

CRESWELL
9 miles E of Chesterfield off the A616

Once a sleepy hamlet nestling amid peaceful farming country, the character of Creswell was irreversibly changed at the end of the 19th century. It was then that Creswell Colliery was opened, and now the village is one of the biggest in the county. There is also a village within a village here as, between 1896 and 1900 a model village of houses and cottages was built. The Model Village was built by the Bolsover Colliery Company in 1896 to house the workforce at the Creswell Colliery. Everybody who lived on the Model worked in the coal mine. It remained as housing for miners until the mid 1980s when the houses were let on the open market. The houses were neglected, repairs were not done and the area became run down. Now with the help of a Lottery Grant, the central park has been almost restored to its original Victorian state with newly planted trees and shrubs, seating and play areas. Many of the houses around the park have been restored and renovated and more will be restored in the in the next phase. The restored Model Village is an excellent example of Victorian social housing for working families.

Lying close to the Derbyshire-Nottinghamshire border, the limestone gorge of the **Creswell Crags** is well worth seeing. Formed thousands of years ago by the erosion of a river which cut through the limestone, this rock, which is porous and subject to erosion underground as well as on the surface, contributes by its very nature to the forming of natural chambers. The subterranean movement of water created a vast network of caves, which were subsequently exposed. Used by Neanderthal man as shelters while out hunting, tours can be taken from the visitor centre, where there is also a display of artefacts found in the area. Testimony to the artistry of the later inhabitants of these caves was the discovery of a bone carved with the head of a horse, which is about 13,000 years old, and can now be seen in the British Museum. The largest cavern, Church Hole Cave, extends some 170 feet into the side of the gorge; it was here that hand tools were found.

Not far from the village and close to the county border with Nottinghamshire is **Steetley Chapel**, thought by many to be the most perfect specimen of Norman architecture in Europe. Whether this is so or not, the elaborate chapel has a rare and unique beauty. Having lain derelict for many years after being desecrated during the Commonwealth, the Chapel of All Saints was restored in the 1880s and at this time some of the wonderful carvings to be seen in the porchway were re-created. Luckily much of the interior remains intact, having survived the test of time. It remains a mystery as to why such a small building should be given such elaborate decoration in the mid 12th century.

WHALEY
8 miles E of Chesterfield off the A632

The **Whaley Thorns Heritage Centre**, situated in a disused school, tells the story of human activity in the area from the Stone Age to the present day. In particular there are displays illustrating the history of coal-mining in this region of Derbyshire and, since the decline of the industry, the efforts that have been made to restore the area to its natural state.

BOLSOVER
7 miles E of Chesterfield off the A632

The approach to Bolsover from the north and east is dominated by the splendid, sandstone structure of **Bolsover Castle**, which sits high on a limestone ridge. A castle has stood here since the 12th century, though the present building is a fairytale "folly" built for Sir Charles Cavendish during the early 1600s on the site of a ruined castle. By the mid 18th century much of the building had been reduced to the ruins seen today, though thankfully the splendid keep has withstood the test of time.

Pevsner remarked that not many large houses in England occupy such an impressive position as Bolsover Castle, as it stands on the brow of a hill overlooking the valley of the River Rother and Doe Lea. The first castle at Bolsover was built by William Peverel, illegitimate son of William the Conqueror, as part of his vast Derbyshire estates. Nothing remains of that Norman building. Now owned by English Heritage, visitors can explore the Little Castle, or Keep, which is decorated in an elaborate Jacobean celebration with wonderful fireplaces, panelling and wall paintings. The series of remarkable rooms includes the Vaulted Hall, the Pillar Room, the Star Chamber, the Elysium and the Heaven Room. Sir Charles' son, William, was responsible for the eastern range of buildings known as the Riding School, an impressive indoor area built in the 17th century, and the roofless but still impressive western terrace. The ruins of the state apartments are also here to be discovered. The whole building later descended to the Dukes of Portland, and it remains a strangely impressive place. However it is threatened by its industrial surroundings. The legacy of centuries of coal-mining beneath its walls is subsidence.

The town itself is industrial, dominated for many years by coal mining, however it was once famous for the manufacture of buckles. The Hudson Bay public house across the road from the castle recalls in its name the fact that it was originally built by Peter Fidler, a Bolsover man, who was a distinguished surveyor with the Hudson Bay Company in Canada during the 18th century. A Peter Fidler Society exists in Canada to this day. Bolsover's oldest public house is probably The White Swan, and is said to have served as the moot hall from the Middle Ages to the early 19th century. Bolsover was granted its market charter by Henry III in 1225.

Naturally, the parish **Church of St Mary's** in Bolsover holds many monuments to the Cavendish family, but it seems amazing that the Church has survived when its recent history is revealed. Dating from the 13th century, the church's monuments include two magnificent tombs to Charles Cavendish, who died in 1617, and Henry Cavendish, who died in 1727. Destroyed by fire in 1897, except for the Cavendish Chapel, St Mary's was rebuilt, only to be damaged again by fire in 1960. It has since been restored. Buried in the churchyard are John Smythson and Huntingdon Smythson, the 17th century architects probably responsible for the design of the rebuilt Bolsover Castle.

SCARCLIFFE
8 miles E of Chesterfield off the B6417

Scarcliffe, recorded as Scardeclif in the *Domesday Book*, takes its name from the escarpment of magnesium limestone on which the village stands. It was settled in Roman times evidenced by the collection of Roman coins found near the village in 1876. The church in this little village is Norman and contains a most magnificent monument of a woman holding a child in her arms. Dating from the 12th or 13th century, the effigy is probably that of Constantia de Frecheville, who died in 1175. Known in Scarcliffe as Lady Constantia, a bell is tolled in her memory

THE ANCHOR INN

Market Place, Bolsover, Chesterfield, Derbyshire S44 6PN
Tel: 01246 241324

Close to Bolsover Castle, just off the market place, you will find the popular **Anchor Inn**. Dating to the 17th century, the hostelry is in the care of Christine and Malcolm Atkinson, who have been at the helm for seven years. They run a friendly pub that is known in the area for serving quality food from a wide-ranging menu of home-made dishes. The house specialities are the mixed grill and the pies (no food Wednesday, Saturday or Sunday evenings). Well stocked bar. Regular karaoke and quiz nights.

The Derbyshire Coal Mines 171

around Christmas. During the industrial revolution coal mining was the main industry and the Lancashire, Derbyshire and East Coast Railway cut through the previously agricultural land including a tunnel between Scarcliffe and Bolsover. The Langwith Colliery closed in 1978 and the railway has long gone.

Poulter Country Park, created from the old colliery spoil heaps, provides scenic walks with excellent views of the surrounding countryside.

HEATH
5 miles SE of Chesterfield off the A617

To the north of Heath, overlooking the M1, are the ruins of what was one of the grandest mansions in Derbyshire, **Sutton Scarsdale**. Built in 1724 for the 4th Earl of Scarsdale, to the designs of Francis Smith, the stonework of the previous Tudor manor house was completely hidden behind the Baroque splendour of the new hall. The magnificent Italian plasterwork can now be seen at the Philadelphia Museum, in Pennsylvania, and demolition of the back of the house has revealed some Tudor brickwork. At the beginning of the 20th century Sutton Scarsdale was owned by a descendent of Sir Richard Arkwright, the famous industrialist. It is this gentleman that D H Lawrence is supposed to have chosen as the inspiration for his character of Sir Clifford Chatterley in the novel *Lady Chatterley's Lover*.

Also close to Heath is the National Trust-owned **Stainsby Mill**. With its machinery now restored to illustrate the workings of a 19th century water-powered corn mill, Stainsby is well worth a visit. Though there has been a mill here since medieval times, the buildings seen today date from 1849 when the then new machinery was first fitted. The large, 17 foot cast-iron waterwheel, which because of its particular design is known as a high breast shot, not only provided power to turn the millstones but also for lifting sacks, cleaning the grain and sieving the flour. Open between the end of March and the end of October, visitors can watch the operations from a viewing gallery.

AULT HUCKNALL
6 miles SE of Chesterfield off the A617

The strange name of this village probably means 'Hucca's high nook of land', and this pleasant place, standing on a ridge close to the Nottinghamshire border, is home to the magnificent Tudor house, **Hardwick Hall**. "More glass than wall", it is one of Derbyshire's Big Three stately homes alongside Chatsworth and Haddon, all three glorious monuments to the great land-owning families who played so great a role in shaping the history of the county. Set in rolling parkland, the house, with its glittering tiers of windows and crowned turrets, offers quite a spellbinding sight. Inside, the silence of the chambers strewn

The Alma Inn

119 Chesterfield Road, North Wingfield, Chesterfield, Derbyshire S42 5LE
Tel: 01246 851094

The Alma Inn can be found in the village of North Wingfield, just off the B6038, and new managers Janet and Pete Thorpe welcome all customers for drinks at lunchtime, in the evening (closed Mondays until 7pm) and all day Friday to Sunday. At the time of writing only Sunday lunches are served, but a more extensive menu will be introduced shortly. There is a lively programme of entertainment with something going on each evening from Thursday to Sunday with quizzes, karaoke and live performers. Accommodation also planned.

Hardwick Inn

Hardwick Park, Nr. Chesterfield,
Derbyshire S44 5QJ
Tel: 01246 850245
Fax: 01246 856365
e-mail: batty@hardwickinn.co.uk
website: www.hardwickinn.co.uk

Hardwick Inn can be located not far from Chesterfield, on the edge of the Hardwick Hall estate, which has a long history going back many hundreds of years. At the end of the 16th century, the manor house was home to Elizabeth, Countess of Shrewsbury, known locally as Bess of Hardwick and it is thought that Bess built the present inn, on the site of an older hostelry, for one of her faithful servants. Constructed of locally quarried sandstone, the mellow building retains to this day many original features, including the leaded windows and gables. In 1959 Hardwick Hall, its surrounding park and woodland, and the inn, were transferred into the care of the National Trust, who continue to be responsible for their care and preservation.

When you step over the threshold, there is a feeling of stepping back in time. The traditional, historic feel has been retained while also providing a comfortable, friendly atmosphere in which to enjoy some fine food and drink. There are two bar areas, three family rooms where children are welcome and meeting rooms available for hire. In winter, the whole area is kept snug and cosy with open, coal fires. It is a relief to know that there are no slot machines or juke boxes to be found here, so you can be assured of a quiet, relaxed visit.

The present landlords, Peter and Pauline Batty, pride themselves on providing efficient, friendly service to all their customers, whether old or new. They stock a first class range of drinks with five real ales available, including such favourites as Theakston's XB, Old Peculiar and Old Speckled Hen. Over 160 malt whiskies and wines galore are also on offer. People come from miles around to sample the food with a wide-ranging menu of home-cooked dishes catering to all tastes and appetites. There is a menu of bar meals and snacks, and there is also a carvery restaurant serving dishes such as roast beef (popular for Sunday lunches), steak and kidney pies (for which the inn is famous), casseroles and fish. There's also a grill, and a changing specials board, which makes the best use of seasonal produce. Booking in advance is advisable.

The Hardwick Inn is a special place, as it is steeped in history and tradition. Children are welcome, and there's nowhere better for a family meal or quiet, relaxing drink.

with rush matting, combined with the simplicity of the white-washed walls, gives a feeling of almost overwhelming peace. The letters E S can be seen carved in stone on the outside of the house: E S, or Elizabeth of Shrewsbury, was perhaps better known as Bess of Hardwick. This larger-than-life figure had attachments with many places in Derbyshire, and the story of her life makes for fascinating reading.

Hardwick Hall

She was born in the manor house at Hardwick in 1520. The house stood only a little distance from the present-day Hall and was then not much more than a farmhouse. The young Bess married her neighbour's son, Robert Barlow, when she was only 12. When her young husband, himself only 14, died a few months later she naturally inherited a great deal of property. Some 15 years later she married Sir William Cavendish and, when he died in 1557, she was bequeathed his entire fortune. By this time she was the richest woman in England, save for one, Elizabeth, the Queen.

The Gallery at Hardwick Hall, with its gorgeous lavender-hued tapestries, has, in pride of place, a portrait of this formidable woman. The portrait depicts a personage who could be mistaken for Elizabeth R, and it seems only right to compare the two. First the "Virgin" Queen who commanded so forcibly the men around her yet never married, and then Bess, who married and survived four husbands. Bess began the building of the house in 1590, towards the end of her life and after her fourth lucrative marriage to George Talbot, sixth Earl of Shrewsbury. It stands as a monument to her wealth and good taste, and is justly famous for its magnificent needlework and tapestries, carved fireplaces and friezes, which are considered as among the finest in Britain.

Though Bess is the first person that springs to mind with regard to Hardwick Hall, it was the 6th Duke of Devonshire who was responsible for the Hall's antiquarian atmosphere. He inherited the property in 1811 and, as well as promoting the legend that Mary, Queen of Scots stayed here, he filled the house with furniture, paintings and tapestries from his other houses and from Chatsworth in particular.

As well as viewing the Hall, there are some wonderful grounds to explore. To the south are the formal gardens, laid out in the 19th century and separated by long walks lined with yew. One area has been planted as a Tudor herb garden and is stocked with both culinary and medicinal plants used at that time. Down in the southeastern corner of the garden is the small Elizabethan banqueting hall, used as a smoking room by the 6th Duke's orchestra, as they were not allowed to smoke in the Hall. There is also, to the back of the house, a lake and lime avenue. Owned by the National Trust, Hardwick Hall is a must for any visitor to Derbyshire and is certainly a place not to be missed. The parkland, which overlooks the valley of the Doe Lea and the M1, is home to an impressive herd of Longhorn cattle among the stag-headed oaks. The ruins of Hardwick Old Hall (English Heritage) also stand in the grounds, and are the interesting remains of Bess's former Tudor mansion.

The village **Church of St John the Baptist**, situated on a back lane, is one of the finest in Derbyshire. Overlooking Hardwick Hall's beautiful parklands, with the square towers of Bess of Hardwick's great house in the distance, the battlemented church exterior does not prepare visitors for its dark, mysterious interior, which reveals the church's much earlier origins. There are many Norman features, including the north arcade, nave and the narrow arches holding up the rare crossing tower. There is more Norman work in the plain capitals of the north arcade.

There are several interesting tombs in the church, such as the large and detailed wall monument just below the east window to the first Countess of Devonshire, dating from 1627. On the floor in front is a simple black slab commemorating the influential and renowned philosopher Thomas Hobbes - author of *The Leviathan* and *De Mirabilibus Pecci: Concerning the Wonders of the Peak* (the latter being one of the first accounts of the Seven Wonders of the Peak) - who died at Hardwick. A much simpler table in the north aisle commemorates Robert

Winsick Arms

Mansfield Road, Hasland, Nr. Chesterfield, Derbyshire S41 0JH
Tel: 01246 206787   Fax: 01246 221204
e-mail: jonathan@winsick.fsnet.co.uk

Though it is on the outskirts of Chesterfield, the hamlet of Winsick still retains a feeling of rural calm. Within the hamlet you will find the **Winsick Arms**, a handsome and rambling inn that was once an old farmhouse. To the rear there is a large, open beer garden complete with a superb children's play area. Located close to Junction 29 of the M1, this makes an ideal stopping off point when travelling through the area.

The Owen family have been in charge since 1996 and in that time have established this as a friendly pub, which is very popular with the locals. The interior is spotlessly clean, with lots of nooks and crannies and comfortable corners where you can sample the range of ales on offer at the bar. There are eight cask ales stocked with Tetleys, John Smiths, Theakstons Best and five rotating guest ales. Food can be ordered from midday until 8.45pm from a printed menu, which has plenty of choice, ranging from sandwiches to hearty, hot dishes. There is also a daily specials board. All dishes are carefully prepared, and the classic steak and kidney pie is one of the most popular options. On Sunday, they serve a three course special lunch which represents amazing value for money. It is advisable to book throughout the weekend.

THE DERBYSHIRE COAL MINES 175

Hackett, a keeper of Hardwick Park who died n 1703. It reads: "Long has he chas'd/ The red and fallow deer/But death's cold dart/At last has fix'd him here."

WINSICK
2 miles S of Chesterfield off the A617

This charming hamlet is just a short drive from the centre of Chesterfield but retains a tranquil rural feel.

GRASSMOOR
3 miles S of Chesterfield off the B6038

Originally named Gresmore ("Grey Copse") according to parish records of 1568, the main employment in the village was for many years coal mining, at Grassmoor Colliery. The first shaft was sunk in 1846 and officially opened in 1880 by Mr Barnes. The colliery closed in 1970. The site of the colliery is now a country park and the start of a pleasant walk called the **Five Pits Trail**, a popular trail running between Grassmoor and Tibshelf, with 8 miles of traffic-free walking and cycling. Originally created in 1971, the paths have been recently re-surfaced. There are many picnic sites along the way past the sites of the old pits, along the line of some of the old railways. Almost all traces of the pits have disappeared, although the head gear remains at Holmewood pit.

PILSLEY
5 miles S of Chesterfield off the B6039

The Herb Garden in Pilsley, featured on the BBC TV programme *Country Gardens*, is one of the foremost gardens in the country. Consisting of four display gardens, the largest is the Mixed Herb Garden, boasting an impressive established parterre. The remaining three gardens are the Physic, the Lavender and the Pot Pourri, each with its own special theme and housing many rare and unusual species. Areas of native flowers and wild spring bulbs can be enjoyed from March to September. On the grounds there is also a lovely tea room serving such delicacies as lavender cake, rosemary fruit slice and cheese and herb scones.

CLAY CROSS
5 miles S of Chesterfield off the A61

This busy market town, situated on a high ridge, is largely a product of the Industrial Revolution. It developed after coal was discovered in the area, when George Stephenson was building a railway tunnel. It grew from a small farming community into an industrial town dominated by the Clay Cross Company. The Company also provided schools, churches and housing. An impressive monument consisting of two large wheels with the inscription "In

ARISTOCRATS CAFÉ
2/3 The Parade, Market Street, Clay Cross, Derbyshire S45 9JE
Tel: 01246 250737

Aristocrats Café can be easily located in The Parade, just off Market Street, in the heart of Clay Cross. An ideal stopping off point while shopping in the town, here you can enjoy some delicious, home-cooked food between 9am and 3.30pm, Monday to Saturday. Run by a local couple, Peter and Judy, it is Peter who is the expert in the kitchen and his all-day breakfasts are very popular. Also open in the evenings for private bookings. Non-smoking throughout. Full disabled access

Clay Cross Church

memory of all North East Derbyshire Miners who lost their lives working to keep the home fires burning and the wheels of industry turning", takes pride of place in the High Street. In 1972 the town earned the title "the Republic of Clay Cross", when the leftwing councillors, including David and Graham Skinner, both related to Dennis Skinner, MP for Bolsover, would not implement the terms of the Tory Housing Finance Act. The Clay Cross Rebels, as they became known, refused to put up council house rents by £1 a week. After a bitter dispute with the Government, which divided the community, they were surcharged, bankrupted and disqualified from office.

TIBSHELF
6 miles N of Alfreton off the B6014

Tibshelf is a large, former coal mining village, with a population of around 3300.

There had been coal mines here for over 650 years until the last two pits, Long pit and Bottom pit, closed 70 years ago. In 1891 over 2000 men were employed in the village mines. Stretching from here north, to Grassmoor, the Five Pits Trail is a scenic route, which passes the old collieries at Tibshelf, Pilsley, Alameda, Williamthorpe and Grassmoor. At first the idea of exploring these old coal workings may not appeal, but since their reclamation by Derbyshire County Council this is now an interesting and entertaining seven mile walk. Suitable for walkers, cyclists and horse riders, the Trail is quite lovely, and offers some splendid views.

With the closure of the pits, which had been largely developed since the middle of the 19th century, the land had fallen into disuse. With the help of the Countryside Ranger Service, Derbyshire County Council manages the Trail and there is also a great deal of support from local groups who have contributed much time and effort to bring this land back to life. The clearing of paths and the addition of plantations, ponds and meadows has ensured that many species of wildlife have been encouraged to return here. Wild plants to look out for include the bush vetch, meadowsweet and the corn poppy. At one time these lovely wild flowers could be seen in abundance in many of Derbyshire's fields and hedgerows.

The church of St John the Baptist has been much restored over the centuries but it still retains an impressive 14th century tower.

STRETTON
6 miles S of Chesterfield on the A61

Stretton village lies close to Ogston Resevoir, which covers an area of over 200 acres and is a favourite place for sailing. The man-made lake is overlooked by the romantic Ogston Hall, which dates from the 16th century and was the ancestral home of the Turbutt and Revell families.

THE DERBYSHIRE COAL MINES **177**

THE WHITE BEAR

Main Road, Stretton, Nr. Alfreton,
Derbyshire DE55 6ET
Tel: 01246 863274

The White Bear can be found on the main A61 Chesterfield road, just a few miles north of Alfreton. It is well worth stopping off here, if only to enjoy the superb panoramic views across the Peak District national park. The pub itself dates back to the 18th century when it was originally a busy coaching inn catering to the many horse-drawn carriages that travelled this route. It is currently under the guiding hands of Martin and Susan and they have created a friendly hostelry which enjoys an outstanding reputation for its fine food. The excellent menu is presented on a blackboard and offers a wide variety of dishes, all freshly prepared and cooked on the premises.

On the day we visited there was goats cheese in flaky pastry, mussels Provencal and Cajun chicken – and that was just the starters! The main dishes featured ostrich, sea bass and venison as well as some steak, chicken and pasta dishes. If you are only after a light snack, there are also sandwiches and jacket potatoes available. You can of course simply have a drink with the bar offering two real ales: Marstons Pedigree and a rotating guest ale. There is ample seating in the cosy interior and some tables outside where you can drink in the view. Closed Saturday lunchtime and all day Monday (except Bank Holidays).

The house was altered extensively in 1768, and then modernised and "medievalised" during Victorian times.

BRACKENFIELD
7 miles S of Chesterfield off the A632

This village was known as Brackenthwaite in the Middle Ages, a name that means "clearing in the bracken". Like Clay Cross, Brackenfield is known today primarily for its proximity to the Ogston Reservoir, created in 1960 by damming the River Amber at the south end of the valley. The site of the former Ogston Mill was submerged under the rising waters. Hidden in the surrounding trees is the ruin of the former **Trinity Chapel**. The church is mentioned in the *Domesday Book*, but was abandoned when the new church was built in 1856. An ancient screen was removed from the chapel and brought to the new church.

THE PLOUGH INN

Matlock Road, Brackenfield, Derbyshire DE55 6DD
Tel: 01629 534437   Fax: 01629 534169

The Plough Inn is a historic inn housed within an attractive building that dates back to the 17th century, and retains much of its traditional charm. Open at every session this friendly hostelry extends a warm welcome to all, while the bar offers a choice of four real ales. The food is superb with a wide ranging menu and specials board available each lunchtime and evening in the restaurant. There is also a separate bar menu. Quiz each Thursday night and occasional live entertainment.

WINGERWORTH
3 miles S of Chesterfield off the A61

The village was settled in Anglo-Saxon times, and is recorded in the *Domesday Book*, as a community of fourteen households. It expanded after the Middle Ages although until the 20th century the population never exceeded five hundred. The Hunlokes were the dominant family in Wingerworth from the reign of Queen Elizabeth I until 1920, acquiring nine-tenths of the land in the parish and becoming lords of the manor. The grand mansion of Wingerworth Hall, which they built in the early 18th century, was demolished in the 1920s. Olave, Lady Baden-Powell, first Chief Guide, was born here in 1889. The village church, although it retains some Norman and 13th century work has had many additions. A tower was added around 1500 and a substantial extension in 1963.

ASHOVER
4 miles NE of Matlock off the B6036

Viewed from the southern rocky ridge known as **The Fabric** (apparently because it provided the fabric for much of the local building stone) and with the monolith of **Cocking Tor** in the foreground, Ashover can be seen as a scattered village filling the pleasantly wooded valley of the River Amber. The name of this village means "ash tree slope" and though there are, indeed, many ash trees in the area, many other varieties including oak and birch also flourish. Ashover was a flourishing industrial town in the past. As well as lead-mining, which dated back to Roman times, there was nail-making, lace, ropes, stocking weaving and malting. One part of the village is called the Rattle because of the sound of the looms rattling in the making of stockings. The main occupation now is farming.

The Barley Mow Inn

Langer Lane, Wingerworth, Chesterfield, Derbyshire S42 6TX
Tel: 01246 541771

The village of Wingerworth is located just off the A61, south of Chesterfield, and this is where you will find The Barley Mow Inn. This attractive, ivy-covered inn dates back to the 1800s, when it was formerly a coaching inn, and has recently been taken over by Stuart and Joy Harris. Extending a warm, friendly welcome to all visitors, the pub is open all day every day for drinks. The well-stocked bar offers two real ales – London Pride and

Bass – together with other popular beers, including John Smiths, Worthington, Stones and Guinness.

A delicious menu of freshly-prepared dishes is served each lunchtime and evening through the week, and at lunchtimes only at the weekend. The menu is presented on blackboards that are displayed around the bar, and all the meals are reasonably priced. There is plenty of seating inside, where you can enjoy the traditional atmosphere, enhanced by the original leaded windows, exposed stone walls and beamed ceilings. In fine weather meals can also be taken outside in the large beer garden, complete with children's play area. Most of the bar area is non-smoking through the day and children are welcome in the bar until early evening. There is a popular pub quiz held each Thursday and Sunday evening. All major credit cards accepted.

The Derbyshire Coal Mines 179

Ashover

Ashover lies just outside the boundary of the Peak District National Park but it still captures the typical character of a Peak village. At the heart of the largest parish in northeast Derbyshire, the village is chiefly constructed from limestone and gritstone, which were both quarried locally. The ruined shell of **Eastwood Hall**, once a large fortified Elizabethan manor house, also lies in the village. Owned, over the years, by several prominent Derbyshire families, including the Willoughbys, the house was blown up by the Roundheads during the Civil War. The ropes were said to be the longest and strongest in the country. The industries, with the exception of quarrying and fluor spar have all died out and the work is now chiefly farming.

The Crispin Inn, next to the interesting parish **Church of All Saints**, claims to date from the time of Agincourt, 1415. However, it is far more likely that, like many other buildings in the parish, it dates from the 17th century. The inn's name reflects one of Ashover's traditional trades: St Crispin is the patron saint of shoemakers and cobblers. The church, with its 15th century tower, houses the alabaster tomb of Thomas Babington and his wife, said by many to be the best in Derbyshire. There are also some handsome brasses. What is surprising is the lead-lined Norman font, described by Pevsner as "the most important Norman font in the country", the only lead-lined font in this area that is so well known for its mining.

HOLYMOORSIDE
3 miles W of Chesterfield off the A632

Surrounded by the attractive moorland and lying in the picturesque valley of the River Hipper, this scattered village has

Chander Cottages

Chander Hill Barn, Chander Hill, Holymoorside, Chesterfield, Derbyshire S42 7BW
Tel: 01246 569416
e-mail: margaretesmith@totalise.co.uk

Close to their own home, itself a converted 16th-century barn, Margaret and Harry Smith have converted another barn into four superb holiday cottages. Surrounding a picturesque courtyard they enjoy views across open countryside towards Chesterfield. **Chander Cottages** sleep either two or four adults and are equipped and maintained to a very high standard. The weekly rates are fully inclusive and short breaks are available out of season. These were recommended to us, and it's not hard to see why.

Kelstedge Inn

Matlock Road, Kelstedge, Derbyshire S45 0DX
Tel: 01246 590448/590305

Within the pleasant village of Kelstedge you'll find the **Kelstedge Inn**. Dating from 1759 it has all the appeal of a traditional country pub and enjoys a corner site at the brow of a steep hill. It is an attractive building of local stone, with an old barn attached, creating a small courtyard to the front where there is car parking. The walls are thick, the windows are small paned and quaint, and it is everything an English pub should be – warm and cosy in winter, and cool and welcoming in summer. The range of drink stocked at its bar will also help keep you cool when temperatures rise. There are two real ales on offer – Tetley's and Marston's Pedigree, plus draught mild, bitter, stout and cider. There is also the usual range of spirits and soft drinks.

In charge are Sylvia and Simon, and under their care the inn maintains an enviable reputation in the local area as a popular place for a drink or a meal. The interior is every bit as attractive as the exterior, with open fires, highly polished wood and comfortable furniture. Just off the main bar is a 25-seater, non-smoking restaurant, which is nice and spacious. Sylvia is the chef, and she presents a varied menu of classic dishes, ranging from light snacks to more hearty meals. If you want a real treat, try the fresh, battered cod, which is very popular with the regulars and all meals are prepared using mainly, locally-sourced produce. Open every lunchtime and evening and all day on Sunday (no food Sunday evening). Major credit cards welcome. A popular pub quiz is held on Tuesday nights in the winter months.

This is a place that offers real value for money. The adjoining barn houses comfortable bed and breakfast accommodation, offering six doubles and a single room, all with en-suite facilities. One room has a four-poster bed, which is ideal for an extra-special, romantic stay. The rates are very reasonable. Ring for full details.

grown into a popular residential area for the nearby towns. The custom of well-dressing in the village was revived in 1979 after a gap of about 80 years. Two wells are dressed, a large one and a smaller one for children, on the Wednesday before the late summer Bank Holiday in August.

The dressers follow the tradition of Barlow, where only flowers and leaves are used and not wool, seed and shells, though they do not stick to biblical themes. In 1990 the well-dressing depicted a scene commemorating the 50th anniversary of the Battle of Britain, one of their most spectacular dressings to date, and won the dressers pictures in the national press.

OLD BRAMPTON
3½ miles W of Chesterfield off the B6050

Situated on a quiet road above a wooded valley, Brampton retains both its medieval church and also its manor hall from the 16th century. The church of **Saints Peter and Paul** is of interest for its battlemented walls, short octagonal spire and Norman doorway and window. Also worthy of note is the large cruck barn, probably the largest in Derbyshire, to be found at **Frith Hall Farmhouse**.

CUTTHORPE
4 miles W of Chesterfield off the B6050

Before the Second World War the well-dressings in this village, which take place on the third Friday in July, had no religious links. After the war the custom died out, but was revived again by three people from nearby Barlow, in 1978. The three dressed wells are blessed during a service of thanksgiving for the pure water.

Near the village are the three **Linacre Reservoirs**, set in the attractive wooded Linacre Valley. Built between 1855 and 1904, until recently they supplied water to Chesterfield. Today the area is home to many species of fish, waterfowl, mammals and plant life, and is considered one of the most important ecological sites in the area. There are very pleasant walks, nature trails and fishing, and a scenic picnic area.

BARLOW
3 miles NW of Chesterfield off the B6051

Barlow is mentioned in the *Domesday Book*, and was the home of Robert Barlow, the first of Bess of Hardwick's four husbands. Although situated outside the limestone area, Barlow has been dressing its main well for longer than most. It is not known for certain when the custom began in the village, though it is known that, like Tissington, the well here provided water throughout the drought of 1615; this may have marked the start of this colourful practice.

Another theory suggests that the tradition in Barlow could date back to the days of Elizabeth I's reign, as the church register of 1572 states that the festival of St Lawrence was celebrated. Whatever the origins of the well-dressings in the village, it is known that they have continued, unbroken even through two World Wars, throughout living memory. The wells are dressed during the second week of August every year.

West of the village, **Barlow Woodseats** are not as uncomfortable as they sound for this is the name of an irregular gabled 16th century house, also called Woodseats Hall (private), which has a cruck barn in its grounds. Home to the Mower family - Arthur Mower was the agent to the Barlow family in the 16th century, and kept a truly remarkable diary from 1555 to 1610. All 52 volumes are now kept in the British Museum. He records the death of Bess of Hardwick in 1608, recalling her as "a great purchaser and getter together of much goods" and notes that she "builded Chattesworth, Hardwick and Owlcotes".

For those interested in Norman churches, there is another in Barlow. At first sight, however, **St Laurence's Church** may appear to be Victorian, but this was the work of enthusiastic remodelling in the 1860s. The interior reveals the true Norman features - the doorways leading from the nave and the short chancel - and there is also a fine alabaster slab in memory of Robert Barley, who died in 1467, and his wife. (The village was originally known as Barley, and the family took their name from it, later changing it to Barlow.) Bess's husband Robert Barlow is also buried here.

HOLMESFIELD
3 miles NW of Chesterfield off the B6054

Holmesfield is an attractive suburb of Chesterfield with its own flavour and rural tranquillity. The parish church of St Swithin was built in 1826 on the highest point of the village, giving spectacular views both north and south.

List of Tourist Information Centres

ASHBOURNE
13 Market Place
Ashbourne
Derbyshire
DE6 1EU
01335 343666
Fax: 01335 300638

BAKEWELL
Old Market Hall
Bridge Street
Bakewell
Derbyshire
DE45 1DS
01629 813227
Fax: 01629 813227

BUXTON
The Crescent
Buxton
Derbyshire
SK17 6BQ
01298 25106
Fax: 01298 73153

CHESTERFIELD
Low Pavement
Chesterfield
Derbyshire
S40 1PB
01246 345777
Fax: 01246 345770

DERBY
Assembly Rooms
Market Place
Derby
Derbyshire
DE1 3AH
01332 255802
Fax: 01332 256137
e-mail: tourism@derby.gov.uk
website: www.visitderby.co.uk

GLOSSOP
The Gatehouse
Victoria Street
Glossop
Derbyshire
SK13 8HT
01457 855920
Fax: 01427 855920

LEEK
1 Market Place
Leek
Staffordshire
ST13 5HH
Tel: 01538 483741
Fax: 01538 483743
e-mail: tourism.services@staffsmoorlands.gov.uk

MATLOCK
Crown Square
Matlock
Derbyshire
DE3 3AT
01629 583388
Fax: 01629 584131

MATLOCK BATH
The Pavillion
Matlock
Derbyshire
DE4 3NR
01629 55082
Fax: 01629 56304

RIPLEY
Town Hall
Market Place
Ripley
Derbyshire
DE5 3BT
01773 841488
Fax: 01773 841487
e-mail: touristinformation@ambervalley.gov.uk

Index of Towns, Villages and Places of Interest

A

Abney 44
  Highlow Hall 44
Abney Grange 44
Aldwark 90
Alfreton 133
  Alfreton Hall 133
  King Street 133
Alport 65
  Harthill Hall Farm 65
  Monk's Hall 65
  River Bradford 65
Alsop-en-le-Dale 92
  Alsop Hall 93
  Viator's Bridge 93
Alstonefield 98
  Tithe Barn 98
Ambergate 137
  Shining Cliff Woods 137
Appleby Magna 129
Arbor Low 93
Ashbourne 83
  Green Man and Black's Head Royal Hotel 84
  Market Square 83
  St Oswald's Parish Church 85
  The Mansion 84
Ashford in the Water 46
  Ashford Hall 47
  Church of the Holy Trinity 46
  Churchdale Hall 47
  Sheepwash Bridge 46
Ashover 178
  Church of All Saints 179
  Cocking Tor 178
  Eastwood Hall 179
  The Fabric 178
Aston-on-Trent 155
  All Saints Church 155
  Aston Hall 155
Ault Hucknall 171
  Church of St John the Baptist 174
  Hardwick Hall 171

B

Bakewell 35
  Bath House 38
  Church of All Saints 37
  Haddon Hall 40
  Lumsford Mill 39
  Old House Museum 38
  Old Town Hall 38
Ballidon 90
Bamford 25
  Bamford Mill 27
  Church of St John the Baptist 27
  Cutthroat Bridge 27
  Derwent Dam 27
  Fairholmes 27
  Ladybower 25
Barlborough 167
  Barlborough Hall 167
  Church of St James 168
Barlow 181
  Barlow Woodseats 181
  St Laurence's Church 182
Barrow-on-Trent 124
  Church of St Wilfrid 125
Baslow 31
  Bridge End bridge 32
  Church of St Anne 31
  Eagle Rock 32
Beeley 59
  Church of St Anne 59
  Hob Hurst's House 59
Belper 143
  Christ Church 145
  Derwent Valley Visitor Centre 144
  George Brettle's Warehouse 145
  North Mill 144
  River Derwent 143
  The River Gardens 145
Birchover 69
  Robin Hood's Stride 69
  Rowtor Chapel 69
  Rowtor Rocks 69
Bolsover 169
  Bolsover Castle 169
  Church of St Mary's 170
Bonsall 78
  Bonsall Brook 79
  St James 78
  Via Gellia 79
Borrowash 152
  St Stephen 152
Boylestone 121
Brackenfield 177
  Trinity Chapel 177

Index of Towns, Villages and Places of Interest   185

Bradbourne 88
Bradley 87
   Bradley Wood 87
   Church of All Saints 87
Bradwell 45
   Bagshawe Cavern 46
   Grey Ditch 45
   Hazelbadge Hall 46
Brailsford 115
   All Saints 115
Brassington 89
   Rainster Rocks 89
   St James 90
Breadsall 112
   All Saints 112
   Breadsall Priory 112
   The Old Hall 112
Breaston 153
   Church Wilne 153
   St Michael 153
Bretby 125
   Bretby Hall 125
Brough 25
Buxton 5
   Axe Edge 8
   Buxton Country Park 10
   Buxton Museum 7
   Buxton Opera House 7
   Cat and Fiddle Inn 8
   Market Place Fountain 8
   Pavilion Gardens 7
   Poole's Cavern 9
   Pym Chair 9
   Spanish Shrine 9
   St Anne's Church 8
   St Anne's Well 5
   The Colonnade 7
Buxworth 11
   Peak Forest Canal 11

C

Calke 121
   Calke Abbey 121
   Staunton Harold Church 123
Calver 31
   Georgian Cotton Mill 31
Carsington Water 80
Castle Donington 155
   Donington Park 155
   St Edward, King and Martyr 155
Castle Gresley 127
   Castle Knob 127
Castleton 19
   Blue John Mine and Caverns 21
   Castleton village museum 21

Crimea Farm 23
Mam Tor 23
Ollerenshaw Collection 21
Peak Cavern 22
Peveril Castle 19, 22
Speedwell Cavern 21
Winnats Pass 19
Cauldon 103
   Staffordshire Peak Arts Centre 103
Chapel-en-le-Frith 10
Charlesworth 14
Chelmorton 53
   Chelmorton Low 53
Chesterfield 161
   Chesterfield Museum and Art Gallery 163
   Crooked Spire 161
   Market Hall 161
   Peacock Heritage Centre 161
   Peak District National Park 161
   The Spread Eagle 163
Chinley 11
   Chinley Viaducts 11
Church Broughton 120
   St Michael 120
Church Gresley 127
   Sir Thomas Gresley 127
Clay Cross 175
Clowne 168
Codnor 142
Combs 10
   Chestnut Centre 10
   Combs Reservoir 10
Coton-in-the-Elms 128
Cressbrook 48
   Cressbrook Mill 48
Creswell 168
   Creswell Crags 169
   Steetley Chapel 169
Crich 136
   Crich Stand 137
   National Tramway Museum 136
Cromford 77
   Cromford Canal 78
   Cromford Mill 77
   Cromford Venture Centre 78
   Cromford Wharf Steam Museum 78
   Leawood Pumping Station 78
   Wigwell Aqueduct 78
Crowdecote 55
   Parkhouse Hill 55
Curbar 30
   Cundy Graves 30
   Curbar Edge 30

Cutthorpe 181
   Linacre Reservoirs 181

D

Dale Abbey 150
   Cat and Fiddle Windmill 151
   Church of All Saints 151
   Hermit's Wood 151
Darley Abbey 112
   Abbey of St Mary 112
Darley Dale 63
   Mill Close Mine 63
   Red House Stables 63
   Whitworth Institute 63
Denby 141
   Denby Pottery 141
Derby 109
   Cathedral of All Saints 109
   City Museum and Art Gallery 110
   Derby Heritage Centre 111
   Derbyshire Constabulary Memorabilia Museum 111
   Industrial Museum 109
   Pickford House 109
   Pride Park Stadium 111
   Royal Crown Derby 109
   Silk Mill 110
   St Mary's Chapel on the Bridge 109
   The Derby Gaol 111
Dinting 16
   Dinting Viaduct 16
Donisthorpe 129
Doveridge 121
Draycott 153
   Victoria Mill 153
Dronfield 165
   Chiverton House 165
   The Hall 165
Duffield 148
   Duffield Castle 148
   St Alkmunds 148

E

Earl Sterndale 55
   Church of St Michael 55
Eckington 166
   Renishaw Hall 167
   St Peter and St Paul 166
Ecton 98
   Ecton Hill 98
Edale 17
   Jacob's Ladder 19
   Pennine Way 17
Edensor 40
   Chatsworth House 40

Ednaston 117
   Ednaston Manor 117
Elton 70
   Castle Ring 70
   Nine Stone Close 71
Elvaston 154
   Elvaston Castle 154
   Golden Gates 154
Etwall 117
   Etwall Hall 117
Eyam 42
   Church of St Lawrence 44
   Eyam Hall 44
   Plague Village 42

F

Farnah Green 145
Fenny Bentley 90
Flagg 53
   Flagg Hall 53
Fritchley 137
Froggatt 30
   Stoke Hall 30

G

Glossop 15
   Church of All Saints 16
   Melandra Castle 15
Grassmoor 175
   Five Pits Trail 175
Great Longstone 41
   Longstone Hall 41
Grindleford 29
   Longshaw Country Park 29
   Padley Chapel 29
Grindon 97

H

Hadfield 16
   Longdendale Trail 16
   Old Hall 17
   Woodhead Chapel 17
Hartington 99
   Beresford Dale 101
   Hartington Hall 101
Hartshorne 121
Hassop 40
   Church of All Saints 40
   Hassop Hall 40
   Monsal Trail 41
Hathersage 27
   Moorseats 28
   North Lees 28
   Stanage Edge 27

Index of Towns, Villages and Places of Interest 187

Hayfield 13
Bowden Bridge quarry 14
Church of St Matthew 14
Kinder Downfall 14
Mermaid's Pool 14
Heage 140
Heage Windmill 141
Heanor 142
Memorial Gardens 142
Shipley Country Park 143
Heath 171
Stainsby Mill 171
Sutton Scarsdale 171
Hilton 119
Wakelyn Old Hall 119
Hognaston 88
Carsington Water 88
Knockerdown Inn 88
Holbrook 147
Holloway 73
Lea Hurst 73
Holmesfield 182
Holymoorside 179
Hope 23
Church of St Peter 23
Hope Agricultural Show 25
Peak's Hole 23
Hopedale 97
Hopton 88
High Peak Railway 88
Hopton Hall 88
Horsley 150
St Clement and St James 150
Hulme End 98
Leek and Manifold Valley Light Railway 98
Manifold Valley 98

I

Idridgehay 147
Alton Manor 147
South Sitch 147
Ilam 95
Church of the Holy Cross 96
Ilam Hall 96
Ilkeston 148
Erewash 148
Erewash Museum 148

K

Kedleston 113
All Saints' Church 115
Indian Museum 115
Kedleston Hall 113

King Sterndale 53
Kirk Ireton 87
Kirk Langley 113
St Michael 113
Kniveton 87

L

Lea 71
Lea Gardens 71
Leek 103
Brindley Water Museum 105
Leek Art Gallery 103
Nicholson Institute 105
River Churnet 105
The Butter Cross 105
The Roaches 106
Tittesworth Reservoir 106
Linton 127
Litton 49
Litton Mill 49
Long Eaton 157
Trent Lock 158
Long Lane 117
The Three Horseshoes 117
Longford 117
St Chads 117
Longnor 56
Church of St Bartholomew 56
Longnor Craft Centre 56
Market Hall 56
Lower Hartshay 140
Lyme Park 12

M

Mackworth 113
Mapperley 149
Nutbrook Canal 149
Mappleton 93
Matlock 61
Church of St Giles 62
Matlock Bath 61
Peak Rail 61
Riber Castle 62
Snitterton Hall 63
Wildlife Park 63
Matlock Bath 73
Chapel of St John the Baptist 74
Great Masson Cavern 76
Great Rutland Show Cavern 76
Gulliver's Kingdom 76
Heights of Abraham 75
High Tor Grounds 75
Life in a Lens 77

Peak District Mining Museum and Temple
  Mine 73
The Aquarium 73
The Model Railway 74
Whistlestop Countryside Centre 74
Mayfield 101
  St John the Baptist 102
Measham 129
Melbourne 123
  Melbourne Hall 124
  St Michael and St Mary 123
Middleton by Wirksworth 79
  Good Luck Mine 79
  Middleton Top Winding Engine 79
Middleton by Youlgreave 68
  Lomberdale Hall 68
Milford 147
Miller's Dale 51
Milton 125
Moira 130
Monsal Head 47
  Monsal Dale 48
Monyash 53
  Lathkill Dale 55
  River Lathkill 55
Morley 150
  Church of St Matthew 150

N

Netherseal 128
New Mills 13
  New Mills Millennium Walkway 13
  Sett Valley Trail 13
  Torrs Gorge 13
Newhaven 93
Norbury 117

O

Oakerthorpe 135
Ockbrook 152
  All Saints' Church 152
  Ockbrook Windmill 152
Old Brampton 181
  Frith Hall Farmhouse 181
  Saints Peter and Paul 181
Osmaston 85
Over Haddon 57
  Lathkill Dale Trail 57
  Mandale Mine 57

P

Parwich 92
  Parwich Hall 92

Parwich Moor 92
Roystone Grange Archaeological Trail 92
Peak Forest 50
  Church of King Charles the Martyr 50
  Eldon Hole 50
  Peak Forest Canal 50
  Peak Forest Tramway 50
Pentrich 139
Pilsley 40, 175
  The Herb Garden 175
Pomeroy 55

R

Renishaw 167
Repton 125
  Church of St Wystan 125
  Foremark Hall 127
  Repton College 127
Riddings 138
Ripley 138
Risley 152
Rosliston 128
Rowsley 59
  Caudwell's Mill 59
  Wind in the Willows 59
Rudyard 106
  Kinver Edge 106
Rushton Spencer 106
  Chapel in the Wilderness 106

S

Sandiacre 151
Sandybrook 90
Sawley 158
  Bothe Hall 158
Scarcliffe 170
Shardlow 154
  Shardlow Marina 155
  Trent and Mersey Canal 154
Sheepbridge 164
  Dunstan Hall 164
Sheldon 53
  Church of St Michael and All Angels 53
  Magpie Mine 53
Shottle 145
South Normanton 133
South Wingfield 135
  Wingfield Manor 135
Spondon 152
  Locko Park 153
Stanley 151
  Stanley's chapel 151

Index of Towns, Villages and Places of Interest

Stanton by Dale 151
  St Michael and All Angels 151
Stanton in Peak 64
  Earl Grey's Tower 64
  Nine Ladies 64
  Rowtor Rocks 65
  Stanton Moor 64
Staveley 167
  Staveley Hall 167
  Staveley Iron Works 167
Stoney Middleton 42
  Lover's Leap 42
  Middleton Dale 42
Stretton 176
Sudbury 120
  All Saints 120
  Museum of Childhood 120
  Sudbury Hall 120
Sutton-on-the-Hill 120
  St Michael 120
Swadlincote 121
Swanwick 137
Swarkestone 124
  Swarkestone Bridge 124
Swinscoe 103

T

Taddington 51
  Five Wells 51
  Taddington Hall 51
Tansley 71
Taxal 10
  Shallcross Hall 10
  St James 10
  Windgather Rocks 10
Thorpe 93
  Beresford Dale 94
  Dovedale 94
  Dovedale Castle 95
  River Dove 94
  Stepping Stones 95
  Thorpe Cloud 94
  Wolfscote Dale 94
Tibshelf 176
Tideswell 49
  St John the Baptist 49
Tissington 90
  Church of St Mary 91
  Tissington Hall 91
  Tissington Trail 92
Tunstead 52

W

Wardlow 48

Warslow 98
Waterfall 96
  St James and St Bartholomew 97
Waterhouses 96
  Hamps-Manifold Track 96
  River Hamps 96
Wensley 68
  Oker Hill 68
  Wensley Dale 68
West Hallam 149
  The Bottle Kiln 150
  West Hallam Hall 149
Wetton 97
  Manifold Valley Trail 97
  Radcliffe Stables 97
  Thor's Cave 97
  Wetton Mill 97
Whaley 169
  Whaley Thorns Heritage Centre 169
Whaley Bridge 11
  Bing Wood 12
  Goyt Valley 11
  Roosdyche 12
  Toddbrook Reservoir 12
Whatstandwell 137
  Shining Cliff 137
Whittington 164
  Revolution House 164
Wingerworth 178
Winsick 175
Winster 70
  Market House 70
  Ore House 70
  Winster Hall 70
Wirksworth 79
  Carsington Water 80
  Heritage Centre 79
  Hopkinsons House 79
  National Stone Centre 80
  North End Mills 80
  Parish Church of St Mary's 80
  Steeple Grange Light Railway Society 80
Wormhill 52
  Wormhill Hall 52

Y

Yeldersley 85
  Yeldersley Hall 85
Youlgreave 65
  Arbor Low 67
  Church of All Saints 65
  Conduit Head 66
  Lathkill Dale 67
  Thimble Hall 66

List of Advertisers

A

Agatino's Restaurant	Heanor, Nr Derby, Derbyshire	142
The Alma Inn	North Wingfield, Nr Chesterfield, Derbyshire	171
The Anchor Inn	Bolsover, Nr Chesterfield, Derbyshire	170
The Anglers Rest	Millers Dale, Nr Buxton, Derbyshire	52
Aristocrats Café	Clay Cross, Derbyshire	175
Ashdale Guest House	Matlock Bath, Derbyshire	75
The Australian Bar Diner	Bakewell, Derbyshire	36

B

Barista Coffee and Patisserie	Glossop, Derbyshire	16
The Barley Mow Inn	Kirk Ireton, Nr Ashbourne, Derbyshire	87
The Barley Mow Inn	Wingerworth, Nr Chesterfield, Derbyshire	178
Bay Tree Restaurant	Melbourne, Derbyshire	122
Bent Farm	Tissington, Nr Ashbourne, Derbyshire	91
Beresford Tearoom	Hartington, Nr Buxton, Derbyshire	99
Blenheim House	Etwall, Derbyshire	116
The Blue Bell	South Wingfield, Derbyshire	135
The Bluebell Inn	Kirk Langley, Nr Ashbourne, Derbyshire	113
The Bluebell Inn and Restaurant	Belper, Derbyshire	145
Buddy's Diner	Chesterfield, Derbyshire	162
The Bulls Head	Repton, Derbyshire	126
Burton Manor Farm Cottages	Over Haddon, Nr Bakewell, Derbyshire	58
Butterley Park	Ripley, Derbyshire	139
Buxton Museum & Art Gallery	Buxton, Derbyshire	8

C

Café Nats and Bar Nats	Buxton, Derbyshire	6
Carsington Cottages	Carsington, Derbyshire	80
Castle Cliffe	Monsal Head, Nr Bakewell, Derbyshire	47
The Castle Hotel	Hatton, Derbyshire	118
The Castle Inn	Bakewell, Derbyshire	36
Causeway House	Castleton, Derbyshire	22
Chander Cottages	Chander Hill, Nr Holymoorside, Derbyshire	179

# LIST OF ADVERTISERS

Chatsworth House	Edensor, Derbyshire	41
Church Farm Cottages	Alsop en le Dale, Nr Ashbourne, Derbyshire	93
The Clock Inn	South Normanton, Derbyshire	133
Coach and Horses Inn	Dronfield, Derbyshire	166
The Cock Inn	Clifton, Nr Ashbourne, Derbyshire	100
The Cock Inn	Mugginton, Nr Weston Underwood, Derbyshire	114
Collycroft Farm	Clifton, Nr Ashbourne, Derbyshire	102
The Crewe & Harpur Arms Hotel	Longnor, Nr Buxton, Derbyshire	56
Crich Tramway Village	Crich, Nr Matlock, Derbyshire	136
Crown Cottage	Eyam, Derbyshire	42

D

The Devonshire Arms	Beeley, Nr Matlock, Derbyshire	60
Donington Grand Prix Collection	Castle Donington, Derbyshire	157
The Duke William	Matlock, Derbyshire	60

E

Earth Brand Café and Antiques	Ashbourne, Derbyshire	84
Eastas Gate	Middleton, Nr Matlock, Derbyshire	68
Eastry Cottage & Hillside House	Castleton, Derbyshire	20
Eyam Tea Rooms	Eyam, Derbyshire	43

F

| The Farmyard Inn | Youlgrave, Nr Bakewell, Derbyshire | 66 |
| Fleur de Lys | Unstone, Derbyshire | 166 |

G

Garden Café	Baslow, Derbyshire	31
Garden Cottage	Idridgehay, Derbyshire	147
The Gate	Tansley, Nr Matlock, Derbyshire	71
The Gate Inn	Lower Hartshay, Nr Ripley, Derbyshire	140
The Gate Inn	Mastin Moor, Nr Chesterfield, Derbyshire	168
The George Hotel	Tideswell, Derbyshire	49
The George Hotel	Youlgreave, Nr Bakewell, Derbyshire	66
Glossop Heritage Centre	Glossop, Derbyshire	15
The Green Man	Leek, Staffordshire	104
The Green Room Restaurant	Belper, Derbyshire	144
The Grouse Inn	Darley Dale, Nr Matlock, Derbyshire	64

H

Haddon Hall	Bakewell, Derbyshire	39
Hardwick Inn	Nr, Nr Chesterfield, Derbyshire	172
Hare and Gate	Leek, Staffordshire	104
Heights of Abraham	Matlock Bath, Derbyshire	76
Hill Top Inn	Belper, Derbyshire	143
Hillcrest House	Thorpe, Nr Dovedale, Derbyshire	95
Hodgkinson's Hotel & Restaurant	Matlock Bath, Derbyshire	74
Holly Bush Inn	Church Broughton, Derbyshire	120
The Hollybush	Netherseal, Derbyshire	128
The Horns Inn	Ashbourne, Derbyshire	83

J

| The Jug and Glass | Lea, Nr Matlock, Derbyshire | 71 |

K

Kegworth House	Kegworth, Nr Derby, Derbyshire	156
Kelstedge Inn	Kelstedge, Derbyshire	180
Kings Croft	Buxton, Derbyshire	4

L

The Ladybower Inn	Bamford, Derbyshire	24
Lakeside Lodge Tearoom	Moira, Nr Swadlincote, Derbyshire	130
The Lathkil Hotel	Over Haddon, Nr Bakewell, Derbyshire	57
Little Mill Inn	Rowarth, Nr Via Marple Bridge, Derbyshire	14

M

The Manifold Inn	Hulme End, Nr Hartington, Derbyshire	99
Matlock Bath Aquarium	Matlock Bath, Derbyshire	75
The Miltons Head	Buxton, Derbyshire	6
Miners Arms	Eyam, Derbyshire	44
The Miners Arms	Brassington, Derbyshire	89
The Mires Café	Wardlow Mires, Nr Tideswell, Derbyshire	48
The Moss Cottage Carvery	Ripley, Derbyshire	139
The Moss Rose Inn	Leek, Staffordshire	104

N

The Nags Head Inn	Castle Donington, Derbyshire	157
The Navigation	Breaston, Derbyshire	153
The Navigation Inn	Shardlow, Derbyshire	155

O

Oddfellows Pool Café & Tea Rooms	Hathersage, Derbyshire	28
The Old Smithy Tea Rooms	Monyash, Nr Bakewell, Derbyshire	54
The Old Talbot Inn	Hilton, Derbyshire	119

P

The Peacock at Oakerthorpe	Oakerthorpe, Derbyshire	134
Pickford's House	Derby, Derbyshire	110
The Plough Inn	Brackenfield, Derbyshire	177
The Priory	Leek, Staffordshire	104

Q

The Queen Anne	Great Hucklow, Nr Tideswell, Derbyshire	44
The Queens Head	Coton-in-the-Elms, Nr Swadlincote, Derbyshire	128
The Queens Hotel	Old Glossop, Derbyshire	16

R

The Rainbow Bistro	Glossop, Derbyshire	15
The Rambler Country House	Edale, Derbyshire	18
The Red House Country Hotel	Darley Dale, Nr Matlock, Derbyshire	64
The Red Lion	Brimington, Nr Chesterfield, Derbyshire	164
The Red Lion Inn	Birchover, Nr Matlock, Derbyshire	69
The Rising Sun Hotel	Bamford, Derbyshire	26
Riverbank Guest House	Matlock, Derbyshire	62
Riversdale Farm	Monsal Dale, Nr Buxton, Derbyshire	48
The Robin Hood	Buxton, Derbyshire	6
Rose Cottage Café	Castleton, Derbyshire	21

S

Scarecrows	Melbourne, Derbyshire	124
Scotland Nurseries Garden Centre and Coffee Shop	Tansley, Nr Matlock, Derbyshire	72
Sheldon House	Monyash, Nr Bakewell, Derbyshire	54
The Shoulder of Mutton	Osmaston, Nr Ashbourne, Derbyshire	86
Sir William Hotel	Grindleford, Derbyshire	29
Spinney Cottage	Birch Vale, Nr High Peak, Derbyshire	14
Stanhope Arms	Stanton by Dale, Nr Ilkeston, Derbyshire	151
The Steam Packet	Swanwick, Nr Alfreton, Derbyshire	138
The Strutt Arms Hotel	Milford, Derbyshire	147
The Swan Inn	Milton, Derbyshire	125
The Sycamore Inn	Parwich, Nr Ashbourne, Derbyshire	92

T

Treeline	Bakewell, Derbyshire	36
The Turks Head	Donisthorpe, Derbyshire	129

U

Underleigh House	Hope, Derbyshire	24
Upstairs Café and Gift Store	Bakewell, Derbyshire	36

W

Websters Restaurant and Take Away	Draycott, Derbyshire	153
The Wheel Inn	Holbrook, Nr Belper, Derbyshire	146
The White Bear	Stretton, Nr Alfreton, Derbyshire	177
The White Lion	Buxton, Derbyshire	4
The White Swan	Hilton, Derbyshire	119
Windy Harbour Farm Hotel	Glossop, Derbyshire	15
Winsick Arms	Hasland, Nr Chesterfield, Derbyshire	174
Wirksworth Heritage Centre	Wirksworth, Derbyshire	79
Wolfscote Grange	Hartington, Nr Buxton, Derbyshire	101

Y

Ye Old Bowling Green Inn	Smalldale, Nr Bradwell, Derbyshire	45
Ye Olde Nags Head	Castleton, Derbyshire	20
Yorkshire Bridge Inn	Bamford, Derbyshire	25

Hidden Places Order Form

To order any of our publications just fill in the payment details below and complete the order form *overleaf*. For orders of less than 4 copies please add £1 per book for postage and packing. Orders over 4 copies are P & P free.

Please Complete Either:

I enclose a cheque for £ ☐ made payable to Travel Publishing Ltd

Or:

Card No: ☐

Expiry Date: ☐

Signature: ☐

NAME: ☐

ADDRESS: ☐

POSTCODE: ☐

TEL NO: ☐

Please either send, telephone or e-mail your order to:

Travel Publishing Ltd, 7a Apollo House, Calleva Park, Aldermaston, Berkshire RG7 8TN
Tel : 0118 981 7777   Fax: 0118 982 0077
e-mail: karen@travelpublishing.co.uk
website: www.travelpublishing.co.uk

	Price	Quantity	Value
Hidden Places Regional Titles			
Cambs & Lincolnshire	£7.99	....	....
Chilterns	£8.99	....	....
Cornwall	£8.99	....	....
Derbyshire	£8.99	....	....
Devon	£8.99	....	....
Dorset, Hants & Isle of Wight	£8.99	....	....
East Anglia	£8.99	....	....
Gloucs, Wiltshire & Somerset	£8.99	....	....
Heart of England	£7.99	....	....
Hereford, Worcs & Shropshire	£7.99	....	....
Highlands & Islands	£7.99	....	....
Kent	£8.99	....	....
Lake District & Cumbria	£8.99	....	....
Lancashire & Cheshire	£8.99	....	....
Lincolnshire & Nottinghamshire	£8.99	....	....
Northumberland & Durham	£8.99	....	....
Sussex	£7.99	....	....
Thames Valley	£7.99	....	....
Yorkshire	£8.99	....	....
Hidden Places National Titles			
England	£9.99	....	....
Ireland	£9.99	....	....
Scotland	£9.99	....	....
Wales	£9.99	....	....
Hidden Inns Titles			
East Anglia	£5.99	....	....
Heart of England	£5.99	....	....
Lancashire & Cheshire	£5.99	....	....
South	£5.99	....	....
South East	£5.99	....	....
South and Central Scotland	£5.99	....	....
North of England	£5.99	....	....
Wales	£5.99	....	....
Welsh Borders	£5.99	....	....
West Country	£5.99	....	....
Yorkshire	£5.99	....	....

For orders of less than 4 copies please add £1 per book for postage & packing. Orders over 4 copies P & P free.

Hidden Places Order Form

To order any of our publications just fill in the payment details below and complete the order form *overleaf*. For orders of less than 4 copies please add £1 per book for postage and packing. Orders over 4 copies are P & P free.

Please Complete Either:

I enclose a cheque for £ _____ made payable to Travel Publishing Ltd

Or:

Card No: _____

Expiry Date: _____

Signature: _____

NAME: _____

ADDRESS: _____

POSTCODE: _____

TEL NO: _____

Please either send, telephone or e-mail your order to:

Travel Publishing Ltd, 7a Apollo House, Calleva Park, Aldermaston, Berkshire RG7 8TN
Tel : 0118 981 7777   Fax: 0118 982 0077
e-mail: karen@travelpublishing.co.uk
website: www.travelpublishing.co.uk

	PRICE	QUANTITY	VALUE
HIDDEN PLACES REGIONAL TITLES			
Cambs & Lincolnshire	£7.99	....	....
Chilterns	£8.99	....	....
Cornwall	£8.99	....	....
Derbyshire	£8.99	....	....
Devon	£8.99	....	....
Dorset, Hants & Isle of Wight	£8.99	....	....
East Anglia	£8.99	....	....
Gloucs, Wiltshire & Somerset	£8.99	....	....
Heart of England	£7.99	....	....
Hereford, Worcs & Shropshire	£7.99	....	....
Highlands & Islands	£7.99	....	....
Kent	£8.99	....	....
Lake District & Cumbria	£8.99	....	....
Lancashire & Cheshire	£8.99	....	....
Lincolnshire & Nottinghamshire	£8.99	....	....
Northumberland & Durham	£8.99	....	....
Sussex	£7.99	....	....
Thames Valley	£7.99	....	....
Yorkshire	£8.99	....	....
HIDDEN PLACES NATIONAL TITLES			
England	£9.99	....	....
Ireland	£9.99	....	....
Scotland	£9.99	....	....
Wales	£9.99	....	....
HIDDEN INNS TITLES			
East Anglia	£5.99	....	....
Heart of England	£5.99	....	....
Lancashire & Cheshire	£5.99	....	....
South	£5.99	....	....
South East	£5.99	....	....
South and Central Scotland	£5.99	....	....
North of England	£5.99	....	....
Wales	£5.99	....	....
Welsh Borders	£5.99	....	....
West Country	£5.99	....	....
Yorkshire	£5.99	....	....

For orders of less than 4 copies please add £1 per book for postage & packing. Orders over 4 copies P & P free.

Hidden Places Reader Reaction

The *Hidden Places* research team would like to receive reader's comments on any visitor attractions or places reviewed in the book and also recommendations for suitable entries to be included in the next edition. This will help ensure that the *Hidden Places* series continues to provide its readers with useful information on the more interesting, unusual or unique features of each attraction or place ensuring that their stay in the local area is an enjoyable and stimulating experience. To provide your comments or recommendations would you please complete the forms below and overleaf as indicated and send to:

The Research Department, Travel Publishing Ltd,
7a Apollo House, Calleva Park, Aldermaston, Reading, RG7 8TN.

Your Name:

Your Address:

Your Telephone Number:

Please tick as appropriate: Comments ☐   Recommendation ☐

Name of *"Hidden Place"*:

Address:

Telephone Number:

Name of Contact:

Hidden Places Reader Reaction

Comment or Reason for Recommendation:

Hidden Places Reader Reaction

The *Hidden Places* research team would like to receive reader's comments on any visitor attractions or places reviewed in the book and also recommendations for suitable entries to be included in the next edition. This will help ensure that the *Hidden Places* series continues to provide its readers with useful information on the more interesting, unusual or unique features of each attraction or place ensuring that their stay in the local area is an enjoyable and stimulating experience. To provide your comments or recommendations would you please complete the forms below and overleaf as indicated and send to:

The Research Department, Travel Publishing Ltd,
7a Apollo House, Calleva Park, Aldermaston, Reading, RG7 8TN.

Your Name:

Your Address:

Your Telephone Number:

Please tick as appropriate: Comments ☐   Recommendation ☐

Name of *"Hidden Place"*:

Address:

Telephone Number:

Name of Contact:

y
Hidden Places Reader Reaction

Comment or Reason for Recommendation: